MW00344564

Assembly Level Programming for Small Computers

Assembly Level Programming for Small Computers

Walter J. Weller

Lexington Books
D.C. Heath and Company
Lexington, Massachusetts
Toronto   London

Library of Congress Cataloging in Publication Data

Weller, Walter J
  Assembly level programming for small computers.

  1. Assembler language (Computer program language) I. Title.
QA76.73.A8W44   001.6'424   75-13436
ISBN 0-669-00049-3

Copyright © 1975 by D.C. Heath and Company

All rights reserved. No part of this publication may be reproduced or transmitted in any form or by any means, electronic or mechanical, including
photocopy, recording, or any information storage or retrieval system, without permission in writing from the publisher.

Third printing July 1976

Published simultaneously in Canada.

Printed in the United States of America

International Standard Book Number: 0-669-00049-3

Library of Congress Catalog Card Number: 75-13436

To Karl, Eric, Lisa, Paul, and
G.V.B., a fine old man who
upset everybody by asking,
"But who will do the work?"

Contents

The counting process. Use of number bases other than ten in historical times. Use of base 8. Digit values as successive powers of the base. Binary place values. Conversion from binary to decimal. Largest number in N binary digits. Equivalent precision of binary numbers. Grouping of bits into words. Shorthand methods of representing binary—octal and hexadecimal. Conversion of hexadecimal to decimal.

The OR, AND, and Exclusive OR functions. Complementation. Nature and effect of shifts. Binary addition and the overflow condition. Negative binary numbers—one's complement and two's complement. Nine's and ten's complement arithmetic. Subtraction as the addition of a negative.

Components of a computer and their nature. Registers and memory. A program as a series of steps. The program counter. Indistinguishability of instructions and data. Classifications of instructions. Memory addressing schemes—absolute—paged—base plus displacement— The "floating" page.

Absolute machine language programming. Octal and hexadecimal loaders. Mnemonic loaders. The assembly process. Definition of symbols. A conversational assembler. Pseudo operations.

tions. Scale factors. Sums of numbers with different scale factors. Rounding and precision loss. Scale factors of products and quotients. Multiplication by special constant fractions. Treating the largest negative number.

Use of more than one word to represent a number—nature of a double precision number. The sign of a double precision number. The sign of the low order part. Propagation of carry/borrow to high order. Double precision addition. Double length shifts. Normalization. Double precision negation.

The nature of multiplication. Operation of a software multiply—the double length product. The hardware multiply instruction. Overflow conditions—squaring the largest negative number. A general multiplication subroutine. Multiplication by special numbers. Products of double precision numbers. Some trigonometric considerations. The nature of division. Operation of a software divide—division as a series of shift and subtract operations. The divide check condition. Use of the hardware divide instruction. Occurrence of the maximum negative number. The double precision divide process.

The automatic scale factor. "Scientific" and floating point notation—exponent and fraction. The normalized form. The bias factor in exponents. Floating point addition and post normalization. Failure of the commutative law of addition for floating point numbers. Floating point precision loss. "Noisy mode" arithmetic. Floating multiplication and division. "Floating" a fixed point number. "Fixing" a floating point number. Other floating point forms—the true hexadecimal exponent.

binary conversion scheme for integers. A conversion subroutine for integers. Conversion of decimal fractions to binary fractions. Precision losses in fraction conversion. A general integer plus fraction conversion subroutine. Conversion of ASCII-hexadecimal to binary.

Conversion of integers by successive subtraction of powers of ten. Conversion of integers by successive division. Editing off leading zeros and fixing the algebraic sign. A general binary-decimal integer conversion routine. Conversion of binary fractions to decimal by successive multiplication. A general integer plus fraction binary to decimal conversion subroutine. Conversion of binary to ASCII-hexadecimal—a short subroutine.

Definition of FIFO and LIFO stacks. Concept of a stack pointer. Autoincrement and autodecrement stack access modes.

Categories of Input/Output instructions—control, sense, and data transfer. Parts of the Input/Output instruction. Concept of a device address. Logical foundation of teletype driver subroutines given in Chapter 13. Testing of ready flags. Controlling peripheral devices. Reading paper tape. Necessary conditions for data transfer. DMA devices. Block transfer instructions and automatic I/O instructions—the "poor man's DMA". Example of automatic output—plotting a histogram.

Nature of interrupts—automatic ready flag monitoring. The interrupt service instruction. Use of a real time clock interrupt. Concepts of arming and enabling. Conditions under which an interrupt can occur. Special properties of instructions when used as interrupt service instructions. Some common interrupt programming errors. Saving and restoring machine status. A software time-of-day clock driven by the real time clock interrupt. The interrupt system used to input and convert data from a keyboard. Priority interrupt systems and the problem of the reentrant programs. The technique of polling.

Concept of block interrupt service. The dual level interrupt scheme. The software time-of-day clock problem reconsidered. Reduction of interrupt service overhead. Use of automatic Input/Output under interrupt control. "Chained" block output examples.

Likely outcome of first attempt to execute a new program. Planning a program so it is easily debugged. Debugging the segments. Integrating the debugged segments. Some probable sources of trouble. Use of a debug program. The technique of breakpointing. Making a binary patch. Use of scratchpad for patching. The method of last resort. Some specific problems and their probable solutions.

List of Tables

Preface

There was a time not very many years ago when almost all programming was done at assembly level, and programmers were expert craftsman, skilled in the stringing together of machine instructions to produce programs. The process of learning to program in those days usually involved working in an installation which had access to a large computer and had a staff of already experienced programmers. There was little or no written instruction, and the novice acquired knowledge by experiment with trial methods and the counsel of his more experienced co-workers. These methods left knowledge firmly, sometimes traumatically, implanted but they were very tedious and drawn out. Each beginner was, to some extent, left to "reinvent the wheel."

As the years passed and computers came into widespread use for well-defined classes of applications for which their cost could be justified, problem-oriented languages arose to cater to the specific needs of these applications. These languages served the needs very well, but the result of their widespread use has been that a generation of programmers has been produced who are unfamiliar with the techniques involved in programming at assembly level.

The appearance of the low cost minicomputer, and more recently the microcomputer, has in a short time made entire new classes of applications economically feasible. We can now begin to consider putting computers into situations which would have been unthinkable even five years ago. These new applications are, in the main, not suitable for implementation with existing problem-oriented languages, The majority of them must be implemented using individual machine instructions, i.e., at assembly level. Thus the need for assembly level programming has increased sharply at a time when the fraction of programmers possessing this skill has declined from earlier years. As the number of potential applications of computers is many times larger today than it was a few years ago, and since the maturing of skilled programmers requires a rather long and prosaic apprenticeship, there seems to be no reason to believe that the demand for assembly level programmers can do anything other than become more acute.

Like any other significant human skill, assembly level programming has two broad components, detailed knowledge of the subject and experience. The ease and facility which comes with experience can be acquired in no other way, but the detailed knowledge which is the common property of skilled programmers can be treated in written form. While there is no substitute for having used a method before, the awareness that a solution to a problem exists and the knowledge of where to find it can be a material aid to a beginner.

For some years now it has seemed to this writer that a guide to some of the common methods ought to exist in printed form. Such a guide could make a material contribution to saving some of the time and pain experienced by beginning programmers in the "reinvention of the wheel." It is to this end, a guide to common assembly level methods, that this book is addressed.

The methods and tricks of assembly level programming are not peculiar to any machine. At base, all computers do the same kinds of things in essentially similar ways, and methods are universal. A square root routine or a random number generator will look different on different computers but the methods used are the same at base. It is the implementation of the method which is peculiar to a given machine. With this in mind it is a severe temptation when writing a book like this to construct a mythical computer with generalized characteristics which would serve the purpose of illustration of methods better than any particular machine. While this might be tolerable or even desirable in an academic or other theoretical situation, it does the beginner no good at all. No matter which machine he is using the examples will not run on it. He must take the step of translating the examples to the machine at his disposal. The only alternative is to select some particular machine, in this way serving a particular group directly, while those using other hardware are no worse off than if a "paper computer" had been invented for the effort.

Selection of a particular machine involves a difficult choice. We are in a very early stage of the evolution of computers and there is a great variety of hardware available and clamoring for attention. Many types of computer architecture are being tried with varying success, and it seems quite probable that not all these types will survive. For a book such as this to be of maximum utility an example machine must be selected which, in the writer's best judgment, represents one of the lines of evolution likely to survive and flourish. Many factors other than technical ones will determine this outcome of course, but most are not tangible enough to deal with. What can be dealt with are the primitive economic factors involved in computer use. The number of potential computer applications is increasing rapidly with falling hardware costs, while the pool of skilled programming talent is growing very slowly. This would seem to indicate that programming ease will play a larger and larger part in the outcome, and in this writer's view ease of programming means a rich instruction set.

It can be argued that a large instruction set poses a learning problem for the beginning programmer, and there is some truth to this. It *is* easier to memorize twenty instructions rather than eighty, but the user is bound by the limitations of the small set in all future situations. Once the larger set is learned, however, the user has the benefit of its power in all situations thereafter. It was with this consideration in mind that the Alpha computers made by Computer Automation were selected as the example machines for this book. The machines have a powerful instruction set and while they do contain design weaknesses, none of them is crippling. The Alpha is not an ideal computer—there is no such thing—but it does represent a very good design compromise which seems likely to enjoy much more widespread use than it does now, particularly if some of its design deficiences are remedied.

Selection of any particular example computer for a book on methods poses some danger, of course, in that exploitation of special features of that machine will lead to a loss of generality and reduced usefulness to those using machinery without the special features. Care has been taken here to avoid this, e.g., programmed multiplication and division are fully developed as separate entities, even though the example machine has hardware for the purpose.

Selection of application areas for discussion poses another decision. Not all application areas can be covered, nor is any single author competent to do so. The application examples shown, therefore, reflect the interest and experience of the writer, i.e., real time control, monitoring, and data acquisition problems. The examples are taken from actual applications and represent real solutions to problems encountered in those applications.

In appropriate places more than one solution is presented. The first, immediately following the definition of the problem, is intended to represent the most obvious solution. It uses only the most elementary capacities of the example computer and is the solution most applicable to a wide range of machines, including the microcomputers. The second and succeeding solutions show better or more efficient solutions which can be more easily understood in the light of the first solution.

This book is not intended to be a theoretical treatise on programming—quite the opposite—it is a how-to-do-it book, an exposition of some of the useful items in the programmer's bag of tricks. If it saves any of the time that would be wasted in the reinvention of these tricks, its purpose will have been well served.

The following individuals contributed to this work by technical discussions and criticisms:

Mr. Don Fitzpatrick
Mr. J. H. Hathwell
Mr. Conrad E. Iungerich
Mr. Albert Shatzel
Mr. Harold Scoblow
Mr. Tom Woods
Mr. Donald B. Johnson

Mr. William McAdams
Mrs. Virginia Klema
Mr. Wayne Johnson
Mr. Harvey Nice

I am also in the debt of Messrs. Ted Singer, Ted Berland, and Jim Currie for aid with various manuscript problems.

Finally, I am most indebted of all to my wife Ruth, whose patience and good humor made the writing possible.

**Assembly Level
Programming for Small
Computers**

1

Binary Representation

The electronic components of which computers are built are devices which can exist in essentially two states—on or off, conducting or nonconducting, one or zero. What we call these states is pretty much irrelevant, but we must deal with the fact that the two state nature of computer components makes itself felt in the use of the computer.

People feel that the decimal system of computation is somehow a "natural" one and that any number base other than ten is artificial. This is an understandable prejudice on the part of creatures who have ten exposed fingers. In primitive enumeration, the fingers are set in one-to-one correspondence with the objects to be counted, and there is a certain subjective "rightness" to expressing counts as corresponding to groups of fingers. This feeling of "rightness" has no more objective base, of course, than that of the little old lady in the religious goods store who insisted that she wanted a King James Bible, "the kind Jesus used . . ." The mental cast which accounts for this is reinforced by the exclusive use of the decimal system in the formative years of our lives until it becomes very clumsy for us to even consider an alternative base.

This attitude has not been shared by all people at all times. There is much historical evidence for the regular use of number bases other than ten in ancient and even relatively modern times. Twenty, for example, was widely used in the ancient world in those areas in which the climate was mild enough to allow people to go barefoot or wear open sandals. Vestiges of this are still to be found in modern language, e.g., the word score in English and the expression quatre-vingt (literally four twenties) for the number eighty in modern French. Traces of the earlier use of base twelve persist in the English words dozen and gross. For those interested in the historical use of bases other than ten there is a fascinating discussion of the subject in Howard Eves' *Introduction to the History of Mathematics*.

Establishing that a preference for the use of ten as a number base is only a cultural prejudice does nothing to ease the problem of becoming comfortable in the use of another base. It is the purpose of this chapter to help ease the transition somewhat. The reader should be forewarned, though, that the feeling of comfortable familiarity can be achieved only by practice.

The two state nature of computer components limits the choice of usable number bases to those in which the total repertoire is two digits. Only one number base satisfies this description, the base two or binary

1

system, and it is in this base that we are compelled to work. Before examining the differences between base ten and base two, it is best to put them in perspective by examining what is familiar about them and about all number bases. Suppose we had evolved with hands like the Walt Disney cartoon characters bearing only four digits on each. To use ten as a base for computation would seem the height of absurdity. The most natural base would be eight. There would be eight distinct single digits: 0,1,2,3,4,5,6, and 7. The numerals 8 and 9 would not exist. Counts greater than eight would be expressed by tallying the number of eights in another column, just as we tally the number of tens in the column to the left of the units. The number we call eleven would be expressed as eight and three, i.e., a one in the eights column and a three in the units column, as:

$$13$$

If the count grew to be greater than eight eights we would move over another column. This column would show the number of sixty-fours. The number that we decimal creatures call seventy-six would be expressed as a sixty-four plus an eight plus four units, as:

$$114$$

and the title of Meredith Willson's famous composition would be "114 Trombones."

Since we are creatures of the decimal system, however, it is necessary to identify which number base is being discussed if more than one is involved. This is done by writing a small subscript immediately after the number, as:

$$203_8$$

The little eight below and after the 203 identifies it as a base eight number. This number by the way is one hundred thirty-one in the decimal system. To state this numerically:

$$203_8 = 131_{10}$$

or:

$$76_{10} \text{ trombones} = 114_8 \text{ trombones}$$

In the base eight system the successive digit positions represent powers of the base itself: 1, 8, 64, 512, etc. These are the values of 8^0, 8^1, 8^2, and 8^3, just as 1, 10, 100, etc., are the values of 10^0, 10^1, 10^2, and so forth.

In the base two or binary system the successive digits represent the successive powers of two, i.e., 2^0, 2^1, 2^2, 2^3, or 1, 2, 4, 8, and so forth. Any number to the zero power is equal to one; 2^0, 8^0, and 10^0 each equal one. Thus the right most digit of an integer number in *any* base is the units digit.

Table 1-1
Powers of Two

Power	Value	Power	Value
0	1	8	256
1	2	9	512
2	4	10	1024
3	8	11	2048
4	16	12	4096
5	32	13	8192
6	64	14	16384
7	128	15	32768

Now let's think about the binary system. As an example, take the binary number:

$$1\ 0\ 0\ 1_2$$

The small subscripted 2 means that this number is binary. The digits from right to left mean units, twos, fours, eights. The right most one is in the units column so the binary number contains a one. The second column from the right, the two's column, is a zero as is the third, the four's column. The last column, the eights, contains a one. The decimal value of this binary number is eight plus one or nine. This is stated as:

$$1\ 0\ 0\ 1_2 = 9_{10}$$

Like a decimal number, a binary number can be expanded to the left indefinitely to produce a number of any size, the value of each binary digit being just twice the value of the one to the right of it. To convert a number from binary to decimal we simply add up the powers of two represented by the place value of each 1 digit in the binary number. In the above example the powers were 2^3 and 2^0. The first sixteen powers of two are shown in table 1-1.

Using table 1-1 it is a straightforward job to convert a binary number to decimal. For each power of two represented by a 1 in the binary number simply add the value of that power. Take the binary number:

$$1\ 1\ 0\ 1\ 0\ 0\ 1\ 0\ 1_2$$

The number contains nine binary digits. In those digits which contain a one the values of the powers are 256, 128, 32, 4, and 1, whose total is 421. This is the decimal value of the binary number, i.e.:

$$1\ 1\ 0\ 1\ 0\ 0\ 1\ 0\ 1_2 = 421_{10}$$

Any other binary number is just as simple to convert to decimal. Take the number:

$$1\ 1\ 1\ 1\ 1\ 1_2$$

This number has a 1 in every position so converting it involves adding up all of the power values from 2^0 through 2^5. This is:

$$
\begin{array}{r}
1 \\
2 \\
4 \\
8 \\
16 \\
+32 \\
\hline
63
\end{array}
$$

Since this six-digit number has a 1 in *every* position it represents the largest number which can be formed using six binary digits. Note that this number, 63, is one less than the next power of 2, 2^6 or 64.

Let's look at another example, the binary number:

$$1\ 1\ 1\ 1\ 1\ 1\ 1\ 1_2$$

Since all of the digits in this eight digit number are 1's it represents the largest number which can be formed in eight digits. Its value is:

$$
\begin{array}{r}
1 \\
2 \\
4 \\
8 \\
16 \\
32 \\
64 \\
+128 \\
\hline
255
\end{array}
$$

Note again that this result, 255, is one less than the following power of 2, 2^8 or 256. This illustrates a general rule, namely:

RULE 1-1. *The largest number which can be represented in N binary digits is:*

$$2^N - 1.$$

To use this rule to find the largest number which can be represented in any number of binary digits just look up the value of the appropriate power in table 1-1 and subtract one. The largest number that can be held in ten digits, for example, is:

$$2^{10} - 1 = 1024 - 1 = 1023$$

This last example furnishes a rule of thumb which is worth remembering. A ten-digit binary number can express a decimal number a little bigger than one thousand. This rough rule can be extended easily for each group of ten binary digits, e.g., a twenty-digit binary number can express a decimal number a little bigger than one million, thirty digits transforms to about one billion, and so forth. Such rules are useful in estimating how many binary digits are necessary to achieve some equivalent decimal precision. A data transfer device such as an analog-to-digital converter which presents a ten-digit binary number to the computer is accurate to about one part in a thousand or 1/10 of one percent.

A more precise rule for finding the equivalent decimal precision of a binary number is to multiply the number of binary digits by .3. This gives the equivalent number of decimal digits as far as precision is concerned. We won't bother with the proof of this, but the rule is:

RULE 1-2. *If D is the number of decimal digits equivalent in precision to an N digit binary number, then:*

$$D = N \log 2$$

or

$$D = .3N \text{ approximately.}$$

Now let's take up a small matter of terminology. In all the examples and discussion so far the expression "binary digit" has occurred a number of times. The need for this expression is obvious, of course, but the expression is clumsy. An abbreviation for it was introduced very early in the computer craft, namely the word "bit" as a contraction of the words binary digit. This abbreviation will be used from now on.

In writing numbers on paper there is no limit to the size of the number which can be written. Extra digits or bits can be added at the left end of the number all the way to the edge of the paper on which it is written. The minicomputer presents a somewhat different situation. Bits are grouped in the computer to form units called *words*. It is the word which is the basic unit of information within the computer. The number of bits which make up a word varies from computer to computer but is fixed for any one computer. The most popular word size for minicomputers is 16, but this varies from 8 to 32. In our example computer the word size, or word length, is 16 bits. One of these bits is required to indicate the algebraic sign of the number, so only 15 are available for the magnitude. The largest number which can be held in 15 bits, by the rule just given, is:

$$2^{15} - 1 = 32768 - 1 = 32767$$

As the reader has probably already noticed, binary numbers are lengthy and clumsy to handle. To get around this difficulty certain "shorthand" methods have been devised. These methods all depend upon the fact that certain number bases can be converted to binary and vice versa easily. The conversion is in fact only a grouping of the digits. As an example take the number 131_{10} which appeared in an earlier example. This number in binary is:

$$1\ 0\ 0\ 0\ 0\ 0\ 1\ 1_2$$

If the digits are grouped into threes starting from the right, we have:

$$1\ 0 \qquad 0\ 0\ 0 \qquad 0\ 1\ 1$$

Reading these groups of digits separately is fairly easy. The left most group is a two, the next a zero, and the right most a three, i.e., the number is read 203. But notice that in the earlier example this 203 is the exact base eight equivalent of the decimal number 131. This is not an accident. For any number base which is an integral power of two, the transformation from binary to that number base consists only of grouping the bits and reading the result as single digits. For base eight the bits are grouped in threes since eight is the third power of two. Base eight numbers have come to be called "octal" numbers, though Webster does not legitimize this term.

Another way of abbreviating binary numbers is to use base sixteen, or hexadecimal. Since sixteen is the fourth power of two, the bits are grouped into fours and read as before. Since four bits can hold a number as large as 15, there is a problem of what to call a group of four bits the value of which is greater than nine. This problem does not occur with numbers like the one in the example above. Grouping the bits by fours, we have:

$$1\ 0\ 0\ 0 \qquad 0\ 0\ 1\ 1$$

The left hand group of bits forms an eight and the right hand group a three, so this number is 83_{16}. But what do we call a number like this?

$$1\ 1\ 1\ 1 \qquad 1\ 0\ 1\ 0$$

The left hand group of bits forms a 15_{10} and the right hand group a 10_{10}, and we don't have names for such groups. This is simply a problem of notation and is solved by assigning letters of the alphabet to groups of bits which represent decimal values greater than nine, as follows:

$$1010 = A$$
$$1011 = B$$
$$1100 = C$$
$$1101 = D$$
$$1110 = E$$
$$1111 = F$$

These bit patterns represent the decimal values ten through fifteen. Using this table, the number above would be FA. Sixteen bit computer words are written in hexadecimal as shown in example 1-1.

Example 1-1

Write the binary number:

$$1\ 1\ 0\ 0\ 1\ 0\ 0\ 1\ 1\ 1\ 0\ 1\ 0\ 1\ 1\ 1$$

in hexadecimal format. First group the bits into fours.

$$1100 \qquad 1001 \qquad 1101 \qquad 0111$$

The first of these groups is a binary twelve or C in the hexadecimal code given in the table above. The second presents no problem as it is less than ten, a 9. The third is a binary thirteen, D in the table, and the last is a 7. Therefore:

$$1100\ 1001\ 1101\ 0111_2 = C9D7_{16}$$

---

or:

Example 1-2

Write the binary number:

$$1\ 1\ 1\ 1\ 0\ 1\ 1\ 1\ 0\ 0\ 0\ 0\ 0\ 1\ 0\ 1$$

in hexadecimal. Grouping the digits as above:

$$1111 \qquad 0111 \qquad 0000 \qquad 0101$$

and reading the necessary values from the table, we have:

$$1111\ 0111\ 0000\ 0101_2 = F705_{16}$$

Hexadecimal can be converted to decimal in a straightforward way. As with any other number base the columns represent multipliers for the power of the base associated with that column. The right most column is the units, the next is 16's, the next 256's and the left most 4096's. The above number is converted as:

$$
\begin{array}{ll}
5 & \text{units} \\
0 & \text{16's} \\
7 & \text{256's} \\
15 & \text{4096's (the 15 being the decimal value of F)}
\end{array}
$$

or

$$15 \times 4096 + 7 \times 256 + 0 \times 16 + 5 = 63{,}237.$$

As can be seen from above, the process is tedious and is usually done best by directly looking up the required number in hexadecimal-decimal conversion tables. These tables are included as an appendix in almost every computer reference manual along with instructions for their use.

The use of binary numbers in their hexadecimal form will seem clumsy at first but this clumsiness disappears quickly with a little practice. Hexadecimal notation is one of the basic tools of assembly language programming and it must be thoroughly understood.

As a small side bonus for the effort, if you tend to forget the combination to locks or other combination security devices try engraving the combination on the back in hexadecimal. *Very* few thieves will bother to try and make sense of it. The combination 14-32-38 transforms to E-20-26, for example. You can never forget the combination this way, and if you do get ripped off you have the comfort of knowing that the thief was another programmer, and a good one.

2 Binary Operations and Arithmetic

Computers perform their work by means of the four fundamental arithmetic operations, plus certain other functions of a decision-making or logical nature. The purpose of this chapter is to give the reader an understanding of how these are performed.

The simplest operation which can be performed is to compare two bits to see if they are the same or different. This is done in many different ways but perhaps the simplest is the so-called *OR* function, sometimes called the logical sum. In this operation two bits are compared to produce a result which depends on the content of the bits. If both bits are zero the result is a zero. If either or both are one the result is a one. Just as there are symbols to represent the four arithmetic operations, there is a symbol for the OR function, namely V (from the Latin "vel," meaning or). To indicate the OR function of two bits whose names are RAIN and SHINE we write:

$$\text{RAIN} \quad \text{V} \quad \text{SHINE}$$

The result of this OR will depend on whether RAIN and SHINE are ones or zeros. There are only four possibilities and they are shown in table 2-1. The result is a one if either or both of the bits in question is a one. This parallels the English language use of the word "or" in the sentence: You can buy the house if you have the cash *or* can get a mortgage. In this case the result (you can buy the house) is true if either of the conditions is true or if both are true.

In the computer the OR function is usually performed on a full word (16 bits) rather than a single bit. This is done by simply taking the OR function of the individual bits in corresponding positions in the two words, as shown in example 2-1.

Table 2-1
The OR function

$$1 \text{ V } 1 = 1$$
$$1 \text{ V } 0 = 1$$
$$0 \text{ V } 1 = 1$$
$$0 \text{ V } 0 = 0$$

Example 2-1

Find the OR function of the two 16 bit words:

$$1100\ 1001\ 1101\ 0111$$

and

$$\underline{1111\ 0111\ 0000\ 0101}$$

$$1111\ 1111\ 1101\ 0111$$

Each bit in the result is the OR of the two bits above it.

The OR function is used for merging two groups of bits together. A common occurrence of this is the requirement for "control" bits for certain peripheral devices. The binary quantity 1001, for example, is the equivalent of a decimal 9, but to get a 9 printed on a teletype requires that certain control bits be merged with the binary quantity. Specifically, the eight bit quantity:

$$1011\ 1001$$

will print the character 9 when sent from the computer to the teletype. This group can be formed by using the OR function to merge the upper four bits with the lower four as follows:

$$0000\ 1001$$
$$\text{V}\ \underline{1011\ 0000}$$
$$1011\ 1001$$

The OR also occurs frequently in situations in which it is necessary to test whether any of a number of conditions is nonzero. In this case a word is kept in computer memory for each of the conditions. If all of these words are ORed together the result will be zero only if all of the words are zero. The OR is sometimes called the *logical sum*.

A second important function performed on binary numbers is the *AND* function. This is sometimes called the *logical product*. It resembles the arithmetic product in that the result is zero if either of the operands is zero. The result of an AND is a one only if both operands are ones. This is shown in table 2-2.

The symbol Λ is used for the AND function. ANDing is used for a very important operation called *masking*. In the example above the OR function was used to merge control bits onto a digit so that it could be sent to a teletype for printing. In the reverse operation a key is struck on the teletype keyboard and a code like the one above is received by the computer. The problem is to remove the control bits so that the binary number itself can be

Table 2-2
The AND function

$$1 \land 1 = 1$$
$$1 \land 0 = 0$$
$$0 \land 1 = 0$$
$$0 \land 0 = 0$$

examined. This is called masking and is done by ANDing the eight bit character with a set of bits which have ones in the positions in which we want to preserve the contents of the character and zeros where we want to discard them. This is shown in example 2-2.

Example 2-2

Remove the control bits from the eight bit teletype character 1011 1001 (the code for a 9 key). It is the right most four bits that are to be saved with the left four set to zeros. This is done by ANDing with a "mask" which contains zeros in the left four bits and ones in the right four bits, as:

$$\quad 1011\ 1001 \quad \text{the teletype character}$$
$$\land \quad \underline{0000\ 1111} \quad \text{the "mask"}$$
$$\quad 0000\ 1001 \quad \text{the result}$$

Each bit in the result is determined by ANDing the two bits above it.

The AND function is often used to determine whether any of a set of conditions is a zero. The result of ANDing a series of quantities together will be zero if *any* of the quantities was a zero. In general, two quantities named TRISTAN and ISOLDE will produce a zero when ANDed if either or both are zero, i.e.,

$$\text{TRISTAN} \land \text{ISOLDE}$$

is nonzero only if *both* quantities are nonzero.

The last important operation of this type is called the *Exclusive OR*. Sometimes called the *logical difference*, this operation yields a one only if the quantities on which it is performed are different, i.e., the first is a zero and the second a one or vice versa. This use of the term OR corresponds to that used in English when a child is told: You may have the ice cream or the gum. The implication in this context is that both, i.e., the ice cream and the

Table 2-3
The Exclusive OR function

$$1 \veebar 1 = 0$$
$$1 \veebar 0 = 1$$
$$0 \veebar 1 = 1$$
$$0 \veebar 0 = 0$$

gum, are out of the question. Though English uses the same word to express both senses of the OR function their meanings are quite distinct. If a question arises as to which is meant in programming context the meaning will be specified by Exclusive or Inclusive, the Inclusive OR being the simple OR function defined at the beginning of this chapter. The Exclusive OR function is defined in table 2-3.

The Exclusive OR is often used to tell whether some quantity has changed. Consider a set of status switches which can be interrogated by the computer. If these switches are read periodically it is possible to tell whether a new reading is different from a former one by performing the Exclusive OR of the two readings. The result will be a zero *only* if the two readings are identical.

Another occasional use of the Exclusive OR is for determining algebraic signs of products and quotients. As will be shown in the pages that follow, the left most bit of a number is a zero if the number is positive and a one if it is negative. It is often necessary to know the algebraic sign of some result, a multiplication or division, without actually knowing the numerical result. This can be done handily by using the Exclusive OR. The sign of a product or quotient will be negative (one) only if the signs of operands are different. Consider the two numbers:

$$1111 \ 1111 \ 1111 \ 1111 \ a \ -1_{10}$$

and

$$0000 \ 0000 \ 1111 \ 1101 \ a \ 253_{10}$$

The product of these two numbers will be negative, $a \ -253_{10}$. The sign of the product can be determined without multiplying by performing the Exclusive OR, as:

$$
\begin{array}{r}
1111 \ 1111 \ 1111 \ 1111 \\
\veebar \ 0000 \ 0000 \ 1111 \ 1101 \\
\hline
1111 \ 1111 \ 0000 \ 0010
\end{array}
$$

The left most bit, the sign bit, is a one; therefore the product would have been negative. This can mean an important time saving on a computer without hardware multiply/divide facilities.

All of the operations discussed so far have involved two binary quantities, but there are important operations that involve only one quantity. The most important of these is what is called complementation and involves simply inverting the value of each bit, i.e., if the bit is a zero make it a one, and if it is a one make it a zero. This is shown in example 2-3.

Example 2-3

Find the complement of the binary number:

$$1101\ 1010\ 0000\ 1000_2$$

We substitute ones for zeros and zeros for ones to get:

$$0010\ 0101\ 1111\ 0111$$

If the above number is written in hexadecimal as DA08, notice that the complement can be gotten by subtracting each of the hexadecimal digits from F_{16} (fifteen). The result is 25F7, which is the hexadecimal form of the binary result.

The last of the simple operations is called shifting. To understand what takes place in a shift imagine a conveyor belt which is partitioned so that a box on the conveyor can occupy only one of the marked spaces and cannot be half in one space and half in the next. Each space on the conveyor can be empty or it can contain a box. Think of those spaces with boxes as having value one, while the empty spaces have the value zero. Further, the conveyor can be moved only in whole spaces, not part of a space. Now let us start this imaginary conveyor going to the right and drive it one space. If there were a box in the right most space, it has fallen off the end. Meanwhile a new space has appeared at the left end. This space will always be empty. As for the rest of the conveyor, all of the remaining boxes have been moved right one space. We can represent the contents of the conveyor as a binary number. If the conveyor is sixteen spaces long the contents might be:

$$0\ 0\ 0\ 0\ 0\ 0\ 0\ 0\ 0\ 0\ 0\ 1\ 0\ 0\ 1\ 0$$

Note that the value of this binary number is 18_{10}. If we move the conveyor right one space we have:

$$0\ 0\ 0\ 0\ 0\ 0\ 0\ 0\ 0\ 0\ 0\ 0\ 1\ 0\ 0\ 1$$

The empty space at the right-hand end has disappeared. The full space which was second from the right has moved into the right-hand position and so forth. At the left a new empty space has appeared. Look at the value of this binary number; it is a 9. Dropping the conveyor analogy, it seems that shifting the number to the right has caused it to be divided by two. This illustrates a general rule, namely:

RULE 2-1. *Shifting a binary number to the right by* N *places causes it to be divided by* 2^N

Going back to the conveyor analogy, if the conveyor is now moved one place to the left, we have the original number back. This illustrates another general rule, namely:

RULE 2-2. *Shifting a binary number to the left by* N *places causes it to be multiplied by* 2^N.

Had the bit shifted out in the right shift been a one it would not have come back. Bits shifted out are lost.

Computers perform several different types of shifts. The examples just given illustrate what is called a logical shift. Another type of shift is that in which bits shifted out of a computer word reenter it at the other end. This is called a circular shift. Other shift types, long and arithmetic, will be explained in detail later in the text.

The most fundamental arithmetic operation is addition. While the reader may be tempted to pass up a section dealing with a subject which on its face seems trivial, there are aspects of computer addition which contain nasty surprises for the unwary. It is worthwhile for a programmer to understand something of how addition is done in a computer to be forearmed against these situations.

On its face binary addition is the simplest possible operation. The sum of two bits can be zero, one, or two and nothing else. All possible sums of two bits are listed in table 2-4.

To add two binary numbers the procedure is similar to the addition of two decimal numbers. Beginning with the right most column add the two digits. If the sum of these is zero or one write it below and continue with the next column to the left. If the sum is a two write the zero below and carry a one into the next column to the left. If a column contains both ones and a carry has been generated from the column to the right of it, the sum will be a three, i.e., $1 + 1 + 1 = 11_2$. In this case write the unit sum in the column and carry the one into the next column. This is illustrated in example 2-4.

Example 2-4

Add the two binary numbers 1010 and 0111. We begin at the right as with decimal addition.

$$1010$$
$$+0111$$
$$\overline{1}$$

The units sum is a one. Do the two's column.

$$
\begin{array}{r}
1 \\
1010 \\
+0111 \\
\hline
01
\end{array}
$$

This sum is a two, so we write the zero and carry the one into the four's column, and

$$
\begin{array}{r}
11 \\
1010 \\
+0111 \\
\hline
001
\end{array}
$$

When the carry is included the fours column adds up to two. Again write the zero and carry the one.

$$
\begin{array}{r}
111 \\
1010 \\
+0111 \\
\hline
0001
\end{array}
$$

Again the carry has caused the sum to become two, so we write the zero and carry the one.

$$
\begin{array}{r}
1111 \\
1010 \\
+0111 \\
\hline
10001
\end{array}
$$

And the addition is finished. The example is easily checked. The original numbers were 1010_2 and 0111_2, ten and seven respectively. The binary sum contains bits in the sixteens and units columns, so its value is $16_{10} + 1 = 17_{10}$.

Table 2-4
Binary Addition Table

$0 + 0 = 0$
$1 + 0 = 1$
$0 + 1 = 1$
$1 + 1 = 10$

In the example above the two four bit numbers were added to produce a five bit result, just as decimal addition often produces a sum with more digits than either addend or augend. This causes no problems in pencil and paper addition as digits can be added to the left indefinitely. In a computer word, however, there is a limit to how far left the sum can expand, namely the left end of the computer word. As noted before the left most bit of a word is not used to contain numerical information but to represent the algebraic sign. This means that only 15 bits can be used for the number. If the result of an addition is a sum greater than the largest number containable in 15 bits the sum "spills" into the sign bit. This condition is called *overflow*. Overflow is not necessarily a catastrophe and means will be shown for dealing with it in Chapter 10.

The last arithmetic operation to be dealt with in this chapter is subtraction. For a number of reasons subtraction is not done directly in computers by subtraction of a digit from a digit with a borrow from the next column if necessary. The borrow may not be confined to one column. If the column borrowed from is already a zero, a borrow is required from still another column. The reader can gain some understanding of the problem by trying a binary subtraction like $10000_2 - 1$ on paper. While our example computer has a subtract instruction, some modern computers do not. In any case an understanding of what happens during subtraction is necessary for the assembly language programmer.

If we cannot subtract directly some other means must be found for finding the difference of two numbers. To put this in symbols, we cannot do this:

$$A - B$$

but if some way can be found to represent a negative number, $-B$ in this case, we can do this:

$$A + (-B)$$

which is the same thing algebraically. The question is how to represent a negative number.

The simplest way to do this is to use the operation discussed earlier in this chapter called complementation. Arithmetic which is done using this representation is known as *one's complement* arithmetic and is used in a number of modern computers, most notably those manufactured by the Control Data Corporation. In these machines the negative of a number is formed by complementing it. Subtraction is done by adding this *one's complement*. This kind of arithmetic is best understood by following an example in decimal. The decimal counterpart of one's complement arithmetic is nine's complement arithmetic. The nine's complement is formed by subtracting each digit of the number to be subtracted from nine. In the problem 45 − 38 the nine's complement of the 38 is formed by subtracting the 3 and the 8 from 9. The entire process is shown in example 2-5.

Example 2-5

Perform the subtraction 45 − 38 using nine's complement arithmetic. The subtraction will be done by adding the nine's complement of 38 to 45, as:

$$
\begin{array}{cc}
45 \\
-38
\end{array}
\quad = \quad
\begin{array}{cc}
45 \\
+61
\end{array}
$$

When we perform the indicated addition we get:

$$
\begin{array}{r}
45 \\
+61 \\
\hline
106
\end{array}
$$

Since we are dealing with two digit numbers the 1 represents a carry out of the highest digit. In any case the sum that remains, 06, is not the right answer, since 45 − 38 = 7, not 6. In nine's complement addition this is solved neatly by something called an "end around carry." The carry out of the high digit is added to the low digit, as:

$$
\begin{array}{r}
45 \\
+61 \\
\hline
106 \\
1 \\
\hline
07
\end{array}
$$

and the two digit result, a 7, is correct. We will not get into the details of how this works, but the reader can be assured that it *does* work.

While the nine's complement system does work, as does the one's complement system, it is not without disadvantages. The number zero has two representations, 00 and 99, in nine's complement and

$$0000\ 0000\ 0000\ 0000 \quad \text{and} \quad 1111\ 1111\ 1111\ 1111$$

in one's complement.

A preferable solution is called the *two's complement system*. In this system, which is used by most minicomputers and our example computer in particular, the negative is formed by first finding the complement and then adding one to it. In the decimal system the corresponding type of arithmetic is called ten's complement. The ten's complement is formed by finding the nine's complement and adding one. The process is shown in example 2-6.

Example 2-6

Perform the subtraction 54 − 19 using ten's complement arithmetic. First we find the ten's complement of 19 by forming the nine's complement and adding one, as:

$$\begin{array}{r} 99 \\ -19 \\ \hline 80 \\ +1 \\ \hline 81 \end{array}$$

Adding this ten's complement to the 54 we have:

$$\begin{array}{r} 54 \\ +81 \\ \hline 135 \end{array}$$

This time we just discard the carry out of the high digit and have the answer directly, the 35, without the end around carry. Further, this system has only one representation for the number zero. To find the ten's complement of zero we find the nine's complement first, a 99, and then add one to get 100. The third digit is discarded and we have 00, just what we started with.

Two's complement arithmetic works in an exactly analogous way. We first form the one's complement by subtracting the number from the maximum number which can be held in this number of bits. Since the largest value which can be held in a bit is 1, subtracting a bit from one amounts to complementing it, since $1 - 0 = 1$ and $1 - 1 = 0$. This is exactly the result we get when we simply invert every bit. Having found the one's complement, we now add one to it to get the two's complement, as shown in example 2-7.

Example 2-7

Find the two's complement of the number:

0011 0001 0101 1101

Begin by finding the one's complement:

1100 1110 1010 0010

and then add 1:

$$
\begin{array}{r}
1100\ 1110\ 1010\ 0010 \\
+1 \\
\hline
1100\ 1110\ 1010\ 0011
\end{array}
$$
the two's complement.

If the reader is unconvinced that this bizarre looking process will yield a workable negative number the result can be checked easily. If the two's complement really is the negative of a number, then the sum of the number and its two's complement ought to add up to zero. Let us try this on the numbers from the example just done.

$$
\begin{array}{r}
0011\ 0001\ 0101\ 1101 \\
+\ 1100\ 1110\ 1010\ 0011 \\
\hline
10000\ 0000\ 0000\ 0000
\end{array}
$$

As before we discard the carry out of the high bit and have all zeros, which is correct. The two's complement system has only one representation for the number zero—all zeros. One peculiarity of two's complement arithmetic does deserve notice, however. For any given word size it is possible to represent one more negative number than positive. The four bit number 0111_2 is a decimal $+7$, while 1000, the maximum four bit negative number is a decimal -8. In a 16 bit computer word the maximum positive number is $+32767$, while the largest possible negative number is -32768. This occasionally leads to confusion, as adding $16384 + 16384$ causes an overflow, but $-16384 - 16384$ does not. It would be an instructive exercise to see what happens when an attempt is made to form the two's complement of the largest negative number. Try it. Overflow occurs in this case.

Multiplication and division will be treated in Chapter 11.

3

Minicomputer Structure and Operations

The power of assembly level programming resides in the ability to specify and manipulate individual computer instructions. Since this programming level is only a slight step removed from the bare structure of the computer itself, the programmer is required to have a fairly thorough knowledge of the operation of the computer at the instruction level. It is toward this understanding that this chapter is devoted.

To begin with, all computers do the same kinds of things—move data from place to place internally, manipulate data to produce results and move data from the external world into the machine and vice versa. Some computers are more able than others at some or all of these tasks, but the fact is that given enough time *any* computer is capable of doing what any other computer can do because they share a basically similar structure. Though the distinction may be somewhat artificial from the standpoint of a hardware designer, it is productive from a programming point of view to think of a computer as composed of three distinct logical parts: a memory, an arithmetic unit, and a control unit. The properties of each of these elements and the functional relations betweeen them are detailed in this chapter.

A memory is a device which holds information and from which the information can be retrieved *repeatedly* without destruction. This paper on which this book is printed fills this definition. Information is printed on the paper, and it can be read any number of times without disappearing. Further, information stored in memory is accessed by referring to its *location*, not the information itself, just as information in a book is referenced by page number, i.e., its location in the book. Another way of thinking of this is by analogy with the boxes in a post office. Contents are retrieved from a box by the box number. A request for the contents of box 105 makes sense in this context, but a request for the contents of the box which contains a specific letter does not. This second request can be fulfilled only by searching all of the boxes.

Computer memory takes many physical forms: magnetic tapes, disks, cores, etc. The functional differences among these forms are concerned chiefly with the speed with which information can be accessed and the manner of its access. In rotary memory systems such as disks and drums the times required for retrieval of information is governed by the speed of the device and the location of the information to be accessed, i.e., if the required information has just passed the read/write head an entire revolution of the device must take place before it is again available. With magnetic tapes, the required information may be at the other end of the tape —requiring a wait of seconds or even minutes until the tape can be positioned properly to access the necessary location. A memory device such as magnetic core in which all parts of the memory can be accessed in the same time is known as a *random access memory*. The new semiconductor memories share this property. A memory device which will hold its information even when power is removed is said to be non-volatile. Magnetic memory devices are non-volatile but semiconductor memories are not.

Memory is organized into groups of bits called *words*, this grouping being specified in the hardware design. The location of each word in the memory is specified by a unique number called its *address*. These addresses begin with zero and continue to the highest numbered memory word. Data are written into and retrieved from memory by referring to the address of the word concerned in the transmission.

The arithmetic unit, also called the arithmetic/logical unit, is similar in function to a calculator. It contains one or more *registers*, each of which is a temporary storage cell capable of holding one computer word. In some computers the registers have addresses, i.e., they may be referred to as part of memory, but this is not usually the case. In our example computer this is not true. In addition to holding one word of information per register the arithmetic unit is capable of adding and (usually) subtracting another word from the contents of a register. Though our example computer can also multiply and divide this is not the usual case with minicomputers. In addition to the arithmetic operations at least one register is usually capable of performing the logical operations (OR, AND, and Exclusive OR) discussed in Chapter 2. The registers may be used for other purposes than pure arithmetic. In many minicomputers some facility is present to allow the contents of a register to participate in the selection of memory addresses to be accessed. This will be discussed in detail in Chapters 7, 14 and 15. Other features of the arithmetic unit include a single bit which indicates the arithmetic overflow condition discussed earlier and may include bits which indicate various other operating conditions.

Breaking the discussion for a moment, let's consolidate what has been said so far. We have a memory capable of holding information and returning it on demand and an arithmetic unit which resembles nothing so much as a primitive hand calculator. Using these facilities alone it would be possible to write a set of instructions for the performance of a calculation, say to add two numbers and subtract a third. Such instructions written down for execution by a human operator might read:

1. Find the first number in memory location 647. Load it into the arithmetic register of the calculator.
2. Find the second number in memory location 477 and add it to what is already in the calculator's register.
3. Find the third number in memory location 650 and subtract it from the contents of the calculator register.
4. Store these results in memory location 500 and stop.

Such procedures are carried out thousands of times per day in offices and laboratories. There is nothing unusual about them. Details may be different, such as specifying in which column and row of the paper to find the numbers rather than giving a memory address, but the procedure is essentially the same.

Now we introduce the critical element, an electronic black box which has the following properties:

1. It contains a register capable of holding an address, called a program register or program counter.
2. It is capable of going to the memory word whose address is contained in the program counter and reading its contents, then adding one to the program counter.
3. It is capable of interpreting the numerical contents of the "fetched" word *as an instruction*.
4. *It can cause the instruction to be performed*, and then go back to step 2.

This electronic black box is the control unit named earlier as the third component. It is this element which integrates the other two elements, memory and arithmetic unit, to form a computer. With these three elements together the computer can execute a series of numerically coded instructions stored in memory without human aid or intervention. Several things should be kept clear about the process just described. First is the concept of a program counter. This is a register which contains the memory address of the *next* instruction to be executed, not the one being done now, but the *next one*. Second, the word which is retrieved from memory is simply an array of ones and zeros, i.e., it is a binary number, but it is interpreted as an instruction—an order to perform some action. Instructions are simply numbers and are not distinguishable from the data upon which they operate and with which they share memory. Finally, this control unit causes the necessary electronic action to effect the execution of the order contained in the numerical instruction it has interpreted. It then retrieves another instruction and the cycle is repeated.

It should be stressed strongly here that the instructions themselves are numbers stored in memory, the nature and order of these numbers detailing the task which the computer is supposed to perform. It follows that it is possible to construct a program purely of numbers, enter it into the computer and cause the task which this program defines to be accomplished. Early machines were programmed in exactly this way. Such programming is almost never necessary today (note the word almost). The construction of numerical programs was immediately realized to be a tedious and error prone process, and aids were developed very early to relieve the programmer of the most oppressive parts of "machine language programming," as it was called.

The computer instructions themselves fall into several broad classes depending on their functions and forms. These classes are:

1. Memory reference. These instructions do a great variety of tasks. Their common property is that they require that a word in memory be accessed to complete their execution. Their principal task is the movement of data between memory and the registers of the arithmetic unit, though not all of them actually transfer data. Moving data to the arithmetic unit may or may not involve performing arithmetic on the data. Those which do not result in a data transfer have functions such as comparison of a register with a number in memory, incrementing a memory word or modifying the program counter. The function of each will be made clear as it arises.

2. Register operate or change. These instructions perform some operation on a number already contained in a register. The complementation and negation (two's complementation) discussed earlier fall into this class. Other functions include transfer of data from one register to another, with or without changes occurring during the transfer. Included as a sub-class are instructions which cause the shifts discussed earlier.

3. Immediates. These instructions resemble certain memory reference instructions in that they transfer data between memory and a register or cause some change to be made on the basis of a number contained in memory. The important difference is that they require no special reference to a memory word for their execution. The numbers which form their operands are contained within the instructions. Though their function may not be completely clear from this brief description, this is a powerful instruction class whose use can allow significant economies to be made in programming.

4. Input and output. These instructions are associated with the movement of data between the computer and the outside "real world." Their functions will be detailed individually as they arise.

In the last three of these classes the object of the action of the instruction is implicit, i.e., it is in the nature of the instruction itself to transfer data, change a register or whatever. In the memory reference class, however, the instruction has a large choice of operands, as many as there are memory words in the computer, and the operand must be specified. This leads to consideration of one of the thornier points of minicomputer design, the specification of the operand address.

Owing to the fact that memory is the most expensive single component of the computer, it is very desirable from a cost point of view to design a machine whose instructions, in the main, occupy only one memory word. Since programs occupy memory just like the data they process, designing a machine which requires more than one computer word to specify an instruction has a gross and immediate cost. Whatever other merits may accrue to double length instructions, the fact is that in machines which use this architecture programs are about twice as long as in those which use a single word for the bulk of instructions. The problem now reduces to designing a scheme in which both the instruction and the address of its operand can be expressed in a single sixteen bit word, and a great deal of ingenuity has been expended in its solution.

In order to address all words in memory for a reasonable size memory directly, enough bits must be used in the address specification portion of the instruction to accommodate the highest numbered address. A typical memory size encountered is 8192 words (a so-called 8K machine). The specification of addresses 0 through 8191 requires 13 bits. This would leave only three bits to identify the instruction and no possible expansion beyond 8K. Three bits can specify eight possible instructions, and while such a machine could be made to work it would not be a very satisfactory device. The available instructions would perforce be limited to a very primitive set in which it would be necessary to write large numbers of instructions to accomplish anything.

The most popular solution to the problem has been an artifice called a *paged memory*. In this scheme memory is divided into subsectors. Instructions which are resident in these subsectors can directly address only data which are contained in the same subsector, plus a common subsector which is addressable from every machine location. This solution is a successful one and has been used many times. Some reasonable number of bits can be allotted for the address, plus a single bit to specify whether the address is to be interpreted as being in the same subsector or page as the instruction or in the commonly addressable page. Many machines have used this addressing scheme, among them the DEC PDP-8 series, the Honeywell (3C's) 16 bit series, the Hewlett-Packard 2100 series and various others. In a paged memory data which are outside the addressable range of a given instruction can be accessed by a technique known as *indirect addressing* in which the full space of a second word is used as another address to "point to" the address to be accessed. Programming such a machine requires that the user pay attention to memory page boundaries which can be a nuisance, but it is no more than that—a nuisance, not a disability.

Another scheme for the solution of the addressing problem is called the *base plus displacement* method. In this method a base register is loaded by the program and its contents used as a bias or offset for the address contained in the instruction. This is the basic scheme used in the IBM 360-370 series. The actual effective address of an instruction is the sum of the contents of the base register and the address portion of the instruction. On a multiregister machine this scheme is a powerful one because several registers can be used to make widely different sections of memory simultaneously addressable.

Yet another addressing scheme, the one used in our example machine, was first extensively used in the now venerable IBM 1800. This method combines the features of the paged memory with those of base plus displacement addressing. Like a paged addressing scheme there is a commonly addressable area of memory. This area, variously called "page zero," the "scratchpad," the "zero sector," and other like names, can be directly accessed by a memory reference instruction located anywhere in the computer. The addressing scheme itself involves the specification of one of several addressing modes. Scratchpad addressing is one of these modes. There is a base register in this scheme and two of the addressing modes specify whether the address or displacement part of the instruction word is to be added or subtracted from the address contained in the base register. Finally, since the execution of instructions causes the location of the instruction being executed to change, the base register also changes. In fact the base register is none other than the program counter itself. This amounts to a paged structure but with the important difference that the page "floats" with the program, making memory addressable in the immediate memory area in which instructions are being executed.

The page size in our example machine is 256 words. Since the addressing scheme allows both forward and backward addressing memory can be accessed 256 words in either direction, a total of 512 words. The addressing mode specification requires two bits. Thus all addressing information is contained in ten bits, leaving six for instruction and other options. One of these six bits is devoted to the specification of indirect addressing leaving five for the instruction itself. Since five bits can express 32 different states room is left for a large and powerful instruction set.

4 The Assembly Program

It was noted in the previous chapter that computer instructions are simple binary numbers and that it is possible to construct a program of numbers, load it into the computer and cause it to be executed. This process of machine language programming (or "banging on the iron" as it is called by certain whimsical people) is very tedious and error prone. The idea of using the computer to aid in programming itself occurred very early in the development of the craft. Perhaps the most elementary idea was that of a simple program to load other programs which had been punched on cards or tape. This would eliminate the tiresome business of keying in instructions individually for commonly used functions. The next most obvious idea was that of an octal or hexadecimal load program. In this version the programmer was freed from the necessity of writing binary instructions. He simply punched or typed hexadecimal or octal characters and the appropriate bit patterns were generated by the load program.

The most sophisticated of these load programs were mnemonic loaders. Using a mnemonic loader the programmer typed an alphabetic code for the instruction. Instead of the binary or hexadecimal equivalent of the instruction which causes the computer's A register to be loaded from a memory location, he would type some code suggestive of the function of the instruction, such as LDA (Load A).

Each of these steps eased the work of programming by making the process less error prone. At each stage more and more of the strictly clerical part of the programming task was taken over by the computer. The difference between programming at these various levels is best shown in an example. Take a program to add two numbers and subtract a third. The two numbers to be added are in memory locations 11_{10} and 16_{10}. The number to be subtracted is in location 14_{10}. In the bare machine language this program is written:

1011000000001011 This loads the A register with the first number from location 11_{10}.

1000100000010000 This adds the second number from location 16_{10}.

1001000000001110 This subtracts the third number located in 14_{10} from the sum of the first two.

27

As should be fairly obvious, programming this way is a grim prospect. This is the process which was referred to earlier as "banging on the iron." With a hexadecimal loader the process is not quite so bad. The same program looks like this:

> B00B   Load the A register from 11_{10}.
> 8810   Add the number from 16_{10}.
> 900E   Subtract the number in 14_{10} from the sum of the first two.

Better, but still no bargain. While this method allows less room for error because the programmer doesn't have to deal directly with long strings of bits, it is still numerical, and there is nothing about B00B which suggests loading the A register. This is still too much "banging on the iron." Finally, the same program using a mnemonic loader:

> LDA   :B
> ADD   :10
> SUB   :E

The addresses are still numerical but the instructions themselves are symbols, and this is a step forward. The colon in front of the address means that the address is hexadecimal. The program which reads these symbolic instructions is somewhat complex, but once it is written it can be punched onto cards or tape and loaded with a simple binary loader. Thereafter all programming can be written at the higher mnemonic level.

Certain clerical problems still crop up at the mnemonic level though. The programmer must continue to keep track of the absolute location of every number with which the program is concerned. Rather than do this it would be better to be able to give a name or label to a number and let the computer keep track of its absolute location in memory. It is irrelevant whether some number is stored in location 50 or 53 as long as the program can access it when it is needed. A program which is capable of doing this is called an *assembly program*. Let's reprogram the above example using assembly language. Suppose we want to call the numbers ERSTE, ZWEITE, and DRITTE. We have:

> LDA   ERSTE
> ADD   ZWEITE
> SUB   DRITTE
>
> ERSTE   DATA 0
> ZWEITE   DATA 0
> DRITTE   DATA 0

Now we've taken the plunge. In order for the symbolic instructions LDA, ADD, and SUB to access the quantities ERSTE, ZWEITE, and DRITTE their addresses have to be specified. This specification is accomplished by writing their names in the left most field. The next field contains the operation code itself, and the third field contains the symbolic name of the operand. The word DATA which appears in the operation code field is not an instruction at all but a flag to let the assembly program know that it must reserve one memory word for a number whose name is ERSTE and the same for ZWEITE and DRITTE. Such expressions as DATA are called pseudo-operations and will be discussed later.

A computer program written in the form shown above is said to be a *source program*. The action of the assembly program is to translate the source program into a form which can be executed by the computer. This process is called *assembly*, and its end product is a machine executable version of the source program. Exactly how this is done cannot be discussed here, but some of the process will become clear later in the book.

The source program is prepared for assembly by keying it directly onto some medium like cards or paper tape or by keying it directly into computer memory. The source program is then scanned by the assembler and the machine executable form, called an *object program*, produced. The keying in of the source program is an important step, in that it involves a rather long and boring task which is error prone. For this reason it is best to avoid using paper tape as the source medium if possible. A single mistake, and there is almost always at least one, means that the entire tape must be redone. One way of avoiding the rather considerable nuisance and trouble of this process is to use Hollerith cards as the source medium. This allows a statement in error simply to be discarded and another substituted in its place with a minimum of trouble. A card reader is an expensive peripheral, however, and there is another way out.

One type of assembly program, called a *conversational assembler*, allows the source program to be typed directly into computer memory where it is retained during assembly. The program can be typed out in whole or part and corrected by eliminating or adding lines. A source tape can then be punched under computer control, i.e., automatically, when the program is correct. This saves all the intermediate tape mess, and the source tape can be reread and changed again if this is ever necessary, with a new updated source tape being produced. Such programs are available for only a few minicomputers, our example machine being one of them. This conversational assembler, called OMEGA, contains a number of clumsy design features but on the whole represents a very large increment of convenience over conventional assembly programs. If such an assembler is available for your machine by all means investigate its use. It will repay the time spent many fold.

The DATA statement was discussed briefly above as one of a class of statements called pseudo operations or pseudo ops. These pseudo ops may or may not cause the assembly program to generate program words, but they furnish necessary information for the assembly process itself. In order to get started a few of them will be discussed here with the remainder appearing as necessary in the later text. These pseudo ops are written in the same fields as the symbolic instructions in the source program and look something like instructions themselves, though they are more in the nature of directives. The first of these specifies where in memory the program is supposed to start. This is the ORG pseudo op, and it is followed by some specification of location, as:

        ORG   :100

This tells the assembly program that the instructions which follow are to begin in address hexadecimal 100 (256_{10}). It is possible to have values other than simple numbers in the operand field of an ORG but this will be discussed later. Another important pseudo op is EQU. It is used to set a name or programmer created symbol to some value and has the form:

    GEORGE   EQU   7

This simply means that for the operand of any instruction which refers to GEORGE the assembler will substitute the value 7. EQU has some more exotic uses as well and these will be covered as the need arises.

There is often a requirement for reservation of a number of adjacent memory words for block data like tables. This is handled by the RES pseudo op. It has the form:

    HENRY   RES   105

This causes the assembly program to allot a block of memory 105 words long. Reference to the name HENRY will access the first word of the block, i.e., the one with the lowest address.

The last pseudo op for which we have an immediate need is the END directive. It simply informs the assembly program that all of the source program has now been processed. It means literally what it says.

We dealt in previous parts of this chapter with the use of names or labels in the left hand field of a symbolic instruction statement, and this now needs more specification. These labels are identifiers for the memory locations with which they are associated. Their form is a matter of the programmer's choice. We have used GEORGE and HENRY above but this was arbitrary. We could have used YIN and YANG, SONNY and CHER, or BOB, CAROL, TED, and ALICE. The idea, of course, is that the programmer should make some choice of labels which is meaningful to the problem he is solving, but there are some limits on what can be used. Labels must be six characters or less in length, e.g., we can use KAPUT but not GOETTERDAEMMERUNG. Also, labels must begin with an alphabetic character, A through Z. Thus the label A12345 is legal but 1A2345 is not. The label so used must appear in the left most field of the symbolic instruction once and only once in the same program. The appearance of the label in this field is said to *define* it. More than one appearance of the same label will cause the assembly program to record an error, namely that the label is *multiply defined*. Attempted reference by an instruction to a label that has not been defined is also cause for an error flag. This is known as an *undefined symbol*, the words label and symbol being used interchangeably.

Symbolic instructions, in addition to referring to defined labels, may contain numbers in their operand fields, e.g., LDA :3 or ADD   :51 are valid. These numbers refer to absolute memory addresses and do not require definition.

5 Memory Reference Instructions

As a large portion of the work done in computers consists of moving data from memory to registers and vice versa the skill with which memory reference instructions are used is of disproportionate importance in the writing of successful programs. About 60 to 70 percent of all the instructions in a program of significant length are of this class. This chapter will serve as an introduction to the use of these instructions although not all of them will be discussed here.

The principal means by which data are moved between memory and computer registers are the load and store instructions. The arithmetic unit of the Alpha computers contains two main registers, A and X. A serves as the main arithmetic register while X is used as an A register extension as well as for other functions related to addressing which will be introduced later. The load and store instructions are LDA and LDX, and STA and STX. They are used in the manner shown below:

label	inst.	operand
	LDA	ALBERT
	LDX	HORACE
	STA	GLORIA
	STX	AGNES
	. . .	

LDA ALBERT causes the A register to be loaded from the programmer defined location named ALBERT, while LDX HORACE loads X with the contents of HORACE. The previous contents of ALBERT and HORACE are unchanged. The previous contents of the registers loaded are lost. The use of all four instructions together is shown in example 5-1.

Example 5-1

Use the load and store instruction to swap the contents of the A and X registers. The problem is solved by storing A in one location and X in another. A is then loaded from the location into which X was stored and X is loaded from the location into which A was stored, as:

label	inst.	operand
	STA	SONNY

```
        STX    CHER
        LDA    CHER
        LDX    SONNY

        . . .
```

The two memory locations, SONNY and CHER, are defined by:

```
SONNY     DATA  0
CHER      DATA  0
```

. . .

The above also underscores the fact that the labels mean nothing to the computer. The locations named SONNY and CHER could have been named LYNDON and HUBERT, DICK and SPIRO, or GERALD and ROCKY with equal effect.

Addition and subtraction are performed by the ADD and SUB instructions. The sum of two numbers can be formed by:

```
        LDA    ALFONS
        ADD    GASTON
```

while the difference of two numbers is found by:

```
        LDA    DICK
        SUB    LIZ
```

In either case if the result generated is greater than +32767 or less than −32768 an indicator called the *overflow bit* is turned on. Results which cause overflow will be algebraically incorrect, though the A register will show a correct result if the sign bit is considered to be simply another magnitude bit. How to handle this situation and still get the right answer will be dealt with in Chapter 10. The use of ADD is shown in example 5-2.

Example 5-2

Find the sum of BOB, CAROL, TED, and ALICE.

label	*inst.*	*operand*
	LDA	BOB
	ADD	CAROL
	ADD	TED

```
ADD    ALICE
 ...
```

The operands BOB, CAROL, TED, and ALICE being defined else-where.

The use of the SUB instruction is shown in example 5-3.

Example 5-3

Find the value of MERRIL + LYNCH + PIERCE + FENNER + SMITH − BEAN.

label	inst.	operand
	LDA	MERRIL
	ADD	LYNCH
	ADD	PIERCE
	ADD	FENNER
	ADD	SMITH
	SUB	BEAN
	...	

Again the operands are defined elsewhere.

A very useful instruction, EMA, allows the contents of the A register to be swapped with the contents of a memory location. This instruction can be used profitably in many situations. Consider the earlier problem of swapping the contents of the A and X registers. The solution required four instructions and two temporary storage locations, a total of six memory words used. Using EMA to solve the same problem:

```
        STX    FUZZ
        EMA    FUZZ
        LDX    FUZZ
        ...
FUZZ    DATA   0
```

Here we use only three instructions and one temporary storage cell, a significant saving. Another use of EMA occurs in situations involving structures called stacks. A stack is a block of memory locations which are moved as a single unit. One type of stack behaves in such a way that entering a new data item into the stack forces another item out. To understand this kind of structure, think of a section of railroad track which can hold exactly four boxcars. Pushing another boxcar into this section of track forces another car out the other end. In a system which simulated this section of a railroad yard, an internal analogy of the external situation could be kept in the computer, as shown in example 5-4.

Example 5-4

Write a program to keep the status of a section of railroad siding four cars long. The siding status is represented as a block of four memory locations, CAR1 through CAR4, each of these memory locations containing the identifying number of the boxcar it represents. We begin with the siding status defined as:

label	inst.	operand	
CAR1	DATA	4327	# of last car to enter
CAR2	DATA	1688	# of next car
CAR3	DATA	5218	# of next car
CAR4	DATA	2740	# of first car to enter

If the identifying number of the car to be pushed onto the siding is available in location NEWCAR, moving the stack is accomplished by:

```
LDA     NEWCAR
EMA     CAR1
EMA     CAR2
EMA     CAR3
EMA     CAR4
```

The identifying number of the car which was pushed out of the siding, 2740, is now in the A register. If the value of NEWCAR was 5315, the stack now looks like this:

CAR1	DATA	5315
CAR2	DATA	4327
CAR3	DATA	1688
CAR4	DATA	5218

We should note before proceeding that the management of stacks is usually done by manipulation of special address words called *pointers*. Further, the later Alpha series machines have built in hardware features to aid stack management which will be discussed in Chapter 19. For a stack of only a few items such as the one in the example the method shown is adequate.

A substantial part of the power of a computer is the result of its ability to make decisions about further computation on the basis of partial results. The principal instruction involved in this decision making is one which allows the contents of a register to be compared with the contents of a memory location, the results of this comparison causing the further course of the program to be modified. The instruction CMS (*C*ompare to *M*emory and *S*kip) performs this function. The contents of the A register are algebraically compared with the contents of the memory location indicated by the operand portion of the instruction. If the number in the A register is less than the number in the memory location the instruction following the CMS is executed. If the contents of the A register are greater than the contents of the memory location, the instruction after the CMS is skipped and the second instruction following is executed. Finally, if the contents of the A register and the contents of the memory location are identical, the *two* instructions after the CMS are skipped and the third executed. This is best shown by example. Suppose the number in the A register is to be compared to a number in a memory location named PANCHO. The instruction behaves like this:

```
CMS    PANCHO
...    if A is less than PANCHO this instruction is
       executed
...    if A is greater than PANCHO this one is executed
...    if A is equal to PANCHO this one is executed
```

This instruction is especially powerful in conjunction with other instructions. Consider the problem of rearranging two numbers in memory locations named FISH and CHIPS. These numbers may be in any order but we want to rearrange them so that the smaller is in FISH and the larger in CHIPS. The problem can be solved by using CMS and EMA together as follows:

```
LDA    CHIPS
CMS    FISH
EMA    FISH
STA    CHIPS
...
```

The solution works this way. We begin with CHIPS in the A register. Comparing CHIPS to FISH, if CHIPS is greater than FISH the instruction after the CMS is skipped and the STA CHIPS is executed. This in effect does nothing, since the contents of A stored into CHIPS puts exactly the same thing there as was there when we started. If FISH and CHIPS are equal both instructions are skipped. If CHIPS is less than FISH the EMA is executed. This stores the smaller number in FISH. After the EMA the STA is executed. Since the EMA has swapped the numbers so that the smaller is in FISH, the larger is now in the A register. Executing the STA stores this larger number in CHIPS, and the problem is solved. This use of CMS and EMA together can be extended to sort lists of any length as will be shown in Chapter 14.

CMS is also useful for keeping historical data. In real time systems it is often desirable to keep a record of the highest or lowest value of some parameter. As each new value is received it is compared with the previous extreme value and replaces that value if it is greater than the previous maximum or less than the previous minimum. Before showing this it will be necessary to introduce two new instructions JMP and NOP.

JMP, meaning jump, is a means of changing the sequence of instruction execution. JMP has an address and the meaning of the instruction is that the next instruction should be taken from the location indicated by the address of the JMP, not from the location immediately following the JMP. It has no effect on memory or the registers. Another way of looking at a jump instruction is that it is a kind of load, except that it loads the program counter rather than a register. NOP is an instruction which does nothing —literally nothing. It occupies a space and takes up one machine cycle when executed. It has no effect at all on register or memory. NOP is somewhat akin in function to the legendary Grandma's Lye Soap—doesn't lather, doesn't foam, doesn't clean, just company in the bathtub. If you are perplexed at the existence of such an instruction be patient for a couple of paragraphs and you will understand.

Finally, before getting back to our history-keeping program, let's look at another feature of the assembly program, the currency symbol $. Use of this symbol in the operand portion of a memory reference instruction is interpreted to mean the location of the instruction in whose operand it appears. It can be combined with a constant to produce various effects. The one we are interested in at the moment is in conjunction with the JMP instruction. A typical use of the currency symbol is in statements of the type:

JMP $+2

The instruction being a JMP means that the next instruction is to be taken from the location specified by the operand of the JMP. The currency symbol $ means the location of the JMP itself. Adding 2 to this means the 2 locations beyond the location of the JMP. This amounts to saying skip the next instruction, which is exactly what happens. A JMP $+5 would mean skip the next four instructions. A JMP $−1 would mean back up one instruction, i.e., do the instruction just before the JMP again.

Now let us return to the history-keeping example. Suppose the highest value of the number called FLORA is kept in location HI and the lowest in location LO. When a new value of FLORA is available it must be compared to the contents of the two cells HI and LO to see if it is greater than the previous HI or less than the previous LO. The instructions to accomplish this are shown in example 5-5.

Example 5-5

Write a program segment to keep a record of historical greatest and least values of the number FLORA.

label	inst.	operand	
	LDA	FLORA	new value of FLORA to A register
	CMS	HI	greater than old maximum?
	JMP	$+2	no, skip the next instruction
	STA	HI	yes, replace old maximum with this one
	CMS	LO	was it less than the old minimum?
	STA	LO	yes, replace the old minimum
	NOP		greater, do nothing
	...		

If the new value was less than the old maximum the JMP is executed and the STA is skipped. If the new value was greater than the old maximum the JMP is skipped and the STA executed. In either case the second CMS compares the new value of FLORA to the historical minimum LO. If FLORA is less than LO the STA is executed and the new value replaces LO. In either case the NOP is executed. If FLORA happens to be identical to LO both the STA and the NOP are skipped and control passes to the next instruction. The function of the NOP can now be seen. It is a kind of "spacer" instruction, inert by itself, but providing for the case in which LO and FLORA are equal.

In writing such programs care must be taken with the initial values. If the initial value of HI was 10000 and of LO −10000, then no history would be recorded at all if FLORA did not exceed these limits. The only safe initial values for HI and LO are the minimum and maximum numbers that the machine word will hold, respectively. Setting HI to -32768 and LO to $+32767$ insures that a value will be recorded the first time the history program is executed. Further, the presence of these extreme initial values after running tells the operator that no data at all have been recorded. Think about it. HI and LO have the initial values:

```
HI        DATA   -32768
LO        DATA   +32767
```

Before leaving this example it should be noted that there is another solution to the problem using the same kind of instructions in a different order. It is:

```
LDA     FLORA
CMS     LO
STA     LO
CMS     HI
JMP     $+2
STA     HI
. . .
```

This illustrates something important about programming. Very often there is no single unique solution to a problem but two or more solutions. Choosing between the two solutions shown above is fairly simple. The second one is shorter and therefore preferable. It performs the same function in six instructions that the first solution did in seven instructions.

A very common requirement is the need to determine whether a number lies between certain preset limits. Some types of equipment require that their operating parameters be kept within limits, a boiler or nuclear reactor, for example. This can be solved in many ways but no solution is nearly as short as that using the CMS instruction, as shown in example 5-6.

Example 5-6

The heat exchange medium for a nuclear reactor is read by the computer from an external source and stored in location TEMP. It is to be determined if TEMP falls between the inclusive limits stored in locations HOT and COLD. If it is outside these limits a jump to location PANIC is to be executed. The easiest solution is:

```
label         inst.    operand

              LDA      TEMP          temperature in A register
```

```
        CMS    COLD        compare to low limit
        JMP    PANIC       less than low limit
        CMS    HOT         compare to high limit
        JMP    $+2         less than high limit, OK
        JMP    PANIC       greater than high limit
```

A better solution is:

```
        LDA    TEMP
        CMS    HOT
        CMS    COLD
        JMP    PANIC
        NOP
        . . .
```

The second solution is preferable because it is shorter.

A very important memory reference instruction, but one whose use is not obvious at first glance, is IMS, meaning *I*ncrement *M*emory and *S*kip. The action of IMS is to increment, i.e., increase by one, the contents of the memory location it addresses. If the location named BEAUTY contains the number 305, after:

```
        IMS    BEAUTY
```

is executed it contains 306. If BEAUTY contained a −5 before the IMS was executed it would contain a −4 afterward. This has more applications than it is possible to illustrate. One of them is shown in example 5-7.

Example 5-7

In a commercial application it is required that counts be kept of the number of individual sales and also of the number of these sales which are less than ten dollars. Write the program to do the necessary counting. The necessary count cells are defined:

label	inst.	operand	
TOTAL	DATA	0	total number of sales
SMALL	DATA	0	count of sales less than $10
SAWBUK	DATA	1000	a thousand cents = $10

Both TOTAL and SMALL are set to zero at the beginning of the business day. As each sale is registered through the point-of-sale terminal the following program is executed. Begin with the amount of the sale in the A register.

```
TALLY    CMS    SAWBUK     was the sale less than $10?
```

IMS	SMALL	yes, bump the small sales counter
NOP		no
IMS	TOTAL	in either case bump the total sales counter
...		

This would allow the merchant to determine the fraction of his sales which were less than \$10 by simply dividing SMALL by TOTAL at the end of the day. Note that the spelling of the label SAWBUK is caused by the six character limit on labels.

If need be every location in memory can be used as a counter in this way. The ability to have large numbers of counters becomes very important in problems involving spectra or frequency distribution determinations. This problem will be taken up in specific examples later in the text. An even more important use of IMS is in allowing a subsection of a program to be repeated some specific number of times using the ability of the IMS to cause a skip when the incremented cell becomes zero. As an example of how this can be used consider the problem of multiplying two numbers by the method of successive addition. To do this it will be necessary to use a new instruction, NAR. The effect of NAR is to form the negative, i.e., the two's complement, of the A register. If the A register were a +5 executing NAR would leave it containing a −5 and vice versa. NAR, meaning *N*egate *A* *R*egister, has a companion instruction NXR which performs the same function for the X register. It will also be necessary to use the instruction ZAR, which means *Z*ero *A* *R*egister. Execution of ZAR leaves the A register all zeros. Now to the problem. Multiplication of two numbers by successive addition is shown in example 5-8.

Example 5-8

Two positive numbers are in locations LAUREL and HARDY. These numbers are small enough that their product can be contained in a single computer word. Find that product by the successive addition method. The problem is solved by starting with a zero A register and adding LAUREL to it the number of times indicated by HARDY or vice versa. The solution is to use the IMS instruction to count the number of times LAUREL must be added. Starting with a negative number in COUNT we add LAUREL and increment COUNT, repeating these steps until COUNT becomes zero.

label	inst.	operand	
STAN	LDA	HARDY	HARDY to A register

```
              NAR                 form the number −(HARDY)
              STA      COUNT      and initialize the step count
              ZAR                 start with zero A
    OLIVER    ADD      LAUREL     add the other number
              IMS      COUNT      bump the count, last time?
              JMP      OLIVER     no, add LAUREL again
              . . .               yes, skip out of the "loop" to
                                  here

              . . .
```

Example 5-8 shows a most important principle, that of *looping*. Looping is the controlled repetition of a section of the program, and it will appear many times between now and the end of this book.

We have already discussed the JMP instruction as a means of changing the program counter and the way in which it can be used in conjunction with the CMS instruction to change conditionally the course of a program. Now we will examine another way in which the execution of a program can be modified as a result of a numerical outcome, the conditional jump instructions. These instructions perform the same function as JMP except that the jump is executed only when some condition is fulfilled. Jumps can be executed on the following conditions:

A register zero, nonzero, positive or negative

The overflow bit on or off (set or reset)

The console sense switch set or reset

X register zero or nonzero

The assembly program provides mnemonics for jumps on all of these conditions as well as useful combinations of some of them. These instructions are:

A register conditional jumps

JAM *Jump if A Minus*

JAZ *Jump if A Zero*

JAL *Jump if A Less than or equal to zero. Note that this instruction combines the jump conditions of the previous two.*

JAP *Jump if A Positive*

JAN *Jump if A Nonzero*

JAG *Jump if A Greater than zero. Note that this instruction combines the jump conditions of JAP and JAN.*

X register conditional jumps

JXZ *Jump if X is Zero*

JXN *Jump if X is Nonzero*

Overflow bit conditional jumps

JOR *Jump if Overflow Reset* (off)

JOS *Jump if Overflow Set* (on). This instruction forces the overflow
bit off when it is executed.

Sense switch conditional jumps

JSR *Jump if Switch Reset* (off)

JSS *Jump if Switch Set* (on)

The use of conditional jump instructions will be amply illustrated
throughout the remainder of this book so only one example will be given
here. Let's reconsider the last example, that of the multiplication of
LAUREL and HARDY by successive addition, in the light of the new
instructions. It can be rewritten as:

label	*inst.*	*operand*	
	ZAR		A register zero
	LDX	HARDY	count in X
	ADD	LAUREL	add the other number
	DXR		Decrement *X* Register. Note below.
	JXN	$-2	add again if X is not zero yet.

Note that this is only five instructions long while the previous example used
seven instructions and a temporary storage cell for the count. The DXR
instruction causes the contents of X to be reduced by one each time it is
executed. The reader may have noticed that neither of these examples will
produce a correct result if HARDY is zero. Why?

There is one final note about the conditional jump instructions, namely
that their jump range is less than that of other memory reference instructions. As noted before normal memory reference instructions have a range
of 256 locations in either direction. Conditional jumps have a range of only
64 locations forward or backward. The easiest way to circumvent this limit
is to test on the opposite condition and skip over a normal JMP instruction.
Suppose it were necessary to jump on zero to a location called GROSS
which was more than 64 locations away. It can be done like this:

	JAN	$+2
	JMP	GROSS
	. . .	

This requires an extra instruction word to accomplish the desired jump.
Most minicomputers have no conditional jump instructions but use condi-

tional skips, i.e., if the tested condition is true skip the next instruction. This is exactly what we have done here. Since the JAN has a jump target only one instruction away the combination amounts to a conditional skip. The careful programmer will not find this necessary very often, since with planning the jump targets can usually be held within the range of the conditional jump, but the technique should be filed away for future use.

The last memory reference instructions to be discussed in this chapter will be the so-called logical instructions, AND, IOR, and XOR. The AND instruction performs the masking function described in an earlier chapter. The contents of the A register are ANDed with the contents of the addressed memory location, with the result left in the A register. The memory location is unchanged. A typical use of AND is shown in example 5-9.

Example 5-9

An eight bit character is received from the teletype attached to the computer. The situation requires that only numeric characters be typed. Write a program to check the character received for validity and mask off the high four code bits to reduce the character to its binary form.

The numeric keys on a teletype generate the eight bit codes:

$$1011\ 0000_2 \text{ through } 1011\ 1001_2$$

$$= B0_{16} \text{ through } B9_{16}$$

If the character received is numeric it will lie between these inclusive limits. Checking for this is easy, as shown in the CMS example. It goes:

label	inst.	operand	
	LDA	KEYIN	character received to A register
	CMS	NUEVE	bigger than 9?
	CMS	NADA	or less than 0?
	JMP	DUMDUM	yes, character not valid
	NOP		spacer

The quantities NADA and NUEVE are defined as follows:

NADA	DATA	:B0	a zero in teletype code
NUEVE	DATA	:B9	a nine in teletype code
	...		

If the program gets past the above test without taking the jump to

DUMDUM the character was valid, i.e., numeric. The upper four bits are masked off by:

AND   LOFOUR

. . .

Where location LOFOUR is defined as:

LOFOUR   DATA :F

or

LOFOUR   DATA 15

Both of the above definitions generate exactly the same binary result. In either case all bits in LOFOUR are zero except the low order (right most) four. These four bits are ones.

IOR is the inclusive OR discussed before, and it is used for "merging" bits in a word. The contents of the A register are ORed with the contents of the addressed memory location and the result is left in the A register with the memory location unchanged. The use of IOR is best shown in an example. Numerical information is often represented as a series of pseudo-decimal digits, each four bits in length. The number 3824 for example is represented as:

$$0011\ 1000\ 0010\ 0100$$

each four bit group containing the binary equivalent of a decimal digit. Such a representation is called *Binary Coded Decimal* or BCD. A BCD digit consists of four bits which have a value between 0000_2 and 1001_2. To print the values of these digits on the teletype requires that a certain configuration of bits be merged with the BCD code, namely the bits 1011 0000. This is done by:

```
        LDA     DIGIT       BCD digit to A register
        IOR     BITS        merge teletype control bits
        . . .
BITS    DATA    :B0         hex equivalent of 1011 0000
        . . .
```

The final logical instruction is XOR, the Exclusive OR, whose operation was explained in a previous chapter. It can be used for many purposes including the ones shown in that previous discussion. The algebraic sign of a product or quotient can be determined without actually multiplying or dividing by:

```
        LDA     F1          first # to A
```

```
XOR    F2          form logical difference
JAM    MINUS       if the product or quotient would
                   have been negative the result of
                   the XOR is negative.
```

Another use of XOR is to determine whether two words are identical. The result of an XOR will be zero if and only if both words are identical. This is shown by:

```
LDA    WORD1
XOR    WORD2
JAZ    SAME
. . .
```

An interesting use of XOR is in the following process. Just what this does will be left to the reader to figure out. It will make a good exercise. If you get through it you will have a good understanding of what the logical instructions do. It goes like this:

Take any two binary numbers A and B:

$$A = 0011$$
$$B = 0101$$

First form the Exclusive OR of the two numbers and write it down. Then form the AND of the two numbers and shift it left one bit, i.e., write an extra zero at its right hand end. If the result of the AND was not zero, then let the new B be the result of the AND and the new A be the result of the Exclusive OR, and repeat the process. Do this until the result of the AND is a zero. When this happens the answer is the current value of A. What does this process do?

Two memory reference instructions have been omitted from this discussion, JST and SCM. These will be covered in later sections as the need for them arises.

6

Register Change, Shift, and Immediate Instructions

Register change instructions, sometimes called register operate or "generic" instructions, perform one or more of the following functions:

1. Zero a register
2. Increment or decrement a register
3. Complement (one's) or Negate (two's) a register
4. Set a register to + 1 or −1
5. Move the contents of one register to the other
6. Perform logical operations between registers.

There are a great many of these register change instructions, some of which are only marginally useful. The most frequently used of these will be discussed here, with certain of the others being introduced later in the text as needed. Reference to some of these instructions has already been made in the last chapter.

Most of the register change instructions occur naturally in pairs with similar instructions performing the same function in both registers. These instructions are:

ZAR - ZXR   Zeros the A or X register

ARP - XRP   Loads +1 into A or X

ARM - XRM   Loads −1 into A or X

IAR - IXR   Increments (adds one) to A or X

DAR - DXR   Decrements (subtracts one) from A or X

NAR - NXR   Negates (two's complements) A or X

CAR - CXR   Complements (one's) A or X

ANA - ANX   Performs the logical AND of the contents of both registers and leaves the result in A or X. The other register is unchanged.

BSA - BSX   These unfortunate mnemonics mean *Bit Set A* and *X* respectively. What they actually do is to Inclusive OR the contents of the two registers, leaving the result in A or X respectively. The other register is unchanged.

BCA - BCX   These instructions use the contents of one register as a mask to clear bits in the other register. In BCA bits which are ones in the X register are used to clear the corresponding bits of the A register, with the result left in A. The X register is unchanged. The previously given example of the stripping of control bits from a teletype character can be accomplished with BCA, as follows:

```
          LDA   KEYIN
          LDX   CMASK
          BCA
          . . .
CMASK     DATA  :FFF0
```

Note that this approach requires one more instruction than the other example and that CMASK is the one's complement of the mask used before. The instruction is of marginal usefulness.

NRA - NRX   These instructions form the "NOR" function of the contents of the A and X registers. The NOR function is the logical complement of the OR function. This means that a bit in the result will be a one only if *neither* of the two operand bits was a one. This is shown below.

The NOR of two binary quantities is formed by finding the OR and then complementing it, as:

```
    00101010
V   00110000
    00111010 This is the OR.
```

Complementing this we have:

```
    11000101
```

This is the NOR of 00101010 and 00110000

For instruction purposes the overflow bit is considered to be a register, though the programmer should clearly understand that it is only a single bit. As discussed before the overflow bit or register can be set (turned on) by an arithmetic overflow condition, the generation of a result greater than +32767 or less than −32768. It is also very useful as a one bit condition indicator. It can be set by certain shift conditions and is also under direct program control by means of the following instructions.

SOV -   Turns the overflow bit on

ROV -   Turns the overflow bit off

COV -   Inverts the overflow bit. If it is a one it is turned to zero. If it is a zero it is turned to one.

LAO - LXO   The overflow bit is set to the same value as the low bit of the A or X register. This amounts, in conjunction with the JOR or JOS instructions, to an even/odd test for the number in the register, i.e., if the low bit of a binary number is a one the number is odd. The function of this instruction is duplicated by BAO - BXO.

SAO - SXO   The overflow bit is set to the same value as the high bit of the A or X register. Since the high bit is the sign this amounts to a sign extension to overflow.

BAO - BXO   These versatile instructions allow any bit of either register to be isolated in the overflow bit *without changing it in the register*. The specified bit is copied from the register into overflow. The bits are numbered 0 through 15 from right to left. To copy bit 7 of A into overflow the instruction:

BAO   7

is executed.

The following instruction subclass allows data to be moved between the A and X registers. The instructions are:

TAX - TXA   The contents of A are copied into X (TAX) or the contents of X are copied into A (TXA). In either case the contents of the source register are not disturbed.

NAX - NXA   The contents of A are moved to X and negated (NAX), or vice versa. The source register is unchanged.

IAX - IXA   The contents of A are moved to X and incremented (IAX) or vice versa. The source register is not changed.

DAX - DXA   The contents of A are moved to X and decremented (DAX) or vice versa. The source register is not changed.

CAX - CXA   The contents of A are moved to X and one's complemented (CAX) or vice versa. The source register is unchanged.

EAX   The contents of A and X are exchanged, the former contents of A ending in X and the former contents of X ending in A.

The next instruction subclass to be considered is the shift subclass. These are really register change instructions in the definition of that term, but their separate hardware implementation has caused them to be classified as a distinct type. Their basic action is to cause the contents of the A or X registers or both registers together to be moved right or left. As discussed in a previous chapter, shifting right effectively divides by a power of two, while shifting left multiplies by a power of two.

Shifts fall into two categories, logical and arithmetic. In logical shifts all bits are treated as simple digits with no special attention accorded the sign bit. Bits which are shifted out of a register are shifted into OV and then lost. Bits shifted in are always zero. As with other register change instructions the shifts occur in pairs, as:

LRA - LRX   Shifts the A or X register right the number of places specified in its operand field. The number in the operand field may not be greater than 8. To shift the contents of the A register right by three places for example, we execute:

LRA   3

Had the contents of A been:

$$0000000000001101_2 = 13_{10}$$

the result after the shift would be:

$$0000000000000001_2 = 1_{10}$$

This illustrates an important point. Shifting right three places caused a division by 2^3 or 8. $13/8 = 1.625$, but since we are dealing with integers the fraction is discarded and we are left with 1. LRX performs the same function in the X register.

LLA - LLX   Shifts the contents of A or X left the specified number of bits. This in effect multiplies the number by a power of 2. To shift the X register left 4 bits we execute:

LLX   4

Had the X register contents been:

$$0000000000000101_2 = 5_{10}$$

after the shift the contents would be:

$$0000000001010000_2 = 80_{10}$$

The value of this result can be verified easily. The 64's bit and the 16's bit are the only nonzero bits, and $64 + 16 = 80$. Since we shifted left four bits we multiplied by 2^4 or 16. As the original number was a 5 the result should be 5×16, and this is correct.

Had the number been:

0111000000000000

the result of the shift would have been:

0000000000000000

a zero! Be careful.

Beside their obvious logical uses shifts can be used in a number of clever arithmetic tricks. The need to multiply by ten arises in conversion of numbers from decimal to binary. This can be done neatly by using shifts to multiply by 2 and 8 and then adding the results. Since $10N = 2N + 8N$ the method is valid. It is shown in example 6-1.

Example 6-1

Convert the two BCD digits 0100 and 0101 to binary. The idea here is that the BCD represents the decimal value 45 and the object of the effort is to get the binary number:

$$101101_2 = 45_{10}$$

as a result. The solution is:

label	inst.	operand	
	LDA	HIDIG	high order BCD digit to A
	LLA	1	multiply it by 2
	STA	SAVE	save this temporarily
	LLA	2	now multiply by 4. Since we multiplied by 2 before this is a total of 8.
	ADD	SAVE	form $8N + 2N$
	ADD	LODIG	now add the low order digit
	...		and we're finished.

It is *very, very* important that a programmer understand the principle behind this example. If it is the least bit hazy go back over it until you do. Skimping at this point will render incomprehensible significant points later in the text.

A modified type of logical shift is the rotary shift. In this type of shift the register shifted is "circular" and includes overflow so that we have an effective 17 bit register. Bits shifted out of one end of the register enter overflow and then reenter the other end of the register. The instructions are:

RRA - RRX These instructions rotate the A or X register right the number of bits specified in the operand. This rotation includes the overflow bit so that a 17 bit rotation must be performed to return to the original register contents. Like the straight logical shifts the largest number which can appear in the operand field is 8. To completely rotate the A register so that its original contents and that of the overflow are unchanged:

```
RRA   8
RRA   8
RRA   1
...
```

RLA - RLX The contents of A or X are rotated left the specified number of places including overflow. Except for the direction of rotation these instructions behave like RRA and RRX.

One of the more exotic applications of shift instructions is shown in example 6-2.

Example 6-2

Write a program to construct the mirror image of the contents of A in X, i.e., if A contains:

$$0000101100111010$$

at the end of the program X should read:

$$0101110011010000$$

i.e., the contents are simply reversed end for end. This problem is solved by putting together several things we have covered here and in the previous chapter. We will perform 16 separate shifts. Rather than write 16 sets of shift instructions we construct a loop using the IMS instruction, as shown in the previous chapter.

label	inst.	operand	
	LAM	16	loads −16 into A. (This is covered later in this chapter.)
	STA	COUNT	initialize the step count
	LDA	VICE	number to be "mirrored" into A
RSVP	LRA	1	shift bit from A to overflow
	RLX	1	rotate it into X
	IMS	COUNT	last step yet?
	JMP	RSVP	no, do it again
	STX	VERSA	
	...		

Bits are shifted out of the low end of the A register and into the overflow. These are then rotated into X in the opposite order. This process is repeated 16 times until the entire word has been reversed. The label RSVP has no significance.

In actual numerical manipulation the arithmetic shifts come into play. In these shifts the sign bit is treated as a special case in that it is *never* changed. Like the logical shifts, arithmetic shifts cause the contents of the registers to be moved left or right but with some important differences. In arithmetic left shifts bits leaving position 14 do *not* enter the sign bit but are lost. In right arithmetic shifts the sign does not participate in the shift. The bits actually shifted are 0-14. Instead of zeros entering the vacated positions, however, the sign bit is copied into these positions. For positive numbers this makes no difference, but the effect on negative numbers must be considered. If the number:

$$1000000000000000_2 = -32768_{10}$$

is arithmetic shifted one place to the right the result is:

$$1100000000000000_2 = -16384_{10}$$

Note that the sign bit has been copied into the vacated shift position. This has some other consequences which will emerge in a moment. Now take the positive number:

$$0000000000000011_2 = 3_{10}$$

and arithmetic right shift it one place to get

$$0000000000000001_2 = 1_{10}$$

This is the result of the natural "rounding down" caused by the truncation of the shifted number, i.e., the integer part of the quotient 3/2 is a 1. If we shift this right once again we get

$$0000000000000000_2 = 0_{10}$$

The number has become zero since we shifted all of the significant bits out and none entered from the left end. Now consider the number:

$$1111111111111101_2 = -3_{10}$$

Shifting this number right with the sign copied into the vacated positions we have:

$$1111111111111110_2 = -2_{10}$$

This time the rounding caused the absolute value of the result to be 2 instead of 1. Shifting once more we have:

$$1111111111111111_2 = -1_{10}$$

This could have been expected, but if we shift once again following the same rules of propagation of the sign bit we have:

$$1111111111111111_2 = -1_{10} \text{ again.}$$

We still have a minus one, and it is apparent that we can keep shifting indefinitely and still keep getting the same result, a minus one. This difference between the shift behavior of positive and negative numbers is a consequence of the nature of the two's complement arithmetic system and must be dealt with on any computer which uses this system. The result of an arithmetic right shift can be predicted by the following rule:

RULE 6-1. *Shifting a signed two's complement number one place to right results in its division by two with the result rounded to the next most negative integer.*

Thus $+3$ shifts to $+1$ and then to zero, but -3 shifts to -2, then to -1 and stays at -1 for all subsequent shifts.

Besides shifting and rotating a single register, there are instructions which shift and rotate both A and X registers together in such a way that they behave as if the high bit of X were connected to the low bit of A. Bits leaving the low end of A on a right shift enter the high bit of X, thus the two registers behave like one long register. On left shifts bits which leave the high end of X enter the low end of A. In either case bits shifted out of the end of the "long register" enter overflow and are then lost while the vacated positions are filled with zeros. The long shift instructions are thus logical shifts. They are LLR and LLL meaning *L*ong *L*ogical *R*ight and *L*ong *L*ogical *L*eft respectively. Unlike their single register counterparts these instructions may have shift counts up to 16. Thus the instruction:

LLL   16

moves the contents of X to A and clears the X register, while

LLR   16

moves the contents of A to X and clears A. These inter-register shifts are useful for many things. In the conversion of BCD to teletype code for example, it is necessary to merge the bits 1011 0000 with each BCD digit, i.e., a BCD nine must be processed as follows to get a bit configuration which will print a "9" on the teletype:

0000 1001	the BCD digit and four extra zeros
V 1011 0000	the teletype control bits
1011 1001	this group of bits prints a "9" on the teletype

Input from digital voltmeters and similar devices is in BCD. It is often desirable to print a DVM reading. A group of four BCD digits can be prepared for printing easily using the shift instructions as shown in example 6-3.

Example 6-3

Write a program to convert four BCD digits in the A register to four ASCII (teletype code) digits in A and X. If we represent the A and X registers as a series of BCD digits with D meaning digit, 0 meaning zero and − meaning irrelevant contents, at the beginning the registers look like this:

```
A          X
DDDD       − − − −
```

If the teletype control bits are represented by B, we want to transform the above to look like this:

```
A          X
BDBD       BDBD
```

each BD group being one teletype (ASCII) character. This can be done with a few shift instructions, as:

label	inst.	operand	A reg	X reg
	. . .		DDDD	− − − −
	LLR	4	0DDD	D− − −
	LRX	4	0DDD	0D− −
	LLR	8	000D	DD0D
	LLA	4	00D0	DD0D
	LLL	4	0D0D	D0D0
	LRX	4	0D0D	0D0D
	. . .			

The teletype control bits are merged by:

	EAX		0D0D	0D0D
	IOR	TBITS	BDBD	0D0D
	EAX		0D0D	BDBD
	IOR	TBITS	BDBD	BDBD
	. . .			

Where TBITS is defined as:

```
TBITS      DATA  :B0B0
           . . .
```

and a job that could have been very clumsy is reduced to only ten instructions! The swapping of the registers (EAX) is necessary because the merging of the control bits can take place only in the A register.

The long rotate instructions function in a manner analogous to their single register counterparts. In a long right rotate bits leaving the low end of the X register enter overflow and then reenter the high end of A. In a long left rotate bits leaving the high end of A enter overflow and then reenter the low end of X. In either case A, X, and overflow behave as if they formed a single 33 bit register. Long rotations left and right are accomplished by the instructions LRL and LRR respectively. The number in the operand field of these instructions is limited to 16.

Long shift and rotate instructions are all of the logical type. There are no long arithmetic shift instructions in the Alpha computers, and this forms one of the significant weaknesses of the machine. Many applications require that numbers greater than the capacity of a single word be manipulated. This requires a facility for performing what is called *multiple precision arithmetic*. Such arithmetic is materially aided by the presence of multi-register arithmetic shift instructions. The subject of multiple precision arithmetic will be covered in Chapter 10.

The final topic of this chapter is the subclass of immediate instructions. These instructions are similar to memory reference instructions in that they move data and perform comparisons with stored values, etc., but with the difference that their operands are not contained in memory words separate from the instructions. The operand of an immediate instruction is part of the instruction itself. One of these instructions, LAM, has already been used in a previous example. Each instruction word is divided into two parts, the upper eight bits being the instruction identifier and the lower eight bits the operand. Since the operand is only eight bits long it can contain no number bigger than $2^8 - 1$ or 255_{10}, but the great majority of constants used in a typical program are small numbers. If the immediate instructions are used for these constants rather than memory reference significant savings in memory consumption can be made.

Since the operand of an immediate instruction is eight bits, these instructions are ideal for handling coded alphabetic and other characters such as occur in teletype communications. This will be shown in examples that follow. The instructions are:

LAP - LXP   These mean *Load A Positive* immediate or *Load X Positive* immediate. The action of this instruction is to load the low eight bits of itself into the specified register. If the constant 47_{10} were required, it can be created in the A register *without* defining a memory location to hold it by:

LAP   47

as contrasted with the way this would be done using memory reference instructions:

```
          LDA    CONST
          . . .
CONST     DATA   47
```

Creation of characters for teletype communication is provided for by the assembly program. The character A is printed by sending the bit configuration:

$$11000001_2 = C1_{16}$$

to the teletype. The assembly program provides an easy means to generate this code in a register by:

```
          LAP    'A'
```

or

```
          LXP    'A'
```

The required constant or character is loaded into the low order (right hand) eight bits of the specified register. The upper half of the register is cleared to zeros.

The generation of negative constants is equally easy. Using the LAM or LXM instructions the specified register is first cleared and the eight bit operand of the immediate instruction is *subtracted* from the zeroed register. This in effect loads the negative of the number which appears in the operand. This was illustrated earlier in this chapter in the example in which the shift instructions were used to create the "mirror image" of a register. The instruction:

```
          LAM    16
```

was used to create the constant -16, which was then used to count the number of times the loop of shift instructions was to be executed. LXM performs the same function in the X register.

Before leaving the LAM and LXM instructions there is an assembler trick which should be discussed. Look at the following table:

			location
	ORG	:3F7	
START	DATA	6	:3F7
	DATA	-44	:3F8
	DATA	29	:3F9
	DATA	31	:3FA
	DATA	18	:3FB
END	DATA	80	:3FC

The ORG pseudo op tells the assembler to locate the string of numbers beginning with START at location :3F7 and up, the final number, 80, being in :3FC. To the assembly program the location symbol START has the value :3F7 and END has the value :3FC. The difference between the values of these two symbols is :3FC − :3F7. Since the first two digits are the same the difference is simply the difference between :C and 7, or $12_{10} - 7 = 5$. The assembly program is capable of evaluating the sums and difference of values of such symbols. The expression:

END-START

in an operand field has the value 5, while END-START+1 has the value 6.

If it were necessary to perform some operation on a table such as the one above, the loop count for the operation could be generated by:

LAM   END-START+1

or

LXM   END-START+1

This would cause the number −6 to be loaded into the specified register. If you are wondering why anybody would bother with such a roundabout route to get a constant, think about this. Suppose that you had written LAM −6 instead. If it were then necessary to change the number of items in the table the LAM −6 would have to be changed too. If the table count were referenced at several places in the program, they would all have to be changed. If one were missed the catastrophe which would result is obvious. If, however, you had used LAM END-START+1 the change would have been made *automatically* by the assembly program leaving no room for error. This illustrates something very important about good programming practice. The purpose of the assembly program is to *help*. Let *it* do all of the work that you can possibly arrange. Application programming is much too complex and detailed to allow your attention to be dissipated in clerical details that can be handled by the assembler. The above is only one of many instances in which clever use of the assembler can actually lock out a source of error.

The next group of immediate instructions allows small constants to be added to or subtracted from a register. They are:

AAI - AXI

and

SAI - SXI

AAI and AXI add the constant in the operand field to the contents of the specified register. The effect is the same as if the number had been added from a memory location by an ADD instruction, except that no memory location containing the constant is necessary. To add 107_{10} to the contents of the X register:

AXI   107

SAI and SXI subtract the number in the operand field from the contents of the specified register just like a SUB instruction. The only restraint on the use of these instructions is that the operand cannot be larger than eight bits. Note that overflow will be set if the result of any of these operations is greater than +32767 or less than −32768, just as with any other arithmetic operation.

The final group of immediate instructions allows an eight bit value in the low half of either register to be compared for equality with an eight bit value contained in the operand of the instruction. These instructions are:

CAI - CXI   These mean *C*ompare to *A* *I*mmediate and *C*ompare to *X* *I*mmediate. If the low eight bits of the register is identical to the operand of the instruction the next instruction is executed. If not the next instruction is skipped.

As with other immediate instructions the value of the operand may be a simple number or an alphabetic character code, i.e., a teletype character enclosed in apostrophes as shown before. This latter use provides a particularly powerful means of searching for specific characters, as shown in example 6-4.

Example 6-4

Write a program to search for the teletype characters A, P, or X. If any of the three is found jump to location BINGO. Begin with the character to be tested in the low eight bits of the A register, and:

label	inst.	operand	
	CAI	'A'	was it an A?
	JMP	BINGO	yes, jump
	CAI	'P'	no, try P
	JMP	BINGO	yes, jump
	CAI	'X'	no, try an X
	JMP	BINGO	found an X, jump
	...		

The action of the CAI instruction is to skip the next instruction if the number in the register is not equal to that in the operand. If they are equal the next instruction, in this case a JMP   BINGO, is taken.

Whole strings of characters can be searched for keywords or expressions in this way as is shown in example 6-5.

Example 6-5

Four teletype characters are contained in the locations ERSTE, ZWEITE, DRITTE, and VIERTE in the low eight bits of each word. The object of the program is to find out if these four characters spell the word FUZZ. If they do jump to location JEDGAR. If they do not jump to location QUIEN.

label	inst.	operand	
	LDA	ERSTE	first character in A
	CAI	'F'	was it an F?
	JMP	$+2	yes, go to next test
	JMP	QUIEN	no, forget the rest
	LDA	ZWEITE	second character to A
	CAI	'U'	was it a U?
	JMP	$+2	yes, try the next character for Z
	JMP	QUIEN	no, a ringer, forget it
	LDA	DRITTE	third character to A
	CAI	'Z'	was it a Z?
	JMP	$+2	yes, try the last one
	JMP	QUIEN	no, forget it
	LDA	VIERTE	fourth character to A
	CAI	'Z'	another Z?
	JMP	JEDGAR	yes, finally
	JMP	QUIEN	no, this is the end

The technique shown above could grow tiresome if one were testing for a key expression such as CHRONOSYNCLASTICINFINDIBULUM, but for short identifiers such as FUZZ it is acceptable.

This chapter and the preceeding one have discussed all classes of instructions except those dealing with the transfer of information between the computer and the external world—the input/output class instructions. These will be discussed at length in Chapters 20 and 21. For now enough groundwork has been laid to begin the discussion of the real subject of this book—minicomputer programming techniques and tricks.

7

Extended Addressing Modes—Indirect and Indexed Addressing

It was explained in Chapter 5 that an instruction can "reach" locations within 256 locations of where the instruction itself is located. While this is adequate for the bulk of work, situations do arise in which it is necessary to access locations not within these limits. To service this obvious need and some others which are not so obvious two additional addressing modes have been provided. These two modes, indirect and indexed, have much in common. They both provide means for accessing a full 32768 words rather than the small 512 word range to which reference is normally restricted. Both modes make use of a quantity called a "pointer" word. It is to the understanding of these pointers that our attention will be directed first.

Every reader has participated at some time or other in the child's game called "treasure hunt." In this game the participants are furnished with clues (addresses) as to the actual location of the "treasure." When the players find the location to which they were directed by the first clue, they find not the treasure but another clue. This chain of clues can continue to any length until the eventual treasure is reached. The extended addressing modes resemble this game very closely in concept. In extended addressing the operand of the instruction does not give the actual location of the data to be accessed, but the address of the word in which the real operand can be found. Like the game of treasure hunt the word which is retrieved in this way may or may not be the data itself but the location of another word. The address of the data item itself, reached at the end of an indefinite number of indirect addresses (i.e., the clues), is known as the *effective address*. In the initial discussion here we will confine ourselves to a single indirect level.

The pseudo operation DATA has already been discussed in connection with the creation of various constant values in example programs. In the previous chapter a table of values was created in memory by:

```
        ORG   :3F7
START   DATA  6
        DATA  −44
        DATA  29
        DATA  31
        DATA  18
END     DATA  80
```

As explained in the previous chapter the assembly program assigns

63

values to the labels START and END. The labels or location symbols have actual numerical values, :3F7 for START and :3FC for END. The instruction LDA START will result in the number 6 being loaded into A. Now we introduce another type of program constant, namely the address pointer, as shown by the statement:

POINTR   DATA START

The DATA word which we have defined, namely POINTR, will contain the number :3F7, i.e., *the address of the symbol whose name appears in its operand field*.

To make use of this pointer word to load the A register the LDA instruction must specify *indirect addressing*, like this:

LDA   *POINTR

The asterisk which precedes the operand field of the LDA specifies that POINTR is *not* the effective address, but the location of the effective address. Executing the instruction above is functionally the same as the LDA START instruction. The pointer itself must be located within 256 locations of the LDA instruction, but the table of values START through END can be anywhere in memory.

Since the address pointer is simply a number in memory it can be manipulated exactly as though it were a piece of data. To find the sum of the numbers in location START and the one after it (the −44) we can execute:

LDA	*POINTR	load the first value (the 6)
IMS	POINTR	increment the address pointer
ADD	*POINTR	and add the second number
...		

In this case we incremented the address pointer from :3F7 to :3F8. This incrementation makes POINTR point to the number after START, i.e., the −44. This technique can be used very effectively to access entire lists of numbers, as in example 7-1.

Example 7-1

Write a program to find the sum of the six numbers contained in the table which begins at location START. Use the method of indirect addressing. We begin by forming a count word as shown in the last chapter, i.e.:

label	*inst.*	*operand*	
	LAM	END−START+1	negative of list length in A
	STA	COUNT	store in temporary count

```
            ZAR                     zero to receive sum
ADDER       ADD    *POINTR          add item from table
            IMS    POINTR           increment  the  address
                                    pointer
            IMS    COUNT            finished?
            JMP    ADDER            no, do it again
            . . .                   finished
```

Before leaving example 7-1 it should be noted that the number in POINTR is :3FD when the program is finished. It cannot be used again to access the same table. For this reason it is the usual practice to copy the pointer into another temporary cell, then do the addressing and incrementing using this temporary cell. This way the original pointer is undisturbed and can be used to reload the temporary address cell each time it is required.

It is possible to have more than one level of indirect addressing, just like the multilevel clues in the treasure hunt game. This works very well in the game but it is a mixed blessing in the computer. It will be shown here for the record (see example 7-2), but the novice programmer would be very well advised to stay away from multilevel indirect addressing until he is very, very sure of himself. It is almost never a productive practice.

Example 7-2

Construct a double indirect addressing scheme with the two address pointers, TINKER and EVERS leading to the data item stored in CHANCE. The contents of CHANCE are to be loaded into A. First the address pointers:

```
label        inst.   operand

TINKER       DATA    *EVERS
EVERS        DATA    CHANCE
CHANCE       DATA    50
             . . .
```

Note that the first address pointer TINKER has an asterisk in its operand field. This indicates that it does not point directly to the data to be fetched but to another address pointer, EVERS. Since EVERS has no asterisk in its operand field it is the last indirect level. It points directly to the data to be fetched, CHANCE. EVERS, therefore, contains the effective address. This Rube Goldbergish construction is used by:

```
LDA    *TINKER
. . .
```

> The computer fetches the contents of TINKER and seeing that it is
> also an indirect address goes one step further to fetch the contents
> of EVERS. As EVERS is not indirectly addressed the last fetch is
> made from CHANCE, and the A register is finally loaded with its
> contents, namely a 50. The operation thus proceeds, in a manner of
> speaking, from TINKER to EVERS, leaving nothing to CHANCE.

Multilevel indirect addressing is a prime source of disaster for the inexperienced. Stay away from it.

Another extremely useful addressing mode is the indexed mode. Like indirect addressing indexed addressing makes use of a pointer, but the pointer is held not in memory but in the X register. To go back to the earlier example in this chapter dealing with a pointer which held the address of a table of numbers, we can load the same address pointer into X by:

LDX   POINTR

Indexed addressing is specified by the presence of the "at" sign, @, in front of the operand. The contents of START can be loaded into A by loading POINTR into X as shown above and then:

LDA   @0
...

This does *exactly* the same thing as the earlier indirectly addressed example. There is only one X register, of course, while indirect address pointers can be set up in any number of memory cells, but indexed addressing has one extra and very important capability. The reader will recall the example given of the addition of the first two numbers in the table using indirect addressing in which the first number was accessed, the pointer incremented, and then the second number accessed. The use of indexed addressing eliminates the necessity of incrementing the pointer. As noted above the presence of the "at" sign in the operand stipulates indexed addressing, but the zero has a meaning too. The zero specifies the low eight bits of the LDA instruction, the so-called displacement field. When indexed addressing is used the displacement portion of the instruction is added to the contents of the X register to form the effective address of the instruction. Just as LDA @0 results in the loading of the contents of START when X contains POINTR, ADD @1 will access the contents of the location which follows START, the one containing the −44. The use of the X register for this function, that of an indexed pointer, results in its being called the *index register*.

It is possible to use indexed addressing for the same kinds of things for which indirect addressing is used. This has a substantial speed advantage which will be discussed below. First, let us reprogram the earlier example in which the sum of the table of numbers was found, as follows:

```
        LAM    END-START+1    same as before
        STA    COUNT          likewise
        ZAR                   likewise
        LDX    POINTR         address pointer to X
ADDER   ADD    @0             add table item
        IXR                   increment address pointer
        IMS    CNT            bump the count, last one?
        JMP    ADDER          no, do it again
        . . .
```

This program takes one more instruction than the previous example but it does not destroy the address pointer. Had the indirect address example saved a copy of the address pointer, which it must if the program is to be used more than once, it would have been one instruction longer. As it is the indexed example will run in about 25 percent less time than the indirect addressing example. Timing of computer instructions has not been discussed so far so we will take a short detour into the subject now.

Memory reference instructions require two computer cycle times for their execution, the first to fetch the instruction itself and decode it, and the second to fetch the operand. If another fetch is required, as it is for an indirect address, then a third cycle is necessary. One cycle is added for each indirect level. In indexed addressing there is no time penalty for use of the index register so that while LDA *POINTR requires 3 cycles, LDA @0 requires only 2. JMP and conditional jump instructions require only one cycle as they do not fetch operands from memory, only the instruction. Register change instructions (except shift) require only one cycle.

Both indirect and indexed addressing can be used with any memory reference instruction except a conditional jump. One such instruction not yet discussed requires that both be used. This is the Scan Memory instruction which will be covered in a later chapter.

A trick which is occasionally useful is the ability to replace an index register address with the contents of that address. Suppose for example that we required the fourth item in the DATA table previously discussed, but in X rather than A. There are several ways to do this. The most obvious would be to add 3 to the address pointer since the fourth item occupies START+3, and use the result as an indirect address, as:

```
label   inst.   operand
        LDA     POINTR     address pointer to A
        ADD     TROIS      add three to it
        STA     PTR        save in temporary cell
        LDX     *PTR       and load X indirect
        . . .
PTR     DATA    0
```

```
TROIS       DATA  3
```

This will work of course, but it requires 6 locations including the constant
TROIS and the temporary address pointer PTR. It can be improved a little
by using an immediate instruction to add the constant, as:

```
            LDA   POINTR
            AAI   3
            STA   PTR
            LDX   *PTR
            . . .
PTR         DATA  0
```

This requires only 5 locations since we got rid of TROIS. Better, but still not
good enough. Try the indexed approach.

```
            LDX   POINTR
            AXI   3
            LDX   @0
```

In this case we have computed an address in X and then replaced the
address with the contents of the cell whose address we computed, in only 3
instructions. It is possible to accomplish the above task in only *2* instructions. This will be left to the reader to puzzle out.

A very useful addressing mode results from the simultaneous use of
both indirect and indexed addressing. When this combination is specified
even greater economies can be made in a variety of situations. This is how it
works. A pointer word is located somewhere in the first 256 memory
locations, the so-called scratchpad. The displacement portion of the memory reference instruction is used as an absolute address to locate this
pointer. The pointer is fetched and the contents of the index register are
added to it to form an effective address. The contents of *this* effective
address are fetched for the operand of the instruction. This will be illustrated repeatedly in the coming chapters, but for a starter reconsider the
example above. If the address pointer POINTR were located in the scratchpad portion of memory, the instruction sequence:

```
            LXP   3              set X to + 3
            LDA   @*POINTR       fetch the number
```

The presence of both the asterisk and the "at" sign signifies the compound
addressing mode, both indexed and indirect. The problem of the addition of
the table of numbers becomes shorter as well. If we redefine POINTR in the
scratchpad so that it points to the location before START, i.e.:

```
POINTR      DATA  START-1
```

then the addition problem reduces to:

```
ZAR                    zero A to receive sum
LXP    END-START+1     number of items in table
ADD    @*POINTR        add the item
DXR                    and decrement X
JXN    $-2             and jump back if X nonzero

  . . .
```

This does the same job as the indexed and indirect examples did separately. It works like this. The X register is used to hold not only the table increment but to count the number of items added. The add loop is finished when the index register is zero. This example will run in half the time of the indirect example and in only 5 locations instead of the 10 required previously. If this is not entirely clear at this point, it should be no cause for severe concern as the technique will be illustrated many times in the pages to come.

There is an old story about a visitor in New York who had become lost despite his tour guide supplied maps. As the tale goes, he stopped one of the local population to get information about the location of his next sightseeing target with the words, ''Excuse me, sir, can you tell me how to get to Carnegie Hall?''. The native, hurrying on, called back over his shoulder, ''Practice, my boy, practice!'' Good programmers, like good fiddle players, physicians, and engineers are produced by experience, not born talent. Though the content of this chapter may seem strange and difficult it will become familiar and easy with experience. It is only the experience that makes the difference between the expert and the novice.

8

Programs and Subprograms

The block of instructions shown below is due to Mr. Tom Woods of Houston. It takes the square root of the number left in the A register.

LXP	1	a one in X
STX	C	save it
SUB	C	subtract the odd number
JAM	$+3	result negative yet?
AXI	2	no, form the next odd number
JMP	$-4	and try again
TXA		move it over
ARA	1	and divide by two
	...	
C	DATA 0	

The functioning of this remarkably brief program is based upon the fact that the integer square root of a number is equal to the number of odd integers which can be subtracted from it before the result goes negative. Thus the integer square root of 16 can be computed by subtracting 1, 3, 5, and 7 from it. When we try to subtract 9, the next odd number, the result is negative. It may be interesting to the reader to follow through the program to see just how it works. The method is not a preferred one for taking the square roots of large integers, but it does work for all positive values and illustrates several things which will be of interest to us in this chapter. If the reader does decide to analyze the above program in detail, it will become apparent that methods such as these are better suited to multi-accumulator machines like the Nova or SPC-16.

The most important thing about the program shown is that it typifies a class of operations which is likely to be performed in many places in an application program. If square roots are required at eight different places in a program, the simplest solution would be to write the above instruction sequence in each place that a square root was required. This would serve the purpose and is indeed sometimes done in situations in which maximum speed is of the essence. It is a very wasteful practice though, and a better solution would be to find some way in which instructions for square root could be written once and for all, this same block of instructions being used by all sections of the program which required them.

There is certainly no problem in loading a number into the A register and jumping to a sequence of instructions which extracts the square root. Jumps are indirectly addressable like other memory reference instructions, and the same sequence could be reached from anywhere in memory. We have the same problem as that of Hansel and Gretl, namely how to get back. What we need here is a kind of jump instruction that would remember where it came from and allow control to be returned to that point after the square root had been extracted. The instruction which does this is the JST or *Jump and STore* instruction. To understand how it works, let us return to an earlier discussion in which the program counter was the subject. Recall that rather heavy emphasis was made at that time of the fact that the program counter always points to the *next* instruction to be executed, not the one currently being executed. This is true no matter what instruction is in progress, including JST. JST like JMP changes the program counter, but during the time it is being executed the program counter still points to the instruction after the JST, and the store part of jump and store refers to the program counter. It works like this. When JST is executed the program counter, i.e., the location of the instruction which follows the JST, is stored in the location indicated by the effective address of the JST. This effective address *plus one* is loaded into the program counter so that the first instruction executed after the JST is located one beyond the effective address of the JST. The location represented by the effective address of the JST has the old program counter stored in it to be used as a return pointer. Now when the square root routine is finished it can return control, with the answer in a register, to the program section which ''called'' it by executing an indirectly addressed JMP *through* the location in which the old program counter is stored. Programs written to function in this way are called *subroutines* or *subprograms*.

The square root program is written as a subroutine, in example 8-1.

Example 8-1

Write a subroutine to extract square roots by the method previously shown. This subroutine should be written in such a way that other programs have a square root ''service'' available to them by executing the sequence:

label	inst.	operand	
	LDA	NUMBER	number whose square root is to be taken
	JST	SQRT	jump to square root routine
	STA	ROOT	save the result
	. . .		

The subroutine SQRT is written:

```
SQRT      DATA   0        storage for old program
                          counter
          LXP    1
          STX    C
          SUB    C
          JAM    $+3
          AXI    2
          JMP    $−4
          TXA
          ARA    1        answer in A register
          JMP    *SQRT    return to "calling" program
C         DATA   0        temporary working storage
```

The location whose label is SQRT is known as the *entry point* of the subroutine, and the subroutine is usually referred to by the label at this entry point, called the *entry point name*. The input number, in this case the number whose square root is needed, is called the *argument,* and the output number, in this case the square root, is called the *function.*

Before leaving this example one more problem must be dealt with, that of the "illegal" argument, here meaning a number whose square root cannot be extracted, i.e., a negative number. It is the responsibility of the subroutine to see that it does not attempt to do the impossible or nonsensical, and some check must be made on arguments to see that this does not happen. The calling program should also be warned that this condition has arisen. One way to do this is to turn the overflow bit on if the argument was illegal and off if it was legal. The overflow control instructions can be used to do this directly, as shown in example 8-2.

Example 8-2

Write a square root subroutine using the previously discussed mathematical method which returns to the calling program with overflow on and A undisturbed if the argument was negative.

```
label     inst.  operand

SQRT      NOP             the entry point
          ROV             overflow off
          JAM    TILT     illegal argument if negative
          LXP    1
          STX    C
          SUB    C
          JAM    $+3
```

```
              AXI   2
              JMP   $-4
              TXA
              LRA   1
   TILT       COV
              JMP   *SQRT
   C          DATA  0
```

Some of this example may seem a little obscure, so a little explanation will be given. The overflow bit is turned off immediately upon entry, (ROV). If the A register is negative a jump occurs to TILT which complements it, (COV), turning it on, and control is then returned to the calling program. If the argument is legal, (positive), the square root is extracted as before. If the reader has not figured it out up until now, when the A register goes negative as the result of the subtraction, the X register contains the *next* odd number beyond the one which was successfully subtracted. If this number is divided by two, i.e., shifted one place right, the result will be the number of odd numbers which occurred before the unsuccessful subtraction. Note that the ARA of the previous exercise has been replaced with an LRA here. Since an odd number always has a one in its low bit a one place logical shift will move this bit into overflow, turning overflow on. Since the square root is positive by definition ARA and LRA do the same thing in this instance, except that an LRA turns overflow on. As the instruction following the shift complements overflow, the result is that overflow is turned off just before the JMP back to the calling program is executed, which fulfills the conditions of the problem.

If the reader has become a little exasperated with this exercise, he may be asking what purpose is served by all this hassle to control the overflow bit in this way. The answer is that it results in a shorter program, one that uses less of the most expensive single computer component—memory. The example could very well been written in such a way as to cause a jump to a special program subsection when an illegal argument was encountered, with this special subsection turning overflow on and returning. If you write this out you will find that the result is only one instruction longer, so you may argue that it wasn't worth the trouble. In a routine which is only 14 words long, one extra instruction increases memory consumption by 7 percent. If the practice were propagated through a long program it could well mean the difference which would force the purchase of another memory module. In 4096 word modules, using the 4097th location is somewhat related in principle to the old story about the girl who was pregnant, only slightly so, but still pregnant. The moral of the story is clear. S-Q-U-E-E-Z-E the computer for everything you can wring out of it. It pays.

In the last example we took up the question of the subroutine's indication to the calling program that an argument is not in the operable range, in that case a negative number. Now we will consider another case of a subroutine whose sole purpose is to check argument range, returning control to one location if the argument was valid and to another if it was not. Such procedures are known by the name of *validity checks*. A common kind of validity check is associated with strings of characters typed by an operator. All operator input should be numeric in our example, but since there may be errors made in typing the validity check is necessary. Teletype code, called ASCII code, is composed of eight bit characters with fixed bit configurations corresponding to specific keys or letters. Striking the 1 (one) key in the top row of teletype keys for example, produces the code:

$$10110001_2 = B1_{16}$$

The codes for the numeric characters zero through nine are the sequential binary numbers 10110000 through 10111001 inclusive. Checking for numeric validity therefore amounts only to seeing that the character in question falls within these limits, B0 − B9 in hexadecimal. Recalling the use of the CMS instruction to check whether a number falls within a set of limits, we define the limits as:

label	inst.	operand
ZILCH	DATA	:B0
NINER	DATA	:B9

and the validity check itself goes:

```
          CMS    NINER        compare to high limit
          CMS    ZILCH        compare to low limit
          ...                 next inst. from here if not within
                              limits
          ...                 and from here ...
          ...                 or here if within limits
```

What is required here is a routine which can be used by a sequence such as:

```
          LDA    CHR          character in A
          JST    VCHECK       go to check validity of character
          JMP    RINGER       return here if not numeric
          ...                 and here if it is numeric
```

RINGER is a location which contains a program equipped to tell the typist that an error has been made. The problem is how to cause a skip of the JMP RINGER instruction if the argument is valid. This is shown in example 8-3.

Example 8-3

Write a subroutine to check the validity of incoming characters. Characters which are numeric should cause a return to the location 2 instructions beyond the calling JST. Nonnumeric characters should cause a return to the instruction immediately following the JST. Using the limits defined before:

label	inst.	operand	
VCHECK	DATA	0	entry point
	CMS	NINER	compare to high limit
	CMS	ZILCH	compare to low limit
	JMP	*VCHECK	a bummer, return immediately
	NOP		spacer instruction
	IMS	VCHECK	increment return address
	JMP	*VCHECK	and return

The address pointer stored in VCHECK is the old program counter. If undisturbed a jump through this pointer will land at the JMP   RINGER instruction back in the calling program. If VCHECK is incremented it points to the location following the JMP   RINGER.

This method of conditionally incrementing the return address is useful for routines which perform classification of data, as shown in example 8-4.

Example 8-4

Write a subroutine which will classify a number left in A upon entry. The routine is to be used by:

label	inst.	operand	
	LDA	NUMBER	number to be classified in A
	JST	SIFT	jump to classification routine
	JMP	MINUS	return here if zero or negative
	JMP	SMALL	return here if positive and less than or equal to 100
	. . .		return here if greater than 100

The subroutine, named SIFT, effects the different return points by selectively incrementing the return address stored in its entry point. It goes:

SIFT	DATA	0	entry point
	JAL	RETURN	zero or minus, return immediately

```
            IMS    SIFT       increment return pointer
            CMS    HUNDRD     less than or equal to 100?
            JMP    $+2        yes, skip the incrementation
            IMS    SIFT       increment return pointer again
   RETURN   JMP    *SIFT      and return
            ...
   HUNDRD   DATA   100
            ...
```

Another subroutine situation arises when the task to be performed requires more data than can be transmitted in the registers. In this case the usual practice is that the JST which calls the subroutine is followed immediately by a series of words containing the addresses of the arguments for the subroutine. *NOTE*, the JST is followed by the addresses of the arguments, *not* the arguments themselves. In a subroutine which has 3 arguments named TOM, DICK, and HARRY the call goes like this:

```
        JST    FIZZ       FIZZ is the subroutine name
        DATA   TOM
        DATA   DICK
        DATA   HARRY
        ...
```

The arguments themselves are defined elsewhere, e.g.:

```
   TOM        DATA 70
   DICK       DATA :50
   HARRY      DATA −28
```

The handling of the arguments on the subroutine end is shown in example 8-5.

Example 8-5

Write a subroutine to find the sum of three numbers. The subroutine is to be used as described above, i.e., if the three numbers to be added are named REPUBS, DEMS, and NAUSEA, the calling program contains the sequence:

```
        JST    SUM        the subroutine name
        DATA   REPUBS     location of REPUBS
        DATA   DEMS       location of DEMS
        DATA   NAUSEA     location of NAUSEA
        ...
```

The subroutine itself can be handled in a number of ways. The most obvious one is:

SUM	NOP		entry point
	LDA	*SUM	address of first argument
	STA	ADR1	save it
	IMS	SUM	bump the pointer
	LDA	*SUM	address of second argument
	STA	ADR2	save it too
	IMS	SUM	bump the pointer
	LDA	*SUM	address of third argument
	STA	ADR3	and save it
	IMS	SUM	bump the pointer for the return
	LDA	*ADR1	load the first number
	ADD	*ADR2	add the second
	ADD	*ADR3	and the third too
	JMP	*SUM	and return with the answer, finally
ADR1	NOP		
ADR2	NOP		temporary address pointer cells
ADR3	NOP		

If this approach seems clumsy, it is. The problem here is that we are dealing with a pointer which contains the address of another pointer. This would be a legitimate place to attempt double level indirect addressing, but since we have already ruled this out, let us try another tack. The "overhead" associated with the above routine is mostly in the creation of the three address pointers ADR1, ADR2, and ADR3. This step can be eliminated by using the index register to hold the address pointer. We can load it with the address of the argument just as A was loaded before, as:

SUM	NOP		entry point
	LDX	*SUM	address of first argument to X
	LDA	@0	load the first argument immediately
	IMS	SUM	bump the pointer
	LDX	*SUM	address of second argument to X
	ADD	@0	add the second number
	IMS	SUM	bump the pointer again
	LDX	*SUM	address of last argument to X
	ADD	@0	add the last number
	IMS	SUM	bump pointer for return

```
    JMP   *SUM        and return . . .
    . . .
```

This second solution to the problem is not only shorter—eleven locations instead of seventeen—but faster—23 cycles instead of 32. This is a significant saving both ways.

Perhaps the most useful form of subroutine is what is called the *external* subroutine. It is written and assembled separately from the actual application program. The user of this routine may or may not know how it works, the only important thing is that he know how to use it. The details of how such an external subroutine is integrated into the user's program are best left to manuals on the subject. In general, all the user needs to know are the name of the entry point of the subroutine and the rules for using it. References to such routines are made by indirect JST's through locations in the user's program which are filled in by the loader program which loads the various segments of the total program just prior to execution. This type of loader program is called a *linking loader* because it is capable of filling in addresses of subroutines and other program segments as they are loaded into the computer. The writing of subroutines for use with a linking loader requires that entry points be specified as externally addressable, for example the entry point name SQRT in the first exercise in this chapter. Another program can use SQRT by specifying that the name SQRT is external to itself. The details of this process are peculiar to each machine, and the subject will be left here.

In all but the most primitive programming situations the loader program also provides the facility for *relocation* of loaded programs. This means that a series of programs can be loaded one after the other with the load program making the necessary adjustments to the program to allow it to operate correctly in the section of memory into which it has been loaded. The usual practice is to load successive program segments into successively higher memory addresses. Most often the two features are combined to form a *relocating linking loader*.

9

Fixed Point Arithmetic—Integer and Fraction

Up to this point we have dealt with all binary numbers as though they were entirely integers or whole numbers. It is very often necessary to work with numbers which represent fractions or mixtures of integer and fraction. It is to the treatment of these situations that this chapter is devoted.

Users of FORTRAN, particularly some of the older versions, have come to regard the term fixed point as being synonymous with integer. This came about because early compilers were unable to generate code to handle fixed point arithmetic for anything except integers, and conversion routines supplied with the compilers universally converted fixed point numbers as pure integer. Broadly speaking though, the term fixed point means any arithmetic situation in which the radix or binary point is not variable. If the binary point is at the right hand end of the word this does mean integer but it need not be so and the assembly level programmer has the freedom of specifying the binary point at any position in the word which is convenient to the solution of the problem at hand. Suppose for example that we were to agree that the binary point is to be fixed in the middle of the computer word, like this:

$$BBBBBBBB.BBBBBBBB$$

where the B's stand for bits. In this representation a measurement of length such as 3 1/4 inches would be represented as:

$$00000011.01000000$$

The integer part to the left of the binary point is interpreted as always, a three. To the right of the binary point the positions represent the negative powers of two. The first few of these are:

$$2^{-1} = 1/2$$
$$2^{-2} = 1/4$$
$$2^{-3} = 1/8$$
$$2^{-4} = 1/16$$
$$2^{-5} = 1/32$$

and so forth. The fraction is made up of a sum of those negative powers represented by ones. The fraction portion of the above number .01000000 has a bit only in the 2^{-2} position, meaning that its total value is 1/4. The value of the entire number is that of the integer plus that of the fraction, or 3

+ 1/4. Using this same notation the measurement 6 5/8 inches would be represented:

$$00000110.10100000$$

Again the integer part is no problem, a four plus a two, totaling six. The fraction part has ones in the 1/2's and 1/8's positions. Its value is therefore 1/2 + 1/8 or 5/8.

The two numbers shown above can be added or subtracted just like any other pair of binary numbers, i.e.:

$$
\begin{array}{r}
00000011.01000000 \\
+00000110.10100000 \\
\hline
00001001.11100000
\end{array}
$$

The integer part of this sum has ones in the eights position and the ones positions, so its value is 8 + 1 or 9. The fraction portion has ones in the 1/2's, 1/4's, and 1/8's positions so its value is 1/2 + 1/4 + 1/8 = 7/8. The complete value of the number, integer plus fraction is therefore 9 7/8. This is the same answer we get by adding the decimal numbers 3 1/4 and 6 5/8.

In performing operations on numbers represented in this way account must be kept of the location of the binary point in each of the different numbers used in the operation. To add or subtract the binary points of both numbers must be in the same position in the word. If they are not one number or the other must be shifted until the points do agree. The result of this will be a sum or difference whose binary point agrees with the number which was not shifted. The position of the binary point in the word is specified by the number of fractions bits allowed for. This number, the number of bit positions to the right of the binary point, is called the *scale factor*. The numbers in the example above have a scale factor of 8. In assembly programs which have the facility for dealing with scale factors means are provided for specification of a scale factor with the number. The above numbers would be programmed by expressions such as:

DATA   3.25B8

and

DATA   6.625B8

Regrettably the assemblers provided with our example machines have no such facility, an unfortunate weakness in software design. For clarity we will use the above notation but the reader should understand that the programmer is responsible for the creation of fixed point constants with scale factors other than zero (integers). This is not difficult but something of a nuisance. The 3.25B8 above is generated by multiplying the number 3.25

by the appropriate power of two, in this case 2^8 or 256. 3.25 times a 256 is 832, so the data statement would read:

DATA 832

This will generate the binary quantity:

0000001101000000

which is the required number.

The operation of adding or subtracting numbers with different scale factors was mentioned above. It is illustrated in example 9-1.

Example 9-1

Write a program section to find the sum of the two numbers:

label	inst.	operand	
EINS	DATA	324	scale factor zero
ZWEI	DATA	1.75B4	scale factor 4
...			

leaving the result in location DREI with a scale factor of 3.

	LDA	EINS	integer to A
	ALA	4	shift for scale factor of 4
	ADD	ZWEI	the second number can be added directly because both numbers now have identical scale factors. The sum has a scale factor of 4. To get scale factor 3 we shift one place . . .
	ARA	1	
	STA	DREI	and store the answer properly scaled.

Care must be used in the selection of scale factors as a situation can arise in which attempts to shift one number left to make its scale factor agree with that of another can cause the most significant bits to be shifted out of the register. Consider the case of the two numbers:

DATA 16385B0   an integer

and

DATA 1.5B1   mixed, with one fraction bit

Attempting to shift the first number left one bit before adding or subtracting would cause the high bit to be lost. Its value would become 1B1 instead of 16385B1, a catastrophe. The other possible solution would be to shift the 1.5B1 right one bit to make its scale factor agree with that of the 16385B1. If this were done the fractional part, .5, would be lost. This involves only a precision loss instead of a disaster so it is the preferable solution. The use of this type of arithmetic involves detailed knowledge of the possible sizes of all of the numbers involved at every step of the process including inter-mediate results. Nevertheless, if the problem can be solved this way it will yield large benefits in both speed and space.

The alternate routes to be taken if the single word fixed point approach is not feasible are to use more than one computer word for each number or to employ an arithmetic scheme in which the differences of scale factors are accounted for automatically. The use of more than one word to represent a number is called *multiple precision*. Arithmetic schemes which keep au-tomatic track of scale factors are called *floating point*. Both of these are discussed in later chapters of this book.

The mechanics of multiplication and division will be covered in the next chapter. The results fall into the topic of fixed point arithmetic and will be treated here. Computer hardware multiplication and division treat their operands as if they were integers, as do software routines which simulate the hardware function. Operation on mixed numbers requires that the scale factors of those numbers be taken into account.

In general, the multiplication of a number N bits long by a number M bits long results in a product $N + M$ bits long. For numbers which are 15 bits in magnitude like those in our example computer this means a product of 15 + 15 = 30 bits, requiring two computer words. As this topic has not yet been covered, the examples shown here will be confined to those in which the results can be held in a single computer word. Consider the two numbers:

$$\text{DATA} \quad 3.5\text{B}2$$

and

$$\text{DATA} \quad 6.75\text{B}2$$

These generate the following binary configurations:

$$0000000000001110_2 = 3.5\text{B}2$$

and

$$0000000000011011_2 = 6.75\text{B}2$$

If the above binary quantities were viewed as integers their values would be

14_{10} and 27_{10}. Hardware multiplication treats them as if they were in fact integers. The product of the above two numbers is:

$$0000000101111010_2 = 378_{10}$$

viewed as an integer. Another way to look at such products is as the result of multiplying:

$$3.5 \times 2^2 \times 6.75 \times 2^2$$

If this multiplication is done on paper the result is 23.625×2^4. The product has a scale factor equal to the sum of the scale factors of the multiplier and multiplicand. If we reinterpret the integer product in light of this we can make some sense of it. Rewriting:

$$000000010111.1010_2$$

the integer part of this has value 23, $16 + 4 + 2 + 1$, while the fraction value is $1/2 + 1/8$ or $5/8$. To restore the product to the same format as that of the factors used to generate it, it must be rescaled, in this case by shifting it right two bits. This yields:

$$00000000010111.10_2 = 23.50_{10}$$

But notice that something else has happened here. A significant bit has been lost in the shift and the result is 23.5 instead of 23.625. Since we insisted on a scale factor of two for the product we have no 1/8's bit and the result is truncated to the next lowest quarter. Such a loss of precision might or might not be significant but the programmer must be aware of it. Significance loss in a series of operations is cumulative and can cause a serious "erosion" of the final results. The effect can be reduced by rounding results, but it can not be eliminated entirely. Rounding is easy on a binary machine since each bit has just half the value of the one immediately to its left. The easiest way to do it is to add one to the last bit which will be shifted out when rescaling, or subtract one if the number is negative. This can be done for the above example by:

```
ARA    1          execute first shift
JAM    $+3        was the number negative?
IAR               no, increment it
JMP    $+2        and skip
DAR               yes, decrement it
ARA    1          and perform the final shift
```

Scaling in division is equally simple. Here again we will confine examples to those situations in which no operand exceeds one word in length. If a dividend S with scale factor N is divided by a divisor T with scale factor M the result is a quotient whose scale factor is $N - M$, i.e.:

$$\frac{S \times 2^N}{T \times 2^M} = Q \times 2^{(N-M)}$$

Consider for example the division of 35B8 by 8B4. These numbers in binary are:

$$00100011.00000000_2 = 35B8$$

and

$$000000001000.0000_2 = 8B4$$

Viewed as integers these numbers are 8960 and 128 respectively and 8960/128 results in an integer quotient of 70_{10}, or in binary:

$$0000000001000110_2$$

Following the rule given above, the scale factor of this quotient is equal to the difference of the scale factors of the dividend and divisor, i.e., $8 - 4 = 4$. Rewriting the result with a binary point:

$$000000000100.0110_2$$

The integer portion is a 4 and the fraction is $1/4 + 1/8 = 3/8$ or .375. The total value is therefore 4.375 which is the correct quotient.

Before going to the next topic the representation of binary fractions requires some special attention. The reader is familiar with the fact that certain fractions can not be written as decimals in a finite number of digits. Every schoolboy has tried to find the decimal value of 1/3 only to discover that the division never ends, i.e.:

$$1/3 = .333333333333 \ . \ . \ .$$

There are many other numbers that share this characteristic, 1/7 for instance. If 1/3 were divided out in a number system whose base was 3 it would be exactly representable as .1. Similarly in base 7 the fraction 1/7 would be exactly representable. The point of this is that certain common decimal fractions such as 1/10 and 1/100 cannot be represented exactly in binary. The value of 1/10 in binary is:

$$.00011001100110011001100110011001100_2 \ . \ . \ .$$

a repeating string of ones and zeros. This fact may make division by ten or its powers somewhat awkward, but it has been responsible for some very clever innovations in fixed point arithmetic. The above fraction can be considered to be the sum of a series of the powers of two represented by the ones bits, i.e.:

$$1/16 + 1/32 + 1/256 + 1/512 + 1/4096 + 1/8192 \text{ etc.}$$

For any binary number N it follows that:

$$N/10 = N/16 + N/32 + N/256 + N/512$$

and so forth. Since the denominators are all powers of two, each of the individual divisions indicated can be accomplished by shifting, and that is the key to a series of special divide methods.

If a number is to be divided by ten it can be shifted to accomplish the divides shown, and the individual results can be totalled to get the result of division by ten. Consider the binary number:

$$0000010000000000_2 = 1024_{10}$$

Calling this number N we perform the indicated shifts:

$$N/16 = 0000000001000000$$

$$N/32 = 0000000000100000$$

$$N/256 = 0000000000000100$$

$$N/512 = 0000000000000010$$

Since the next set of shifts would result in a zero we stop here. Adding the above numbers we get:

$$0000000001100110_2 = 102_{10}$$

which is the integer portion of the quotient that would be the result of the division of 1024 by 10.

The series shown above can be written in another form, namely:

$$N/10 = N/8 - N/32 + N/128 - N/512 \ldots$$

with the signs of each term alternating between $+$ and $-$ and the denominators alternate powers of two.

$$N/10 = \frac{N - N/4 + N/16 - N/64 + N/256 - N/1024 \ldots}{8}$$

This last expression is just the one above it with 1/8 factored out of it. This leads to a very interesting way of dividing by ten, as shown in example 9-2.

Example 9-2

Write a subroutine to divide the contents of the A register by ten and return with the integer quotient in the A register.

label	inst.	operand	
DBYTEN	DATA	0	entry point

```
              LXM   5          set up loop count
              STX   CNT        save it
              TAX              and move to X
LOOP          ARX   2          shift for next power of two
              NXR              adjust sign of this term
              STX   T          store it for the addition
              ADD   T          form partial series sum
              IMS   CNT        last iteration?
              JMP   LOOP       no, form the next term
              ARA   3          divide by eight
              JMP   *DBYTEN    and return
CNT           DATA  0
T             DATA  0
              . . .
```

The original number is kept in A to use as the first term and transferred to X. On each iteration X is first shifted right to form the magnitude of the next term and then negated, since alternate terms have alternate signs. This method is good to about 1/5 of 1%, and the precision can be increased by simply increasing the loop count. Increasing it to more than eight will serve no purpose since the number thereafter will have been shifted entirely out of the X register, and the process can only add zeros to the sum in A.

The above method is superfluous on our example machine since it has multiply/divide hardware, but on machines which have no such hardware it can be important. A divide which can be done in this way is much faster than a full software divide. The series for division by other common numbers is given below.

Division by 3:
$$N/3 = N/4 + N/16 + N/64 \ldots$$

Division by 5:
$$N/5 = N/8 + N/16 + N/128 + N/256 + N/2048 + N/4096 \ldots$$
or:
$$N/5 = N/4 - N/16 + N/64 \ldots$$

Division by 7:
$$N/7 = N/8 + N/64 + N/512 + N/4096 \ldots$$

Division by 9:
$$N/9 = N/16 + N/32 + N/64 + N/1024 + N/2048 + N/4096 \ldots$$
or:
$$N/9 = N/8 - N/64 + N/512 \ldots$$

Division by 11:

$$N/11 = N/16 + N/32 - N/512 - N/1024 + N/16384 + N/32768 \ldots$$

The reader can find such a series to fit almost any special divisor in just a few minutes with a hand calculator and a table of the powers of two. None of these methods is true division of course, but simple multiplication by a fraction. The case of true multiplication and division plus some more of these tricks will be shown in chapter 11.

Finally, a word of warning about fixed point fractions. We have already dealt with the problem of the presence of one more integer in the negative direction than in the positive direction in a two's complement system. This poses a special problem for numbers which are pure fraction, such as those programmed with a B15 specification. B15 means that there are 15 bits to the right of the binary point—only the sign being to the left. In such a scheme the binary number:

$$0111111111111111_2$$

represents the largest positive fraction, $.999969\ldots_{10}$. If we take the two's complement of this fraction, namely:

$$1000000000000001_2$$

this represents the negative of the same value, but the presence of the low order 1 indicates that it is possible to have one number more negative than this, i.e.:

$$1000000000000000_2$$

Since the first negative fraction represented the largest fraction possible, the second must represent something 2^{-15} larger in magnitude, the number -1. This is the integer -1 and not a fraction at all. This poses certain programming problems that need to be kept in mind when working in such formats. Adding:

$$\begin{array}{l} 0100000000000000_2 = 0.5_{10} \\ \underline{0100000000000000_2 = 0.5_{10}} \\ 1000000000000000_2 = -1 \text{ !!!! and overflow !!} \end{array}$$

while adding:

$$\begin{array}{l} 1100000000000000_2 = -0.5_{10} \\ \underline{1100000000000000_2 = -0.5_{10}} \\ 1000000000000000_2 = -1.0_{10} \text{ and } no \text{ overflow.} \end{array}$$

In other words, it is legal to add $-.5$ and $-.5$ but not $+.5$ and $+.5$! Think about it.

10 Multiple Precision Schemes

The case often arises in which a number is too large to be held in a single computer word or requires an intermediate precision greater than that achievable within a single word. In such cases two or more words are used to contain the number. Numbers which are represented in this fashion are called *multiple precision* numbers. The case in which two words are used is known as *double precision*. In this chapter we will be dealing with certain instances of double precision with generalization to further multiple precision where necessary.

A double precision number is one which requires between 16 and 30 bits for its expression. It is represented in the magnitude bits of two computer words, usually adjacent memory locations, with the algebraic sign of the number in the sign bit of the most significant or *high order* half. The sign bit of the least significant or *low order* half is always zero, whether the number itself is positive or negative. This last statement is of pivotal importance in dealing with double precision numbers, so it will be restated: *The sign bit of the low order half of a double precision number is always zero.*

The largest positive number which can be held in a signed computer word is:

$$0111111111111111_2 = 32767_{10}$$

To express a larger number than this, say 32768, it is necessary to use a second word. The number is then expressed in two words, as:

0000000000000001	0000000000000000
high order	low order

The number $2^{16} - 1$ or 65535_{10} is expressed:

0000000000000001	0111111111111111
high order	low order

Note that the sign of the low order part of this number is a zero, as it *must* always be. Since a double precision quantity occupies 30 bits it is capable of holding a number as large as:

$$2^{30} - 1 = 1,073,741,823$$

By our previously discussed formula the decimal precision equivalent to 30 bits is:

$$30 \log 2 = 30(.3) = 9 \text{ decimal digits}$$

Double and multiple precision numbers are simply fixed point numbers with extended ranges and they behave just as single precision fixed point numbers do. The only important practical difference is that operations on such numbers must be done on parts. Addition and subtraction must be done in halves, with the low order parts first added or subtracted and the carry or borrow propagated to the sum of the high order halves. It is for the propagation of the carry or borrow that the sign bit of the low order word is kept zero.

To understand how this carry and borrow propagation is done consider the subtraction of two identical single word quantities, the largest negative number, one from the other. The purpose of this exercise is to show that the sign bit really behaves just like an ordinary arithmetic bit.

$$
\begin{array}{r}
1000\ 0000\ 0000\ 0000 \\
-\ 1000\ 0000\ 0000\ 0000 \\
\hline
0000\ 0000\ 0000\ 0000
\end{array}
$$

Since all bits are zeros except the sign bit the only bits involved in actual subtraction are the sign bits. The result is zero of course, which is proper for any number subtracted from itself. Now examine the subtraction:

$$
\begin{array}{rl}
0000\ 0000\ 0000\ 0000 & \text{a zero} \\
-\ 0100\ 0000\ 0000\ 0000 & 16384_{10} \\
\hline
1100\ 0000\ 0000\ 0000 &
\end{array}
$$

Only the highest magnitude bit is involved here. It is is subtracted from the zero above it a borrow is caused from the bit position to the left, namely the sign bit. This forces the sign bit to turn negative. Since a positive number is being subtracted from zero the result must be negative, so this sign bit is proper. The point of this is that a borrow has been taken from the sign bit causing the sign of the result to become a one. Had the original sign bit been a one the borrow would have caused it to become zero. It is this inversion which allows the sign bit to be used to propagate a borrow or carry into a higher word. The original state of the sign bit can be one or zero, but conventional practice has been to set it to zero.

Double precision addition can be done in many ways. The best method for any situation will depend on the circumstances, in particular whether or not both registers are available for use. One short, simple method is shown in example 10-1.

Example 10-1

Two double precision numbers are located in XHI, XLO, and YHI, YLO. Form the correct double precision sum in the A and X registers. Overflow should be set if the sum exceeds 30 bits, but reset otherwise.

label	inst.	operand	
	LDA	XLO	low order of first number to A
	ADD	YLO	form low order sum
	LLR	15	this moves the magnitude of the low order sum to X, while leaving the sign, i.e., the carry, in the low bit of A.
	LRX	1	this vacates the sign bit of X as demanded by double precision format.
	ROV		overflow off
	ADD	XHI	high order of first number + carry
	ADD	YHI	high order sum in A. If there was an overflow the OV bit is set here.
	. . .		

Double precision operations are usually confined to subroutines in order to save the duplication of programming and waste of memory space. This makes these operations somewhat slower but poses no problem if speed is not critical. Double precision subroutines are conventionally written so that one operand is in the A and X registers upon entry. The other operand is indicated by an address pointer following the calling JST. For a double add routine to perform the addition of XHI, XLO, and YHI, YLO the sequence of calling instructions would read:

	LDA	XHI	high order addend in A
	LDX	XLO	low order addend in X
	JST	DBLADD	execute double add subroutine
	DATA	YHI	address pointer to double augend

The address pointer points to the high order word of the augend. Conventionally the high order word occupies the lower memory address with the low order word in the location immediately following it. Workings of a typical double add subroutine are shown in example 10-2.

Example 10-2

Write a double precision add subroutine to the specification given above. The result should return in A and X with the low order sign vacated. Overflow should be set only if the operation generated a result which cannot be held in 30 bits. In this and *all* other multiple precision routines it is the responsibility of the subroutine to be *sure* that the sign of the low order half is left zero.

label	inst.	operand	
DBLADD	DATA	0	
	STA	T	save high order addend
	TXA		low order addend to A
	LDX	*DBLADD	fetch augend address
	STX	ADR	save augend address
	ADD	@1	form low order sum
	LLR	15	this instruction transfers A to X leaving the carry bit in A. As the former contents of X was the augend address pointer, the low bit of X is the former high bit of the augend address pointer. Since this bit is always zero the low bit of X is now zero. X can be properly formatted and OV turned off by a single instruction, namely
	LRX	1	A is now one or zero depending on whether or not there was a carry from the low order sum.
	ADD	T	carry + low order addend
	ADD	*ADR	final sum in A. The overflow bit is now properly set.
	IMS	DBLADD	increment return address
	JMP	*DBLADD	and return
T	NOP		high order addend save
ADR	NOP		augend address save
	...		

The low order sum is formed by using indexed addressing. With the augend address pointer in X the low order augend can be accessed by specifying displacement 1. The shift right leaves the carry in A and the high order addend and augend are added to this. Since the overflow bit was turned off by the formatting shift any overflow which exists was caused by the subsequent additions, i.e., it is real.

As multiple precision numbers are simply extra length fixed point numbers the need arises for double precision shifts, i.e., arithmetic shifts in which the double precision number is shifted right or left as a single entity. Such operations are called *long arithmetic shifts*. In long arithmetic shifts the sign bit of the low order register, X, does not participate. Bits leaving the magnitude portion of X in a left shift immediately enter the low bit of A. Bits leaving the low bit of A in a right shift immediately enter the high magnitude bit of X, "hopping" over the sign bit. As with short arithmetic shifts the sign bit of the A register is propagated into the vacated bits. For shifts longer than 15 bits right the sign bit is propagated into the lower register. A long arithmetic left shift of one place is shown below:

A	X	
0100000000000010	0111000100000001	before
0000000000000101	0110001000000010	after

Several things have happened here. The high magnitude bit of X has entered the low bit of A as the contents of both registers were shifted. The former high magnitude bit of A has been lost and a zero has entered the low bit of X. A long arithmetic right shift is shown below:

A	X	
1001000000000001	0110001000000010	before
1100100000000000	0111000100000001	after

Again the sign bit of the low order word did not participate in the shift as the low magnitude bit of A entered the high magnitude bit of X directly. The low bit of X is lost, and the sign bit of A has been propagated or copied into the vacated position immediately to its right.

Some minicomputers like the Honeywell 16 bit series have hardware facilities for performing shifts like those shown. This contributes substantially to the outstanding arithmetic power of these machines. Most others, including our example machine, have no such hardware facility so we will have to perform the equivalent function using other program instructions. The left shift is easy, as shown in example 10-3.

Example 10-3

Write a program segment to perform a one bit long arithmetic left shift.

label	inst.	operand	
	ALA	1	A register 1 bit left, sign undisturbed. At this point the low bit of the A register is a zero.

STA	T	save it
ZAR		zero A to receive the high magnitude bit of X
LLX	1	move the high magnitude bit of X into the sign bit so it can be moved to A
LLL	1	this moves the high bit of X to the low bit of A
LRX	1	reformat the X register
IOR	T	this merges the arithmetically shifted A register with the bit brought in from X

For long left shifts of more than one bit the ALA and the LLL shift counts can be increased, but keep in mind that ALA cannot have a shift count greater than 8. If long shift counts greater than 8 are required more than one ALA will be necessary. The right shift is even easier when only one bit is involved as is shown in example 10-4.

Example 10-4

Write a program segment to perform a one bit long arithmetic right shift.

label	inst.	operand	
	LLX	1	position X register contents
	LLR	1	shift both registers right. This vacates the A register sign which would leave an incorrect result if the original number were negative.
	LLA	1	move A back where it was
	ARA	1	and propagate the sign

Again, longer shifts can be accomplished by changing the shift counts of the LLR and ARA instructions, but the same safeguards must be observed as noted above since the shift count of the ARA cannot exceed 8. The omission of long arithmetic shifts in the hardware design of the Alpha computers is a significant design weakness of these machines.

The Alpha computers do feature one specialized kind of long arithmetic shift, not one which is useful for the kinds of tasks which we have been discussing, but for another arithmetic mode. In using double or other multiple precision modes we have sought to extend the ranges of fixed point numbers with which we can deal effectively. In some situations it is impossible to do this as intermediate results may generate numbers of unpredictable range. In these cases numbers are represented as pure fractions accompanied by a scale factor, in the same way that the decimal number 45 can be represented by:

$$.45 \times 10^2 \qquad \text{or} \qquad .045 \times 10^3$$

Either of the above representations is numerically correct, but the left one is preferable since it has a significant digit immediately to the right of the decimal point, i.e., no leading zeros. A number which has no leading insignificant digits is said to be *normalized*. In a positive binary number a leading insignificant digit is a zero while in a negative binary number a leading insignificant digit is a one. The condition for a normalized binary number therefore is that the bit immediately to the right of the sign bit be different from the sign bit itself. The reader can satisfy himself on this point by writing out a few short signed binary numbers on paper.

The process of getting a normalized number is called normalization and it is accompanied by the generation of a scale factor for the number, i.e., a count which tells how many places the number had to be shifted to achieve normalization.

A double precision number can be normalized by the use of the NRM instruction. A memory cell is loaded with zero to hold the count of shifts performed during the normalization, and the A and X registers are loaded with the double precision number to be normalized. The low order portion of the number in the X register is shifted left one bit to eliminate the low order sign. The NRM instruction has as its operand the cell which was previously set to zero. The NRM is then executed causing A and X to be shifted left until the most significant bit of A is different from the sign bit of A. If this cannot be done, as in the case of a double precision -1, 31 shifts are executed and then the instruction terminates. For each shift executed the previously zeroed count cell is decremented once. At the end of a normalization it contains a negative number indicating the number of normalizing shifts which were executed.

NRM is one of three instructions in the Alpha machines (other than stack instructions) which are double length, the others being MPY and DIV. These instructions require two computer words each, the first word being the instruction itself and the second an address pointer indicating the location of the operand. The full use of NRM will be discussed in the chapter on floating point arithmetic. Multiplication and division of double precision numbers will be covered in the next chapter.

The final double precision operation to be considered here is that of negation, the formation of the two's complement of the double precision number. Going back to the definition of the two's complement, it is formed by finding the one's complement, i.e., invert every bit, and then adding one. Though there is a special hardware instruction to perform negation for single word quantities, (NAR − NXR), negation could be done in two steps by:

CAR	form one's complement
IAR	then increment

and this division into two steps is how a double precision number is negated. First the two halves of the number in A and X are one's complemented:

```
CAR
CXR
```

Now the low order part must be incremented. Since this may involve a carry into the high order part it is executed like a double precision add with carry propagation. First we clear the low order sign by:

```
LLX    1
LRX    1
```

then increment:

```
IXR
```

If incrementation caused a carry into the sign bit the sign bit must be cleared again and the high order half incremented to reflect the carry:

LLX	1	carry to overflow
JOR	$+2	skip if no carry
IAR		increment high order for carry
LRX	1	

The above will work but it leaves the overflow bit off even if the negation was not valid. Recall in an earlier chapter that the negation of the maximum negative number cannot be done. The attempt yields the same number and overflow is turned on. A complete double negation routine should check for this and turn overflow on if an attempt is made to negate the maximum double precision negative number:

$$1000000000000000\ 0000000000000000$$

A little careful thought will yield a way around this difficulty. The question to be considered is this: If, after the low order sign has been cleared, the X register is incremented, under what circumstances can a carry out of the highest magnitude bit occur? If this is written out on paper the answer becomes apparent immediately. The carry can only occur if *all* of the low order magnitude bits are ones. Further, if a number which is all ones is incremented the result, except for the carry out of the high bit, will be zero. It follows that a carry into the high order half only occurs if the result of incrementing the low order half is a zero after the low order sign is cleared. Since clearing the low order sign by shifting also clears the overflow bit, the result of incrementing the high order half will force overflow to reflect the true overflow condition, on if the number was the maximum negative number, but off under all other circumstances. A subroutine which shows the application of this is shown in example 10-5.

Example 10-5

Write a subroutine to perform the negation of the double precision number in A and X on entry. Overflow should be off on return if the negation was valid and on if it was not valid.

label	inst.	operand	
DNEG	DATA	0	entry point
	CAR		complement high order
	NXR		negate low order
	LLX	1	clear the sign bit of X
	LRX	1	and overflow
	JXN	$+2	is X all zeros?
	IAR		increment high order for carry
	JMP	*DNEG	and return . . .

---

11 Multiplication and Division

Multiplication is a process learned by most people as a rote procedure in the lower grades by memorizing a large number of specific cases called the multiplication tables. These specific cases are then applied to more complex situations by a set of rules, also memorized. The student is thus left in the position of being able to perform the actual computation (at least before the "new math") but with no real understanding of what multiplication is.

This is no real functional disability until he is required to perform the process using a number base with which he is not familiar. This single fact is probably responsible for the sale of more minicomputer multiply/divide hardware than any other. The purpose of this chapter is to give a sufficient understanding of these two processes that the reader will be able to perform them on *any* computer, with or without hardware.

When the decimal product 347 times 24 is written the meaning of the indicated operation is:

$$347 \times 4 + 347 \times 20$$

The factor of twenty is introduced because the 2 occupies the tens place in the multiplier. In the execution of this multiplication we do not actually multiply by twenty but by two, achieving the same effect by indenting the partial product one place to the left. This amounts to a decimal left shift of one place, i.e., a multiplication by ten. If there had been a third digit the next line of the partial product would have undergone a two place shift corresponding to multiplication by one hundred because the third digit represents the hundreds place. A similar situation applies to binary multiplication. Take the indicated product:

$$111_2 \times 11_2$$

This is interpreted to mean:

$$111 \times 1 + 111 \times 10 \qquad \text{all numbers binary}$$

The place values correspond to powers of two rather than ten but the operation is otherwise the same as multiplication in decimal. When we go to actually carry out this multiplication though, one important practical difference emerges, namely, there is no multiplication table of any size to memorize. A multiplier digit may be one or zero and nothing else. As with the decimal example the lines of the partial product are indented to corre-

101

spond with the position of the multiplier digit. Development of the partial product lines is much simpler than in decimal. If the multiplier digit is a one, copy the multiplicand, properly indented, into the partial product line. If the multiplier digit is a zero ignore it and go on to the next digit. Developing this product just as a decimal product would be developed will help make the process clear. All the numbers are binary.

```
  111  the multiplicand
×  11  the multiplier
  111  multiplier times units digit
  111  multiplier times two's digit
10101  completed product
```

This product is 21_{10}, which might have been expected from multiplying 7 times 3. The indentation of the partial product lines is strictly a matter of format. We could have indented the first line to the right one bit rather than the second line to the left. The result would be the same as long as the *relative* positions of the partial product lines remained unchanged. Let's write it this way:

```
   111
×  11
   111
   111
 10101
```

The product is the same. If a three digit multiplier were used we would indent the first partial product line two bits to the right, the second one bit to the right, and the third not at all. This can be seen if we multiply 1010_2 by 111_2 (ten times seven), as:

```
   1010  the multiplicand
×  111   the multiplier
   1010  first partial product line
   1010  second partial product line
   1010  last partial product line
1000110
```

This number is $64 + 4 + 2 = 70$. This kind of exercise is all right on paper but attempting to add three binary numbers in this way is risky since a sum of four can result if all three bits are ones and a carry is propagated from a low order column. To avoid this situation we develop the sum as we go, shifting each partial product line to the right one bit before adding the next partial product line to it. These shifts are not really shifts as we have thought of them because the bits shifted out to the right are not lost but preserved as bits of an ever lengthening partial product. This is exactly the situation that would result from shifting bits out of one register and into another, as from A to X in a long shift.

Now let's try a multiplication on a computer. To keep the visual clutter down we will use four bit words with no sign bit. All four bits are magnitude bits. If we assume that the multiplication is done on a computer like our example machine, then shifting bits out of the low end of the X register with a logical shift will cause them to enter overflow where they can be tested easily to see whether they are ones or zeros. The idea of the exercise that follows is that it should simulate exactly the paper multiplication shown above. We begin by zeroing the A register and loading the multiplicand into X. The X register is then logically shifted one bit right so that its low bit occupied OV (overflow). If the multiplicand is 5 and the multiplier 7 the registers now look like this:

A   X   OV

0000 0010 1

We will use the A register to receive the partial product with long shifts moving this partial product a bit to the right each cycle. The low bits of the partial product are therefore saved in X. These long shifts also serve the function of moving the next multiplicand bit into OV for testing. The bits of the X register vacated by the multiplicand are thus used to contain the developing product. As each bit appears in OV it is tested. If it is a zero nothing more is done and both registers are shifted right one bit in preparation for the next multiply step. If OV contains a one the multiplier is added to A and then both registers are shifted. This is done as many times as there are bits in the multiplicand word, in this case four.

			A	X	OV
JOR	$+2	test multiplicand bit	0000	0010	1
ADD	MPLR	a 1, add multiplier to A	0111	0010	1
LLR	1	double shift right	0011	1001	0
JOR	$+2	test, a zero, ignore it			
ADD	MPLR	...			
LLR	1	move everything right	0001	1100	1
JOR	$+2	test multiplicand bit			
ADD	MPLR	a 1, add multiplier	1000	1100	1
LLR	1	move everything right	0100	0110	0
JOR	$+2	skip if OV zero			
ADD	MPLR	...			
LLR	1	move everything right	0010	0011	0
JOR	$+2	skip if OV zero			
ADD	MPLR	...			
...		finished	0010	0011	0

The final answer is $00100011_2 = 35_{10}$, the correct product of 7 and 5. Notice though that the product cannot be held in one of our four bit computer words. Multiplier and multiplicand were both three bits long and the product is six bits long. This is an instance of the general rule stated in a previous chapter, restated here:

> The product of two numbers, one N bits long and the other M bits long, is $N + M$ bits long.

It can be seen now that the multiplication shown above is the exact analog of the "pencil and paper" multiplication done with decimal numbers, though the format is a little different. A multiply done this way without using the hardware multiply feature of the computer is called a *software multiply*.

The exercise above deviated a bit from what takes place in the real computer in that no allowance was left for the sign bit. In the real computer only 15 multiply steps are executed but there are 16 bits in the register. This leaves one irrelevant bit in the low order position of the low order product word, while a significant product bit occupies the sign bit of the low order product. Both problems are solved by an LRX 1 after the last multiplication step. A full software multiply is given in example 11-1.

Example 11-1

Write a subroutine to find the product of two 15 bit positive integers which are contained in the A and X registers upon entry.

label	inst.	operand	
TIMES	DATA	0	entry point
	STA	MPLR	save multiplier
	LAM	15	set up number of
	STA	CNT	multiply steps
	LRX	1	first multiplicand bit to OV
	ZAR		zero A to receive product
	JOR	$+2	test multiplicand bit, skip if zero
	ADD	MPLR	a 1, add the multiplier
	LLR	1	move partial product and multiplicand right
	IMS	CNT	last step?
	JMP	$-4	no, do another one
	LRX	1	adjust low order product, vacate low order sign

```
         JMP   *TIMES      return
CNT      NOP               step count cell
MPLR     NOP               multiplier cell
```

The product which results from executing the example just given will be thirty bits in length. The most significant 15 bits occupy the A register and the least significant bits occupy the X register. The algebraic sign if there were one would be the sign bit of the A register, but since both numbers were stipulated to be positive the sign bit is zero. As with any double precision number the sign bit of the X register is *always* zero and nonsignificant, whatever the algebraic sign of the product.

Our example machine has a hardware multiply facility of sorts which will perform the multiplication of positive integers as shown above, but it is a little tricky for negative numbers. The multiply instruction MPY works like this. The multiplicand is loaded into the X register with the multiplier occupying a memory location. If the A register is not zero the positive contents are added to the product as an offset. Note that the offset in A *must* be positive. If A is zero the simple product will be developed. While the multiplicand in X may be positive, zero, or negative, the multiplier in memory *must* be positive. MPY is one of three instructions on this machine which require two memory locations. The first location specifies the instruction itself and the second is an address pointer, pointing to the multiplier. This is a little complex so let's take it in steps. First the product of two positive integers, exactly the same as the software multiply shown above, is accomplished as shown in example 11-2.

Example 11-2

Write a subroutine to find the product of two positive integers which are in A and X upon entry. This program should use the hardware MPY instruction:

```
label      inst.   operand

TIMES      NOP               entry point
           STA    MPR        store the multiplier
           ZAR               A is zeroed
           MPY    MPR        form the product
           LRX    1          adjust the low order part
           JMP    *TIMES     and return
MPR        NOP               multiplier cell
           . . .
```

To multiply two numbers with no restriction on algebraic sign is a little more complicated. The largest product which can be generated by two positive numbers is:

$$(2^{15} - 1)^2 = 2^{30} - 2^{16} + 1$$

and this fits into 30 bits with no problem. Similarly the product of the largest positive and largest negative integers is:

$$-2^{15}(2^{15} - 1) = -2^{30} + 2^{15} = -(2^{30} - 2^{15})$$

This presents no problem. The square of the largest negative number, however, results in a product that cannot be held in thirty bits, i.e.:

$$(-2^{15})^2 = +2^{30}$$

By our previously given rule the largest number which can be held in 30 bits is $2^{30} - 1$, so an overflow condition is possible in multiplication and this possibility must be tested for. The problem is to use our hardware multiply instruction to find all possible products. This is shown in example 11-3.

Example 11-3

Write a subroutine to find the product of two integers which are in the registers upon entry using the hardware **MPY** instruction. Return the high order 15 bits of the product in A and the low order 15 bits in X with overflow off if the product can be found. If the product cannot be found, i.e., square of the largest negative number, return with the best approximation in A and X and OV on.

To use the hardware **MPY** order, the multiplier *must* be positive. The multiplicand contained in the X register can be positive or negative. The first part of the job is to accomplish this by swapping the two numbers if necessary. If both are negative they can be negated without changing the product since the product of two negative numbers is positive. If the negation of a negative number yields another negative number then that number is -32768, the largest negative number, since this is the only case in which this can happen.

label	inst.	operand	
MPY	NOP		entry point
	JAP	OK	multiplier is positive, jump
	EAX		swap multiplier and multiplicand
	JAP	OK	is this one positive?
			If control reaches here both of the numbers were negative.

Since the product of two negative numbers is positive we change nothing by negating both numbers, as the product will be the same. If one or both of the numbers was the maximum negative negating will not change it. If only one was the maximum negative number then the multiplication can be done, but the sign will be wrong. This is treated as a special case at locations A1 and A2 below. If both were the maximum negative number then the product cannot be held. This is treated as another special case at NMAX below. We first negate both numbers and if both are now positive we can proceed with the multiplication.

	NAR		
	NXR		both numbers should now be positive
	JAM	A1	at least one is still negative
	EAX		one is positive, try the other
	JAM	A2	the other is negative
			If control reaches here the multiplication can be executed normally, as
OK	STA	MPR	save the multiplier
	ZAR		zero A to receive partial product
	MPY	MPR	do the multiplication
	LRX	1	reformat the low order half
END	ROV		overflow off for normal return
	JMP	*MPY	and return
A1	EAX		first number still negative, try the other
	JAM	NMAX	both negative, illegal product
A2	LLL	16	If control reaches here one and one only of the numbers

was -32768. The product is simply the other number times -32768. Since 32768 is 2^{15} the product can be formed by simply transferring the other number to the high order product and setting the low order part to zero. This is done in one instruction, the LLL 16. Since it has the wrong sign we negate, as:

	NAR		
	JMP	END	and return normally
NMAX	AXM		AXM sets all bits of both registers
	LRA	1	clear high order sign
	LRX	1	clear low order sign and set overflow
	JMP	*MPY	and return with "best" approximation and overflow set
MPR	NOP		

It should be understood that the procedure shown in the example is necessary only in cases where the numbers whose product is to be found can have the value -32768. If the numbers cannot reach this value the problem becomes simpler:

MPY	NOP		entry point
	JAP	OK	multiplier positive, O.K.
	EAX		swap and try the other one
	JAP	OK	this one is positive, proceed
	NAR		negate both numbers
	NXR		
OK	STA	MPR	store multiplier
	ZAR		zero A and
	MPY	MPR	multiply
	LRX	1	format low order product
	JMP	*MPY	and return
MPR	NOP		
	...		

This procedure can be used in the majority of cases. The extra checking in the example was made necessary by the possible presence of the number -32768. In most applications the nature of the data being processed precludes this, e.g., data from peripheral devices is almost never 15 bits in magnitude.

In working with fixed point numbers, particularly integers, the problem of multiplication by some constant which is not an integer is often encountered. There are several ways to solve this. The most obvious is to represent the constant as a fixed point number with the radix point far enough to the left that sufficient fraction precision is maintained. Thus the constant:

$$3.1416\text{B}10$$

is equivalent to the binary word:

$$000011.0010010001$$

The double precision product must be rescaled by the scale factor of the constant after the multiplication in order to restore the answer to integer format. Since our assembly program has no facilities for the creation of such constants, we must resort to an artifice to accomplish the same thing. The trick is to multiply by some number which when rescaled will give the desired factor. If the above constant were viewed as an integer its value would be 3217_{10}, i.e.:

$$\frac{3217}{(2^{10})} = 3.1416, \text{ approximately}$$

Schemes like this depend on the divisor being an even power of two so that the division can be accomplished by a simple shift. This rules out approximations like 22/7 for pi and also the very good approximation 355/113 = 3.1415929.

Some useful constants are listed in table 11-1.

Table 11-1
Ratios for Common Constants

Number	Fraction	Decimal value	Real Value
pi	201/64	3.140625	3.141592653
pi	3217/1024	3.1416015	3.141592653
1/pi	163/512	0.3183593	0.3183098
pi^2	1263/128	9.8671875	9.8696043
$\sqrt{}$pi	1815/1024	1.7724609	1.7724538
e (base of natural logarithms)			
	5567/2048	2.7182617	2.7182818
e "	87/32	2.7187500	2.7182818
1/e	47/128	0.3671875	0.3678794
$\sqrt{}$e	211/128	1.6484375	1.6487213

Multiplication of double precision numbers usually involves the treatment of these numbers as fractions rather than integers. The product of two 30 bit numbers is 60 bits long, and if the numbers are integers the full 60 bit quadruple precision number must be retained. In such cases as this it will almost always pay to use floating point techniques. For fractions, however, there are significant advantages to using double precision fixed point. The high precision trigonometry used in astronomy and crystalography can be accomplished very efficiently this way. A precision of 30 bits corresponds to a resolution of about .001 second of arc for trigonometric purposes. Double precision multiplication is accomplished by the use of the identity:

$$(A + B)(C + D) = AC + AD + BC + BD$$

in which A and B are the high and low order halves of the multiplier and C and D are high and low halves of the multiplicand. Since the high and low order parts of the operands are of different magnitude ranges the magnitudes of their products must be taken into account when adding to form the final double precision product. Assuming that both double precision quantities are pure fraction the AC term involves the high order parts of the two operands and the double precision product of A and C will enter into the two highest order product words. The BD term involves the product of two numbers whose greatest value is $2^{-15} - 2^{-30}$. The maximum possible product of these terms is the square of the above number, i.e.:

$$(2^{-15} - 2^{-30})^2 = 2^{-30} - 2^{-44} + 2^{-60}$$

and this product must therefore be added to the third and fourth order terms of the double precision product. Assigning magnitudes in the same way for the other terms, and designating the high and low order terms of each of the cross-products by the prefixes H and L, the terms of the partial product are placed in the following positions for summation:

1st order	2nd order	3rd order	4th order
HAC	LAC		
	HAD	LAD	
	HBC	LBC	
		HBD	LBD

With the individual products in the magnitude positions indicated above a quadruple precision addition is performed to form the full 60 bit product. If this sum is then truncated to 30 bits, the maximum error which will result from discarding the two low order terms is:

$$2^{-30} - 2^{-60}$$

an error of less than one part per billion. If the number were a trigonometric sine or cosine the largest possible error which can result in taking the inverse function will be about 9 seconds of arc. The error of 9 seconds of arc will occur only in the immediate vicinity of 90° for arcsines and 0° for arccosines.

Before leaving the subject of trigonometry and high precision it will be worth our while to look at the way in which the angles themselves are represented. The usual method of representing angles is as a mixed number, integer degrees plus fraction, or integer radians plus fraction. In a single precision scheme this means that the angle is represented like this:

SII.FFFFFFFFFFFFF   for radians

or

SIIIIIIII.FFFFFFF   for degrees

where *S* is the sign, *I* is the integer, and *F* is the fraction. The maximum precision representable in the radian scheme, fixed by the 13 bit fraction length, is 1 radian (57.29°) divided by 8192 or about 25 seconds of arc. Using the degrees and fractions scheme the maximum precision is 1/128 of a degree or about 28 seconds of arc. There is another alternative, however. If angles were represented as fractions of a circle the full precision of the available bits can be utilized. The angle 180° would be represented as:

0.100000000000000

i.e., one half of a circle. The maximum precision available in this representation is 180/32768 or a little less than 20 seconds of arc. This shows that the choice of representation can have an effect on precision. This causes no trouble when computing trigonometric functions since the constant multipliers of the sine and cosine series can be adjusted at assembly time to allow the routines to take arguments in fractions of a circle. The scheme has one other rather striking advantage. Angles can be added or subtracted in any number without regard for the value of overflow or the sign bit. This is shown by the following example:

270° = 3/4 of a circle = 0.110000000000000

180° = 1/2 of a circle = 0.100000000000000

The sum of these two is 450° or 90° when it is reduced modulo 360°. Adding the binary fractions:

$$
\begin{array}{r}
0.110000000000000 \\
+ \ 0.100000000000000 \\
\hline
1.010000000000000
\end{array}
$$
and overflow is turned on.

If we simply vacate the sign bit and ignore overflow we have:

0.010000000000000 = 1/4 circle or 90°

Vacating the sign bit reduces the angle by one full circle, 360°, and the remaining fraction is the correct sum. Had these angles been represented as degrees or radians the addition would have been much more complicated, with checks being made afterward to detect overflow and reduce the angle modulo 360° or 2 pi radians.

Turning now to the second subject of this chapter, division, it is again necessary to examine the "pencil and paper" process in order to understand what goes on in a computer divide. To begin take the division of the decimal number 47 (the dividend) by the number 3 (the divisor). This division is indicated by:

$$3\overline{)\;47}$$

As we learned by rote in school, we begin by matching a number of "trial" dividend digits to the size of the divisor. Since the divisor (the 3) is one digit long we start by dividing the first dividend digit (the 4) by this single divisor digit. This division yields a 1 which we write in the result (the quotient) above the line, as:

$$\begin{array}{r} 1 \\ 3\overline{)\;47} \end{array}$$

Now the divisor is subtracted from the first dividend digit as many times as is indicated by the quotient digit, in this case once. The subtraction is indicated by writing the subtrahend under the first divisor digit:

$$\begin{array}{r} 1 \\ 3\overline{)\;47} \\ -3 \\ \hline 1 \end{array}$$

The indicated subtraction is performed and a new dividend is formed by "bringing down" the next digit from the old dividend, as:

$$\begin{array}{r} 1 \\ 3\overline{)\;47} \\ -3 \\ \hline 17 \end{array}$$

The process is now repeated with the next quotient digit being the number of times that the divisor can be taken from the new dividend, in this case 5. The 5 is written in the next quotient position and the new subtrahend is formed below by multiplying the new quotient digit by the divisor:

$$
\begin{array}{r}
15 \\
3)\overline{47} \\
-3 \\
\hline
17 \\
-15 \\
\hline
2
\end{array}
$$

The result of the subtraction, the 2, is written below. Since there are no more dividend digits to be "brought down" the division is finished. The number left at the bottom is called the *remainder*.

Now let's look at this same division in a little different format, in particular, let's simplify the business of the new dividend mentioned above. The entire process could be made more compact if we were to simply rewrite the dividend to reflect this step. This means that the step:

$$
\begin{array}{r}
1 \\
3)\overline{47} \\
-3 \\
\hline
17
\end{array}
$$

can be simplified to:

$$
\begin{array}{r}
1 \\
3)\overline{17}
\end{array}
$$

and the step:

$$
\begin{array}{r}
15 \\
3)\overline{47} \\
-3 \\
\hline
17 \\
-15 \\
\hline
2
\end{array}
$$

is reduced to:

$$
\begin{array}{r}
15 \text{ R2} \\
3)\overline{17}
\end{array}
$$

Now we'll try the same division but in binary. The division of 47 by 3 is indicated by:

$$
11)\overline{101111}
$$

We again begin by taking a number of dividend bits equal to the number of digits in the divisor, in this case two. Since the first two bits of the dividend are 10, i.e., a decimal 2, the divisor cannot be subtracted from these two bits at all, so we write a zero in the quotient and include another dividend bit, as:

$$
\begin{array}{r}
0 \\
11\overline{)101111}
\end{array}
$$

The problem now is to divide 101_2 by 11_2, i.e., 5/3. The quotient bit is a 1, and the 3 is subtracted from the 5 directly in the abbreviated format shown above:

$$
\begin{array}{r}
01 \\
11\overline{)010111}
\end{array}
$$

Since the leading zeros in both quotient and the new dividend have no significance we can eliminate them and rewrite:

$$
\begin{array}{r}
1 \\
11\overline{)\ 10111}
\end{array}
$$

Please note that this last operation is the equivalent of a left shift. The significance of this will be apparent in a minute. We now repeat this process until the remaining "new dividend" is smaller than the divisor at which time the division is finished.

This binary division has one feature that makes it simpler than decimal division, namely that it is never necessary to multiply the divisor by a quotient digit to form a subtrahend. The subtrahend can have only two values—zero or the value of the divisor—depending on whether the quotient bit was a zero or a one. As before the operation of "bringing down" a digit was eliminated by the direct subtraction from the dividend, then shifting in a bit to form the new dividend. It is probably becoming clear just how computer division works. The divisor is compared to the high bits of the dividend and a bit is set to one in the quotient if it is less than the high bits of the dividend, otherwise to zero. If the quotient bit was a one the divisor is subtracted from the high bits of the dividend, and the new divisor is formed by shifting in another bit.

As with the multiplication examples earlier in this chapter, the process is shown most simply in a short word with no algebraic sign to complicate things. The precise mechanics of the division depend on the dividend being held in both registers, i.e., it is considered to be a double precision number. The high order bits in A are compared to the divisor which is held in memory. If the divisor can be subtracted from the high order dividend, it is subtracted and the quotient bit is set to one. Otherwise no subtraction is done and the quotient bit is set to zero. The new divisor is then formed by shifting a bit into A from X. Since this left shift vacates the lower bit of X this space is used to hold the quotient. Quotient bits are generated by setting the overflow bit to one or zero, then using a *Long Rotate Left* instruction to do the shifting. This is similar to the trick used in the multiplication example in which product bits were moved into the space vacated as the multiplicand was shifted right. Again there is *no* sign on either of the registers in this example. The cycle of tests, subtracts, and shifts is repeated as many times as there are bits in the computer word. Example 11-4 shows the division of 31 by 5. We begin with the double precision dividend held in the 4 bit A and X registers:

program			A	X	OV
ROV			0001	1111	0
CMS	DVSR	compare to divisor			
JMP	$+4	skip if high dividend less than divisor			
NOP					
SUB	DVSR	subtract if greater or equal			
SOV		and set quotient bit to one			
LRL	1	move everything left one bit	0011	1110	0
CMS	DVSR	compare to divisor . . .			
JMP	$+4	skip if less			
NOP					
SUB	DVSR	subtract if greater or equal			
SOV		set quotient bit to one if the subtract took place			
LRL	1	move everything left one bit	0111	1100	0
CMS	DVSR	compare again . . .			
JMP	$+4	skip if less			
NOP					
SUB	DVSR	subtract . . .	0010	1100	0
SOV		and set quotient bit to one	0010	1100	1
LRL	1	move everything left one bit . . .	0101	1001	0
CMS	DVSR	compare again . . .			
JMP	$+4	skip if less			
NOP					
SUB	DVSR	it's equal, do the subtract	0000	1001	0
SOV		set quotient bit to one	0000	1001	1
LRL	1	move everything left one bit	0001	0011	0
CMS	DVSR	compare the last time			
JMP	$+4	skip if less			

Example 11-4

```
NOP
SUB    DVSR     as before . . .
SOV
RLX    1        shift in final quotient bit     0001  0110  0
. . .            finished
```

The quotient in the X register is $0110_2 = 6_{10}$, and the remainder in A is $0001_2 = 1_{10}$, the proper result. The remainder in A is the number left when all possible multiples of the divisor have been removed from the dividend. A division performed in this way without the aid of divide hardware is known as a *software divide*.

Now that we have covered the process of raw binary division, some constraints on the process must be considered. Up to this point the examples have been "paper" type divisions in which we could simply tack more digits onto a number which was becoming too large. In a real computer, however, we must deal with the problem of a fixed word size. Conventional practice holds that the quotient should be containable in a single computer word. With a software divide performed like the one in the example above the whole process is under program control and the quotient can be developed to any length which is required. Divide hardware enforces this restriction, however, and tests for the possibility of a quotient which cannot be held in a single word before performing the divide. The criterion applied is that the high order half of the dividend, considered as an integer, must be *less* than the divisor. If the high order part of the dividend is greater than or equal to the divisor, the result would be a quotient which cannot be held in a single word. If this condition obtains the hardware refuses to perform the divide and an indicator, usually overflow, is set to signal the failure. This condition is known as the *divide fault* or *divide check* condition. A software divide routine which attempts to simulate the function of the divide hardware must test for the divide check condition and set the overflow indicator accordingly.

Turning now to a real computer we will use the method developed above to perform a divide on our example machine, as shown in example 11-5.

Example 11-5

Write a program to divide the double precision dividend contained in memory locations HIDVDD and LODVDD by the divisor contained in location DVSR. Assume that both dividend and divisor are positive numbers. If a divide check condition arises turn overflow on and terminate the effort. Otherwise perform the division and turn overflow off. Leave the quotient in X and the remainder in A.

label	inst.	operand	
DIVIDE	LAM	15	
	STA	CNT	initialize divide step count
	LDX	LODVDD	load low dividend
	LDA	HIDVDD	load high dividend
	CMS	DVSR	test for divide check condition
	JMP	$+3	o.k., do the divide
	JMP	TILT	dividend greater than divisor, no good
	JMP	TILT	dividend equal to divisor, no good
	LLX	1	pack dividend to eliminate low order sign
D2	LRL	1	dividend left one bit
	CMS	DVSR	can we subtract?
	JMP	D3	no, leave quotient bit zero
	NOP		yes . . .
	SUB	DVSR	subtract divisor from high dividend
	SOV		set quotient bit to one
D3	IMS	CNT	last divide step?
	JMP	D2	no, do it again
	RLX	1	yes, bring in the last quotient bit
	ROV		overflow off for normal divide
	JMP	$+2	skip over divide check instruction
TILT	SOV		divide check, set overflow
	. . .		

Note should be taken of two things about this divide before leaving the example. First, it was unnecessary to turn overflow off before starting. Since the conditions of the problem stated that the dividend is positive this is taken care of by the first left shift. Second, we could have developed the quotient directly in X by using IXR and not bothered with overflow at all. The LLX which packed the low dividend left vacated the low bit of X before the divide started. But both of these points are minor. The above method will work on *any* computer, with or without divide hardware.

The Alpha computers contain hardware to do most of the work of division. The same result as the last example can be had by the sequence:

	LDA	HIDVDD	high order dividend to A
	LDX	LODVDD	low order dividend to X
	LLX	1	pack to eliminate low order sign

DVD   DVSR   and divide
. . .

The quotient appears in X and the remainder in A. The hardware divide demands that both divisor and dividend be positive numbers so the programmer must provide for the algebraic signs of the result. This can be done using the exclusive OR function as shown before. The sign of the quotient is the logical difference of the signs of the dividend and divisor. The sign of the remainder is set so that the relation:

$$\text{(quotient) (divisor)} + \text{remainder} = \text{dividend}$$

This works out to mean that the sign of the remainder must be the same as that of the dividend.

In working with the general divide the case of the maximum negative number, the bane of the two's complement arithmetic system, comes back to haunt us again. If the high order half of the dividend is the maximum negative number the divide is impossible since a quotient larger than one computer word would result whatever the value of the divisor. If the divisor is the maximum negative number the divide is trivial. The magnitude of the quotient in this case is the same as the high order dividend, the magnitude of the remainder being the low order dividend. This amounts to simply swapping the contents of the two registers, remembering to adjust the algebraic signs in accordance with the rules just stated.

Like the MPY instruction, DVD occupies two words, the first specifying the instruction itself and the second containing an address pointer which specifies the location of the divisor. In both cases the address contained in the second word may be direct or indirect.

Division of a multiple precision number by another multiple precision number occurs almost exclusively in dealing with high precision fractions. In such cases the remainder is ignored. If a true multiple precision divide is required it will be necessary to perform a software simulation of the divide process shown above at the precision required. If you really *need* to do this it can be done, but it is very tedious. For double precision results a quadruple precision dividend is formed, and the divide carried out using simulated quadruple precision shifts, double precision compares, and double precision adds. Division is accomplished by the same process as shown in this chapter, but remember that 30 divide steps must be executed.

If the application does not demand a full 30 bit quotient there is another way out of the problem that does not require the tedium and suffering of the true double precision divide. This method or its equivalent is used by all but the most fanatical devotees of precision and produces a quotient which is accurate to 29 bits. It involves only single precision multiples and divides and is based on the relation:

$$\frac{A + B}{C + D} = \frac{A}{C} + \frac{B}{C} - \frac{DA}{C^2} - \frac{DB}{C^2} + \frac{D^2A}{C^3} + \frac{D^2B}{C^3} \cdots$$

which is the result of dividing out $(A + B)/(C + D)$. The quotient goes on with succeeding terms involving higher and higher powers of C and D. Since the powers of the high order terms like C decrease in size much less rapidly than the powers of the low order terms like D, the values of the terms of the series decrease quickly, so quickly in fact that only the first three terms are required for 29 bit precision. An example showing this kind of division is a little too long for a book of this type, but a careful reading of the listings in manufacturer supplied manuals will give the reader the idea of how it is done. Should the reader decide to attempt such a program remember that the outcome of the division is not affected by multiplying both divisor and dividend by the same number. This fact is of use in preserving the maximum precision of the process. The divisor is "normalized" by shifting it left until a significant bit occupies the highest magnitude position. The dividend is then shifted left the same number of places.

12 Floating Point Arithmetic

In the section on fixed point arithmetic and fractions the process of scaling a fixed point number was detailed. Going back to this for a moment, recall the necessity of keeping track of the location of the radix or binary point of every number upon which operations were to be performed. Doing this allowed operations on mixed or fractional quantitites to be performed using the normal arithmetic instructions of the computer.

Situations do arise, however, in which it is impossible to know in advance what the magnitudes of the numbers will be, and fixed point techniques cannot be applied successfully. In these cases we modify the fixed point system by carrying with each number its own scale factor which indicates the location of the radix point within the number. Some computers have hardware to perform this task, while others relegate the work to subroutines. The result is the same in either case. The management of the magnitudes of numbers is taken over by some source other than the inline instructions written by the programmer. The purpose of this section is to acquaint the reader with the methods by which such arithmetic is done. Arithmetic which is performed in this manner has been given the generic name *floating point arithmetic*.

Most readers will be familiar with the so-called "scientific" notation for numbers by which a single digit is carried to the left of the decimal point and a scale factor is included with the number. In this system the number 126.7 would be written:

$$1.267 \times 10^2$$

Floating point notation works in a very similar way. Instead of keeping one digit to the left of the decimal or radix point, however, the number is written as a pure fraction and a scale factor. The number 126.7 in floating point notation would be written:

$$.1267 \times 10^3$$

In the first part of this section floating point principles will be illustrated by decimal floating point numbers with a transition to binary when the fundamental ideas have been presented. For these illustrations a six digit floating point decimal number will be used. The first (left most) two digits will represent the scale factor or *exponent* and the final four digits the significant part of the floating point number. In addition to these six digits a sign will be specified. In this notation the number above would be written:

$$+03\ 1267$$

The radix point in this number is understood to be between the exponent and the significant digits, making the number pure fraction, to be multiplied by the power of ten shown in the exponent. Note particularly that the first digit to the right of the decimal point is nonzero. A floating point number which has a significant, i.e., nonzero digit in this position is said to be in the *normalized* form. Remember this because it will come up again and again. A number which is not in the normalized form is put into this form by shifting the fraction left and decreasing the exponent by one for each place shifted until a significant digit occupies the highest fraction digit. This process, called *normalization*, goes like this. The number 310 can be expressed in many ways, two of which are:

$$.3100 \times 10^3 \quad \text{or} \quad +03\ 3100 \text{ in floating point}$$

and

$$.0310 \times 10^4 \quad \text{or} \quad +04\ 0310 \text{ in floating point}$$

The second floating point expression for this number is in the so called unnormalized form and before being operated upon it must be normalized. To shift the fraction left by one decimal digit amounts to multiplying it by ten. This is compensated for by decreasing the exponent by one for each place shifted.

The floating point form shown above fails to allow for very small numbers and this problem must be addressed. The smallest number which can be expressed in the above form is:

$$.0001 \text{ or } +00\ 0001$$

The exponent of zero means 10^0 or 1 since any number to the zero power is equal to one. What we lack here is some means of expressing the *negative* powers of the number base in the exponent, i.e., 1/10, 1/100, etc. This problem is solved in decimal computers by expressing the exponent as an *excess 50* number. This means that the exponent is to be interpreted as if 50 were subtracted from it. An exponent of less than 50 means a negative power of ten, that power being the difference between 50 and the exponent. This sounds complicated but it is really very simple as the following examples show:

$$1/10 = .1 \times 10^0 = +50\ 1000$$
$$1/100 = .1 \times 10^{-1} = +49\ 1000$$
$$1/1000 = .1 \times 10^{-2} = +48\ 1000$$

This scheme allows the full number of digits in the fraction to be used for significance. The largest and smallest nonzero numbers which can be expressed this way are:

$$+99\ 9999 \text{ or } .9999 \times 10^{49}, \text{ the largest}$$

and

$$+00\ 1000 \text{ or } .1000 \times 10^{-50}, \text{ the smallest}$$

The floating point number zero is expressed as:

$$+00\ 0000$$

As the purpose of using floating point arithmetic is to be rid of the hassle of keeping track of the radix point, this is done automatically by the floating hardware or subroutines. To add two floating point numbers whose exponents are different, the exponent of one is adjusted while shifting its fraction until the two exponents are identical. The two fractions are then added. This amounts to the pencil and paper operation of aligning the decimal points before adding. To add the two numbers:

$$+52\ 2800 \quad (a\ 28)$$

and

$$+51\ 3100 \quad (3.1)$$

the exponents of the two numbers must be made to agree before the fractions can be added. There are two ways to do this. The first is to shift the fraction of the larger number left and decrease its exponent. This is impossible since it would run the fraction into the exponent. There is simply not room to accomplish this. The other way is to shift the fraction of the smaller number right while *increasing* its exponent. By this means the 3.1 can be changed from the above form to $+52\ 0310$. The two numbers now look like this:

$$+52\ 2800$$

and

$$+52\ 0310$$

Since the exponents are now equal the fractions can be added directly as:

$$
\begin{array}{r}
+52\ 2800 \\
+52\ \underline{0310} \\
3110
\end{array}
$$

The exponent, $+52$, is automatically attached to the resulting fraction and the result is $+52\ 3110$ or 31.10 which is correct. Sums or differences of floating point numbers can be generated which cause the exponent to change, however. Consider the following case:

+53 1000 one hundred in floating point
−51 1000 a one

The exponent of the smaller number, the one, is increased and the fraction shifted right to yield the following addition:

+53 1000
−53 0010
+53 0990 i.e., 100 − 1 = 99

This leaves the result in an unnormal form. The floating point hardware or subroutines adjust for this automatically and normalize the result to:

+52 9900

The other situation in which the exponent may be changed is shown by the following:

+51 9000 a nine
+51 1000 a one

In this case neither exponent needs adjusting so the add can be performed directly, but the addition results in a carry out of the highest fraction digit. The floating point hardware or subroutines compensate for this by shifting the result right and increasing the exponent to yield:

+51 9000
+51 1000
+52 1000 or ten, the correct result.

Binary floating point notation is the exact analog of the decimal floating point notation, with a binary fraction being multiplied by a power of two. The exponent is also divided into a positive and negative range by the use of an "excess" system as with the decimal. If the exponent portion is eight bits long the exponent can run from 2^{127} to 2^{-128}, the zero power exponent being:

$$1000\ 0000_2 = 80_{16}$$

A binary floating point 1 for example is expressed as:

sign   exponent   fraction
0   1000 0001   1000 0000 0000 0000 . . .

meaning $\frac{1}{2} \times 2^1$. The equivalent range of decimal exponents is about $10^{\pm 38}$. Binary floating point occupies at least two computer words per number. The thirty-two bit double word is allotted as one bit for the algebraic sign, seven or eight bits for the exponent, and the remaining twenty-three or twenty-four for the significant portion of the number, the fraction. Twenty-three bits yields almost seven decimal digits of precision. This does *not* mean that arithmetic done with such numbers will yield results which are good to seven decimal digits, and this is a subject which must receive some attention. Consider the following three numbers and their floating point equivalents:

number	floating
5.135	+51 5135
4.074	+51 4074
6.381	+51 6381

Adding the first two of these:

```
+51 5135
+51 4074
+51 9209  or 9.209
```

Now add the third to the sum of the first two:

```
+51 9209
+51 6381
+52 1559  = 15.59
```

a shift right having taken place because a carry occurred out of the high digit.

Now let's add them in the opposite order, the last pair first and then the first number. Adding the last pair:

```
+51 4074
+51 6381
+52 1045
```

Again a right shift of the fraction has taken place because a carry occurred out of the high fraction digit. The exponent has been increased to compensate for this event. Now take the first number and add it to this sum:

```
+52 1045
+51 5135
```

This cannot be added directly because the exponents are different. Shifting the fraction of the smaller number right one digit and increasing its exponent we have:

```
+52 1045
+52 0513
+52 1558  = 15.58
```

In other words, adding in different orders gives different sums!!!

What has failed here is the commutative law of addition. In ordinary numerical processes it is always true that:

$$A + B + C = C + B + A = B + C + A = A + C + B$$

This commutative law does *not* hold for floating point arithmetic. The cause of this is fairly easy to see with a little close attention to what goes on in floating point addition. In the first sum we added the numbers in such a way that the exponent of the sum was the same as the exponent of the number to be added next. When the third number was added no pre-shift was necessary to equalize the exponents and the fractions could be added directly. In the second case the numbers were added in such an order that the sum of the first pair added had an exponent one larger than that of the number yet to be added. This required that the fraction of the number yet to be added be pre-shifted before the addition. This caused a significant digit to be lost before the addition even took place.

It could be argued that the difference, $15.59 - 15.58$ is small and could be ignored, but this avoids the obvious question of what happens when large numbers of floating adds or subtracts are done as required in such processes as numerical integration. The error in the earlier operations is propagated into the later ones and compounded by the errors in these later operations until the significance of the result is eroded beyond usefulness.

This "erosion" produces some surprising results which are shown in table 12-1. The significance loss gets worse as the fraction of the floating point word gets shorter, and the difference caused by the order of operations is clear. The numbers in the table are the results of summing the first 20,000 numbers of the form .001, .002, .003, .004, ... The correct sum can be computed analytically. The *forward sum* represents the best floating point result that can be gotten at the listed fraction length. The *backward sum* is the worst possible result.

Looking at the results for 23 bits, the forward sum, the *best* result which can be expected is 199894.06 or 115.94 different from the correct result. The error is in the *fourth* significant digit even though the fraction precision was 23 bits, almost seven decimal digits. Rounding of the intermediate results can produce a little improvement in this but not as much as adding another bit.

The error is the result of several factors, one of which is the fact that .001 is not precisely representable in binary, as will be usually true with decimal fractions. The worst case, the backward sum, shows almost twice the error of the best case. Since the same numbers were used in forming each total the difference must be due to the order in which the summing was done, smallest to largest and largest to smallest.

There is at least one quick moral to be drawn from the above results. *DON'T* use floating point for computing with numbers which represent

Table 12-1
Floating Point Precision Loss

Length of fraction,	True sum	Forward sum	Backward sum
27 bits	200010	200002.75	199995.77
26 bits	"	199995.51	199981.54
25 bits	"	199981.02	199953.08
24 bits	"	199952.03	199896.19
23 bits	"	199894.06	199782.50
22 bits	"	199778.06	199555.12
21 bits	."	199545.25	199101.00

money!!! The early lore of the computer field is filled with stories of bank programmers who enriched themselves by diverting the difference between a true sum and a floating point sum into their own accounts, and the financial institutions have long since become wise to the trick.

There is one obvious solution to the problem of floating point error, and that is to use more bits in the fraction. It was with this solution in mind that many of the large early computers were designed with large word lengths. The IBM 700-7000 series machines used a 36 bit word, sign bit, eight bit exponent, and twenty-seven bit fraction. This gave a precision of a little more than eight decimal digits and was adequate for almost all of the scientific and engineering applications for which the machines were used. Even greater floating point precision was achieved by the Control Data Corporation machines which used word lengths of from 48 to 60 bits. The ultimate of these "number crunchers" was the IBM 7030, the legendary STRETCH machine, which employed an additional twist in the quest for higher precision, the so-called "noisy mode" technique.

When two floating point numbers are added or subtracted the fractional result may have no significant bit or bits in the upper fraction positions. This is the condition we have previously named "unnormal." Normalization of the results is part of the floating point operation process, but the resulting left shift of the fraction introduces zeros at the right end. "Noisy mode" arithmetic introduced ones instead of zeros. This option could be selected by the program and turned on and off at will, so a problem could be run both ways, with zeros introduced during normalization and again with ones. The two results could then be compared and an idea of significance loss estimated from the difference between them.

An excellent book has been written on the subject of significance loss, J. H. Wilkinson's *Rounding Error in Algebraic Processes*. This should be read by everyone concerned with floating point arithmetic and ought to be in the personal library of every programmer.

Floating point multiplication and division are simpler and are not subject to the precision losses suffered during addition and subtraction. Multiplication is accomplished by simply finding the product of the fractions and adding the effective exponents, since:

$$(A \times 2^n)(B \times 2^m) = A \times B \times 2^{n+m}$$

Since A and B in this case are pure fractions there is no scaling problem. Division is similarly simple, again because the operands are pure fractions. The dividend is simply divided by the divisor and the difference of the two effective exponents attached to the result, which follows from the expression:

$$\frac{(A \times 2^n)}{(B \times 2^m} = \frac{A}{B} \times 2^{n-m}$$

There are two other operations associated with floating point numbers, that of "floating" a fixed point number and that of "fixing" a floating point number. Floating a fixed point number means converting its value to the equivalent floating point value. If the fixed point number is an integer, this involves attaching an exponent to it whose effective value is the number of fraction digits in the floating point number. This is illustrated in example 12-1.

Example 12-1

Convert the decimal fixed point integer 9 to a floating point number in a six decimal digit word. The original integer looks like this:

000009

The number of fraction digits in the floating point word is four so we attach an exponent whose effective value is four, i.e., 54 in the excess 50 systems, as:

+540009

But this is not in a normal form. To get it into the normal form simply add a floating point zero to it. Since the result of a floating point operation is automatically normalized, the following happens:

$$
\begin{array}{r}
+54\ 0009 \\
+00\ 0000 \\
\hline
+51\ 9000
\end{array}
$$

The conversion of a floating point number to a fixed point number involves the use of special operations called *unnormalized floating operations*. These operations are performed in exactly the same way as ordinary floating operations, but the result is not normalized. Conversion of a number from floating to fixed point integer form, called *fixing,* is done by forcing the exponent of the floating number to assume a value equal to the number of digits in the fraction. In this way the fraction portion of the number is positioned in such a way that if the exponent were removed the remaining number would be the integer portion in fixed point form. This is better illustrated than discussed further. Take the number in the last example, +519000, and add the floating constant +540000 to it, as:

$$+51\ 9000$$
$$+54\ 0000$$

Since the exponents disagree the fraction portion of the number with the smaller exponent must be shifted right and the exponent incremented until they do agree. When this is done the result looks like this:

$$+54\ 0009$$
$$+54\ 0000$$

Since the number being added, +540000, has all zeros in its fraction the effect of the addition is to simply copy the fraction part of the first number into the sum, as:

$$+54\ 0009$$
$$+54\ \underline{0000}$$
$$54\ 0009$$

The unnormalized floating add stops here. No attempt is made by the hardware to normalize the result. If the exponent is now discarded (masked off in a binary word) the result is:

$$000009$$

a fixed point 9. If the fixed point number were required to have one decimal place, i.e., scale factor of 1, the number +53 0000 would have been used in the unnormalized add. This would look like:

$$+51\ 9000$$
$$+53\ 0000$$

Forcing the exponents equal gives:

$$+53\ 0090$$
$$+53\ 0000$$

with the remainder of the process being the same as above to give 000090 as a final answer.

Even with the relatively large range of values expressible in the floating point format overflows do occur, though not in the significant portion of the number as occurs in fixed point, since if the fraction overflows compensation is achieved by shifting the fraction right and adjusting the exponent. If the exponent cannot be held in the space allotted to it, however, we have reached the end of the floating point read. This condition is called *exponent overflow* and means that the procedure by which the problem is being solved will have to be rethought. The opposite condition, in which the number becomes too small to be expressed, is called *exponent underflow*. It results in a zero, and the consequences are not as serious as for overflow.

One final topic must be considered before leaving the subject of floating point arithmetic. In recent years a form of floating point arithmetic has come into fashion which is different from that presented here in some important respects. It arose out of a desire to extend the range covered by floating point numbers. There are several obvious ways to do this, the most obvious being to use a longer floating point word containing a larger exponent. The most common binary word size at that time was 36 bits, that of the IBM 700-7000 series computers. In an effort to keep word size as an exact multiple of eight bits to accommodate the then new eight level code systems a choice had to be made between extending the computer word to 40 bits or decreasing it to 32, i.e., 4 characters. The choice of a 32 bit word length was made, but this caused an even greater problem in both the extension of exponent range and preservation of precision. A compromise solution was adopted that allowed exponent range to be extended with some loss of precision. It works this way. In ordinary binary floating point the binary fraction is multiplied by some power of two, expressed in the exponent, to form the actual value of the number. In the modified form the fraction is still binary and the exponent is a seven bit binary number, but this exponent actually represents a power of sixteen. This means that a change of one in the exponent implies a multiplier of sixteen rather than two as before. In a straight binary floating point system a one is represented as $\frac{1}{2} \times 2^1$. In this modified system it is represented as $1/16 \times 16^1$, as shown below:

sign	exponent	fraction
0	100 0001	0001 0000 0000 0000 0000 0000

An important consequence of this is that a number expressed this way in general may have leading nonsignificant zeros, i.e., it cannot be truly normalized since to decrease the exponent by one requires a shift of 4 places in the fraction. The range of the exponent is extended greatly by this artifice to about $10^{\pm 76}$, but the 24 fraction bits are not all available for use as shown above. For the number above this makes no difference, but for a number such as 1.1 it means a loss of 3 bits out of the available 24, giving a 21 bit precision. The effect of this has been to curtail sharply the fraction of problems which will produce satisfactory results using single precision floating point.

Because of some concern over the effect of this, IBM released a study of the differences in results obtained using the former 36 bit precision and the new 32 bit precision. This study was hopefully entitled "Utility of the 32 Bit Word for the Scientific User." In this study 26 application programs were run under both conditions. The identification of the problems is sketchy and 6 of the 26 are completely unidentified. Of the 26, one problem, an analysis of variance, would not produce satisfactory results at either precision. Of the remaining 25, 6 produced agreement which was said to be exact, 5 more produced a sufficient agreement to be acceptable (marked "yes" in ths study), and the remainder were judged either "probable" or "no." Thus only 11 of the 25 tested programs yielded results which could be certified as satisfactory at the short precision. The conclusion of the study expresses a positive note, namely that if a problem were found to run satisfactorily at the short precision, time could be saved by doing so, but if in doubt, a greater precision should be used.

For those who wish to read the details of the IBM study the publication number is C20-1628-0.

13 Using the Teletype

The teletype is the most common of all minicomputer peripheral devices. It is slow and noisy, but for all the complaints which are lodged against it, it is an amazingly versatile machine. The teletype provides a keyboard and printer and both reads and punches paper tape. Service is almost universally available, and the machines keep running in environments which would ruin more sophisticated devices. An even greater advantage is that it is cheap, and it is this attribute which is chiefly responsible for its popularity.

The very versatility of the teletype contributes to the difficulty encountered by the beginner in programming for it. This chapter is an attempt to short circuit some of this difficulty by presenting the reader with a general explanation of programming procedures plus a set of subroutines which will allow the teletype to be used effectively until his competence is advanced to the point of real understanding.

The computer and teletype communicate with each other by means of eight bit codes. Each of these codes represents some function performed by the teletype. The code 11000101_2 represents the letter "E," while 10000111 represents the ringing of the teletype's internal bell. Other codes are associated with the return of the teletype print carriage, advancing the paper, etc. Codes sent from the computer to the teletype cause the functions associated with them to be performed by the teletype. Codes sent from the teletype to the computer are interpreted as signals to the computer that the function associated with the code has been performed on the teletype. A complete list of teletype codes and the function associated with each is given at the end of this chapter.

The assembly program aids in teletype communication by providing automatic generation of the bit patterns associated with each of the teletype functions. This can be done in two convenient ways. The first is by means of the DATA statement used earlier. The teletype codes, called ASCII codes, associated with the letters OK are generated in an assembled program by the statement:

        DATA   'OK'

The letters which are to be encoded are enclosed within apostrophes in the operand field of the DATA statement. The above DATA statement causes the binary word:

        1100 1111 1100 1011

133

to be included in the assembled program. The left most 8 bits of this word $1100\ 1111_2 = CF_{16}$ represent the letter O, while the right most 8, $1100\ 1011_2 = CB_{16}$, represent the K.

If more than two characters are required the TEXT pseudo operation is more convenient. It is used as follows:

TEXT   'THERE ONCE WAS A LADY NAMED ALICE'

This is a string of 33 characters. The assembly program will generate the binary code for each of the 33 and pack the 8 bit codes, two per computer word, into 17 successive program locations. Since the number of characters is odd, a blank code is added as a final character.

Codes for which there is no printed function cannot be generated this way and must be treated as numerical data. To advance the paper and ring the teletype bell the codes :8A and :87 must be sent to the teletype. To create a memory word containing these codes use the DATA pseudo operation, as:

DING   DATA   :8A87

The colon before the number means that it is to be interpreted as hexadecimal. Advancing the paper one line does *not* return the teletype carriage. Unlike a typewriter, the teletype treats carriage return and paper advance as two separate functions. Consulting the table at the end of the chapter, the codes for carriage return and line feed (paper advance) are :8D and :8A. To create a word which contains these codes we use:

NXTLIN   DATA   :8D8A

In most printing schemes the character in the left most part of the word is printed first. For this reason the carriage return code is placed in the left part of the created word. Carriage return from the extreme right-hand carriage position requires more time than the advance of paper or printing a character. If a carriage return were issued to the teletype followed immediately by a printing character, say X or 5, the character would be printed while the carriage was in the return motion. Had it been at the extreme right position the X or 5 would appear in the middle of the line, smeared by the motion of the carriage. For this reason the line feed character is issued after the carriage return. The paper can then be advanced while the carriage is returning. These two motions do not conflict, and since the line feed code causes nothing to be printed no problem of a "smeared" character arises. On some older teletypes even this provision is not enough and a "fill" character must be supplied after the line feed. The function of this fill character is simply to waste one print cycle while waiting for the return of the carriage to be completed. The fill character most commonly used is binary code 1111 1111, called the "rubout" code. In no circumstance should a program ever be written which depends on teletype timing. The 1/10 second is strictly a nominal time and individual teletypes may deviate from this by as much as 20 percent.

The teletype routines at the end of this chapter are written in the closed form described in the chapter "Programs and Subprograms." The routine whose entry point name is RKB is used to read one ASCII character from the teletype. It is used by:

JST   RKB

The contents of the registers on entry to RKB are irrelevant. On return the A register will contain the 8 bit ASCII code for the key which was struck. The X register will be unchanged. RKB has no definite execution time as it must wait until a key is struck on the teletype keyboard. The character code for the key is in the low 8 bits of the A register. The upper 8 bits are zeros. If the key struck was Carriage Return (CR), RKB will cause a line feed to be sent to the teletype automatically before returning control to the calling program.

The routine with entry point name CHOUT (*CH*aracter *OUT*) is entered with an ASCII character code in the low 8 bits of the A register. This code is sent to the teletype to print the appropriate letter or symbol or to perform a control function. If a Carriage Return is sent out via CHOUT a line feed will be supplied automatically, making the teletype behave like a conventional typewriter in which return and paper advance are a single operation. To use CHOUT to print a *B* on the teletype:

LAP   'B'   load character "B" into the A register
JST   CHOUT   go print the character

The timing of CHOUT is that of the teletype itself, nominally 1/10 of a second.

Finally, PRT (*PriNT*) will cause an entire line or group of lines to be printed with a single execution. It is used by entering with the *address* of the word containing the first character to be printed in the A register. This address is a pointer used to access the characters to be printed. Strings of characters printed by PRT *must* end with a backslash character (\). This character is labeled FORM on some keyboards and is blank on others. In any case the character is that obtained by typing *L* with the shift key depressed. The backslash character is not printed. It is used by CHOUT to determine the end of the character string. Suppose it were necessary to print:

THERE ONCE WAS A MAN FROM NANTUCKET

on the teletype. This can be done by creating a TEXT string with the necessary characters and an address pointer which points to the word containing the first character of the message, as:

```
POINTR    DATA  MSGE
MSGE      TEXT  'THERE  ONCE  WAS  A  MAN  FROM
                NANTUCKET\'
```

Note that the string beginning at MSGE is enclosed in apostrophes and ends with a backslash. If a Carriage Return character is encountered in the string being printed a line feed will be supplied automatically. To print the line in the TEXT statement:

```
          LDA     POINTR       message address to A register
          JST     PRT          print the string
          . . .
```

A carriage return and line feed are supplied before the line is printed. If carriage return characters are encountered in the string being printed, line feeds are supplied automatically. This furnishes a useful way to perform multiline printing with a single entry, as in the following:

```
label      inst.   operand
LPTR       DATA  $+1
           TEXT  'THERE ONCE WAS A HERMIT NAMED DAVE'
           DATA  :8DFF carriage return and rubout
           TEXT  '(second line)'
           DATA  :8DFF carriage return and rubout
           TEXT  '(third line)'
           DATA  :8DFF
           TEXT  '(fourth line)'
           DATA  :8DFF carriage return and rubout
           TEXT  'BUT THINK OF THE MONEY I SAVE\'
```

The entire limerick can be printed by:

```
          LDA     LPTR         message address to A
          JST     PRT          print it
          . . .
```

Since a line feed is supplied automatically after each carriage return (:8D) the above is printed with single space between lines. If the DATA statements in the above had been DATA   :8D8A, i.e., carriage return and line feed, the message would have been double spaced.

The above described routines are presented here for utility only. The details of their operations and the general methods for communicating with other peripheral devices will be given in chapter 20.

```
**********************************
* TELETYPE HANDLER ROUTINES *
**********************************
*
* KEYBOARD READ ROUTINE
*
RKB        DATA    0            ENTRY POINT
           SEL     TTY          SET AUTO ECHO
           SEL     TTY+1        SELECT KEYBOARD
           SEN     TTY+1        KEY STRUCK YET?
           JMP     $-1          NO
           INA     TTY          YES, BRING IT IN
           STA     PRT          SAVE IT
           CAI     :8D          WAS IT A CARRIAGE RETURN?
           JST     CHOUT        YES, SUPPLY THE LINE FEED
           LDA     PRT          PICK UP THE CHARACTER
           JMP     *RKB         AND RETURN
*
* CHARACTER PRINT ROUTINE
*
CHOUT      DATA    0            ENTRY POINT
           OTA     TTY          PRINT THE CHARACTER
           SEN     TTY+1        FINISHED YET?
           JMP     $-1          NO
           CAI     :8D          WAS IT CARRIAGE RETURN?
           JMP     $+2          YES
           JMP     *CHOUT       NO, RETURN
           LAP     :8A          PICK UP THE LINE FEED
           JMP     CHOUT+1      AND PUT IT OUT
*
* LINE PRINT ROUTINE
*
PRT        DATA    0            ENTRY POINT
           STA     RKB          SAVE STRING ADDRESS
           LAP     :8D          PICK UP CARRIAGE RETURN
           JST     CHOUT        PUT IT OUT
           LDX     RKB          ADDRESS POINTER TO X
           LLX     1            FORM BYTE ADDRESS
           SBM
           LDA     @0           PICK UP CHARACTER
           CAI     '\'          WAS IT A BACKSLASH?
           JMP     END          YES, RETURN
           JST     CHOUT        NO, PUT IT OUT
           IXR                  BUMP BYTE ADDRESS POINTER
           JMP     $-5
END        SWM
           JMP     *PRT         RETURN
TTY        EQU     :38
           END
```

ASCII TELETYPE CODE

SYMBOL	HEX CODE	SYMBOL	HEX CODE
@	C0	BLANK	A0
A	C1	!	A1
B	C2	"	A2
C	C3	#	A3
D	C4	$	A4
E	C5	%	A5
F	C6	&	A6
G	C7	'	A7
H	C8	(	A8
I	C9	)	A9
J	CA	*	AA
K	CB	+	AB
L	CC	,	AC
M	CD	−	AD
N	CE	.	AE
O	CF	/	AF
P	D0	0	B0
Q	D1	1	B1
R	D2	2	B2
S	D3	3	B3
T	D4	4	B4
U	D5	5	B5
V	D6	6	B6
W	D7	7	B7
X	D8	8	B8
Y	D9	9	B9
Z	DA	:	BA
[	DB	;	BB
\	DC	<	BC
]	DD	=	BD
↑	DE	>	BE
←	DF	?	BF

CONTROL CODES

CARRIAGE RETURN	8D
LINE FEED	8A
BELL	87
RUBOUT (ALL 1'S)	FF
NULL (ALL 0'S)	00

14 Handling Arrays of Data—Address Modification

Data received by a computer are often associated with one another in such a way that they can be considered items in a data set. Dealing with sets of data efficiently requires that the entire set be accessible with the minimum of programming overhead. For this reason sets or blocks of associated data are usually stored in adjacent memory locations, i.e., memory locations whose addresses are contiguous. A set or block of data stored in this manner is called an *array* or *vector*. For an array which requires five locations, there are several ways to reserve space. The most obvious is:

label	inst.	operand
BLOCK	DATA	0
	DATA	0
	DATA	0
	DATA	0
	DATA	0

The DATA statement can generate the same result as the above with a single line, as:

BLOCK	DATA	0,0,0,0,0

In each of the above cases the label BLOCK refers to the first location of the array of five, that with the *lowest* memory address. If the numbers in the array had to be set to particular values, this can be done, for example, by:

BLOCK	DATA	5,−7,92,36,−8

In this case BLOCK refers to the cell containing the 5, BLOCK+1 to the cell with the −7, and so forth, BLOCK+4 referring to the cell containing the −8. For an array which does not have to be initialized to different values there is another, more convenient, way of doing the job, namely:

BLOCK	RES	5

or if all of the array items are to be set to the *same* value, say −24:

BLOCK	RES	5,−24

The RES statement, meaning *RES*erve, sets aside an array of five locations under the name BLOCK. When this array has been filled with data from some source it will be necessary to do something with the data. Examples

139

dealing with the addition of numbers in an array have already been given in a previous chapter, showing the relative efficiencies of indirect, indexed, and the compound indexed-indirect addressing modes. The purpose of this chapter will be to elaborate upon the earlier examples and illustrate more complex array handling situations.

A frequent requirement is to find the maximum and minimum values contained in an array. This arises in such situations as generation of report data in which the greatest and least values of the item being reported are to be appended to the report. To find maximum and minimum it is necessary to compare each item of the array to some standard, and replace the standard with the array value if the array value exceeds the standard. To do this we will define two locations called MAX and MIN and compare each array item to these two cells. If the array item is less than MIN it will become the new MIN. If the item is greater than MAX it replaces MAX to become the new maximum standard. After all of the items have been so compared MAX and MIN will contain the largest and smallest items from the array, respectively. To start the process it is necessary to initialize MAX and MIN to some values such that some array item is bound to be larger than MAX and smaller than MIN. To understand why this is necessary, consider what would happen if MAX were set to 1000 and MIN to -1000. If all of the array items fell between the limits ± 500, MAX and MIN would still be 1000 and -1000 after all the array items had been compared to them. The conditions can be satisfied if we initialize MAX to the largest negative number and MIN to the largest positive number. This means, in the case considered above, that the first array item compared to these limits will replace both of them as soon as it is compared. Another way to satisfy the conditions is to set both MAX and MIN to the same value as some item in the array, any item. As successive array items are compared anything greater than MAX will replace this item and anything less than MIN will replace it. This is shown in example 14-1.

Example 14-1

Find the maximum and minimum values in the 100 word array whose name is FUNGUS. First we define the necessary pointers and temporary storage words, as:

label	inst.	operand	
FUNGUS	RES	100	an array named FUNGUS
FADR	DATA	FUNGUS	address pointer pointing to FUNGUS
CNT	DATA	0	
MAX	DATA	0	

```
MIN          DATA  0
             ...
```

and the program:

```
             LDA   FUNGUS    first array item store in
             STA   MAX       both MAX
             STA   MIN       and MIN
             LAM   100       count of items in array
             STA   CNT       to temporary count cell
             LDX   FADR      let's use indexed addressing
FLOOP        LDA   @0        pick up array item
             CMS   MIN       compare to minimum, is it
                             less?
             STA   MIN       yes, save new minimum
             CMS   MAX       compare to maximum, is it
                             greater?
             JMP   $+2       no, forget it
             STA   MAX       yes, save new maximum
             IXR             bump address pointer in the X
                             register
             IMS   CNT       last array item?
             JMP   FLOOP     no, get the next one
             ...             yes, we're finished
```

Very often more information is needed about the values of array items than the simple maximum and minimum, and the necessary information can be extracted only by setting all of the array items into ascending or descending order. This process, called *sorting,* is very common in commercial data processing and much effort has been expended in finding ways to do it efficiently. We will confine this discussion to illustrating the principle involved in one of the most common methods called a *bubble sort.*

Sorting an array means putting it into ascending or descending order. The example which follows puts the array into ascending order, though sorting the other way is no more trouble. If the array is sorted into ascending order then the value of the Nth array item is by definition less than the value of the $N + 1$st item. It is this which will be used to accomplish the sort. The general procedure is to compare an array item with the next array item. If the first item is greater than the second the two are swapped. This is done for the entire list. Each time a swap is made a counter is incremented. The process is repeated until each item in the list can be compared with the next without a swap taking place, i.e., the swap counter is still zero at the end of the pass. When this happens the array is in order. Note that for an array N items long, only $N - 1$ comparisons are made since each item can be compared only with $N - 1$ other items in the array.

From the earlier discussion of indexed addressing, remember that the effective address of an indexed instruction is determined by adding the displacement part of the instruction to the contents of the X register. If the X register contains the address of the first (lowest address) item in the array, the instruction:

```
LDA    @0
```

will fetch the first item in the array, while:

```
LDA    @1
```

fetches the second, and:

```
LDA    @2
```

fetches the third. This amounts to an "offset" to the address contained in the X register. Such use of index offsets is not confined to LDA, of course. The first item in an array can be compared to the second by:

```
LDA    @0         fetch first item
CMS    @1         compare to second
JMP    STWO       less, skip
JMP    $+2        greater, swap the two items
JMP    STWO       equal, skip
EMA    @1         swap A and second item
STA    @0         restore first item
```

If the X register is now incremented (IXR) it will contain the address of the second array item. LDA @0 will fetch the second array item while CMS @1 will compare it to the third item. This small group of instructions is the heart of the bubble sort process, as shown in example 14-2.

Example 14-2

Write a program to sort an array of 100 numbers into ascending order using the bubble sort method described above. The temporary storage words and address pointers are defined as:

label	inst.	operand	
TUBSRT	RES	100	the array to be sorted
ADR	DATA	TUBSRT	address of array to be sorted
CNT	DATA	0	count cell
TRGR	DATA	0	this cell is incremented each
	. . .		time a swap of two array items

occurs. When a complete pass through the list is made without incrementing this cell the array is in order.

The sorting program is:

SZERO	ZAR		set the swap count to zero at
	STA	TRGR	the beginning of each pass
	LAM	99	# of comparisons * array length − 1
	STA	CNT	
	LDX	ADR	address pointer to index
SONE	LDA	@0	pick up array item
	CMS	@1	1st item greater than 2nd?
	JMP	STWO	no, less, leave it in place
	JMP	$+2	yes, swap the items
	JMP	STWO	no, swap on equal. If this were allowed the sort could not be completed by our criteria, since the swap trigger TRGR would be incremented on every pass if the array contained two equal items.
	EMA	@1	perform the swap
	STA	@0	. . .
	IMS	TRGR	increment the swap count
STWO	IXR		bump the item address
	IMS	CNT	last one?
	JMP	SONE	no, do the next one
	LDA	TRGR	yes, any swaps on this pass?
	JAN	SZERO	if yes, do it all over again
	. . .		if no, the sort is finished

The reader should take notice of the fact that it is not possible to assign a definite time to the execution of the above sort program. The number of passes through the array that must be made is determined by the initial ordering of the array. Even if the array is in perfect ascending order to begin with one pass is made to verify that no swaps are necessary. Nevertheless, the method does work and it is adequate for short lists of numbers in which memory space is more important than time. The sort routine shown above can easily be written as a subroutine which can perform sorting on lists located anywhere in memory as a service to other programs. Only two items of information need to be transmitted to such a subroutine to perform its task, the address of the first item in the list to be sorted and the number of items in the list. If the address is transmitted in X and the number of items in A, we have the sort subroutine shown in example 14-3.

Example 14-3

Construct a sort subroutine to be used by a calling program executing the sequence:

label	inst.	operand	
	LDX	VADRS	address of array to be sorted in X
	LDA	NUMBER	# of items in the array
	JST	SORT	execute the SORT subroutine
	...		return here with the array sorted
VADRS	DATA	VECTOR	address of VECTOR
VECTOR	RES	100	the array to be sorted
NUMBER	DATA	$-VECTOR	number of items in the array VECTOR (the reader will be left to evaluate the meaning of the expression $-VECTOR)

The SORT subroutine itself looks like this:

SORT	NOP		the entry point
	STX	ADR	save the array address
	JAM	$+2	force the array count negative
	NAR		...
	IAR		form − (NUMBER − 1), the # of comparisons
	JAZ	RETURN	garbage if this is zero
	STA	NCMPS	save for subsequent passes
SZERO	ZAR		
	STA	TRGR	zero swap count, as before
	LDA	NCMPS	
	STA	CNT	initialize comparison counter
	LDX	ADR	array address to index
SONE	LDA	@0	pick up array item
	CMS	@1	greater than next item?
	JMP	STWO	no, less, skip the swap
	JMP	$+2	yes, proceed with swap
	JMP	STWO	no, equal, skip the swap
	EMA	@1	perform the swap

```
          STA    @0        . . .
          IMS    TRGR      and increment the swap count
STWO      IXR              bump the address pointer in X
          IMS    CNT       last comparison?
          JMP    SONE      no, do it again
          LDA    TRGR      yes, were any swaps made?
          JAN    SZERO     repeat if swap count nonzero
RETURN    JMP    *SORT     if zero, the array is sorted, re-
                           turn
ADR       NOP              storage for array address
NCMPS     NOP              storage for # of comparisons
                           per pass
TRGR      NOP              swap counter
CNT       NOP              comparison counter
```

Now we will consider a little more difficult problem—that of handling more than one array at a time. The need for such operations is common. A typical requirement is that a member of an array be operated upon in conjunction with the corresponding member of another array. One array might contain the number of hours worked by the employee whose number is the number of the array item while the other array contains the hourly rate. In this case a number in the first array is to be multiplied by its counterpart in the second array to arrive at a paycheck figure.

A problem which arises in spectroscopic and photographic processes is the determination of the total energy transmitted by a filter whose absorption varies with the wave length of incident light when the source of the light varies in intensity in different wave lengths. To do this it is assumed that the transmission of the filter is linear over some small wavelength interval, say 10 Angstroms. We divide the interval of interest into subintervals 10 Angstroms wide. The energy emitted by the light source is divided into corresponding subintervals. The total transmitted energy in any subinterval is then the amount of incident energy in that subinterval times the percent transmission of the filter in the same subinterval. The total energy passed by the filter for the entire wavelength region is simply the sum of all of these products. If the individual transmissions were expressed in integer percents this sum must be divided by 100.

This problem, while a little complex, is a desirable one for an example since it forces us to draw upon several other skills discussed earlier and integrate them into a complete solution to the problem. The individual products may be longer than 15 bits, so we must cumulate the sum in double precision. As there are two arrays involved and only one index register we are forced to the use of indirect addressing. The double precision, multiply and divide operations are done by subroutines, so the techniques of subroutine call are exercised. The solution to the problem is shown in example 14-4.

Example 14-4

The spectral interval 9000 to 9500 Angstroms is divided into 50 subintervals each 10 Angstroms wide. It is required to determine how much total energy will be passed through a layer of water vapor (the filter) from an infrared source. The spectral characteristics of the source are already known and tabulated in the array named SOURCE. The percent transmission of the layer of water vapor is also predetermined and tabulated in the array named FILTER. Find the total energy transmitted by the layer of water vapor. Arrays and constants are defined by:

label	inst.	operand	
SOURCE	RES	50	array of energies in the subintervals
FILTER	RES	50	array of transmission percents in the subintervals
SADR	DATA	SOURCE	address pointer for SOURCE array
FADR	DATA	FILTER	address pointer for FILTER array
ADRF	NOP		temporary pointer
ADRS	NOP		temporary pointer
CNT	NOP		temporary count cell
SUM	RES	2	double precision sum cumulation cells
	...		
START	ZAR		
	STA	SUM	zero the double precision sum
	STA	SUM+1	
	LDA	SADR	initialize temporary pointers
	STA	ADRS	...
	LDA	FADR	...
	STA	ADRF	...
	LAM	50	initialize subinterval count
	STA	CNT	
ELOOP	LDA	*ADRS	pick up energy in this subinterval
	LDX	*ADRF	and percent transmission in this subinterval

```
        JST    MPY           and go to the multiply sub-
                             routine
```

Control returns from MPY with the double precision product in A and X. We add it to the double precision sum by:

```
        JST    DBLADD
        DATA   SUM
        IMS    ADRS          increment  energy  array
                             pointer
        IMS    ADRF          and transmission percent
                             array pointer
        IMS    CNT           last subinterval?
        JMP    ELOOP         no, do the next one
        . . .
```

When control reaches here the double precision sum of all of the products is in SUM and SUM+1, placed there by the DBLADD routine. The sum is also still in A and X, however, in the exact form required for a double precision dividend. The division by 100 is accomplished by referencing a divide subroutine, as:

```
        JST    DIVIDE
        DATA   HUNDRD
        . . .
```

At this point the problem is finished if no divide check occurs.

As a final exercise on array handling the problem of a structured array will be treated. Structured arrays have the property that array items occupy more than one computer word. In a commercial application, for example, a single array "item" might consist of five words containing the following information:

Employee number

Hourly rate

Number of years employed

Number of sick days this year

Number of overtime hours this year

If the X register contained a pointer which pointed to the beginning of one of these five word blocks, the employee number could be accessed by:

```
        LDA    @0
```

and the number of overtime hours this year by:

LDA   @4

Learning to handle arrays like this furnishes an opportunity to learn a very convenient assembly program trick involving the use of the EQU pseudo op. EQU is used to set the value of one symbol equal to that of another. If, for example, it was discovered that two temporary storage locations in a program were never in use at the same time, the waste of one of them could be eliminated by deleting it from the source program and setting its former symbol equal to the value of the one retained. If for example DICK were to be eliminated in favor of GERRY, the source statement defining DICK would be deleted and the statement:

DICK   EQU   GERRY

inserted at some point *after* the source statement which defined GERRY. Thereafter all references to DICK would be assembled as if they had referred to GERRY instead. Note that the EQU must be inserted *after* the definition of GERRY. Anything in the operand field of an EQU *must* have been previously defined.

The field of an EQU can contain a number instead of a symbol. Numbers need no previous definition as their meaning is unambiguous. Thus a symbol can be set to some fixed value by an EQU statement like:

ADOLPH   EQU   175

and any instruction which refers to ADOLPH will reference the number 175 in the appropriate way.

Returning now to the question of a structured array containing multiword files, the five file items can be given symbolic names by the EQU artifice shown above, as:

EMPNO	EQU	0	the employee number
HOURLY	EQU	1	the hourly rate
YEARS	EQU	2	number of years employed
SICK	EQU	3	number of sick days
OVRTIM	EQU	4	number of overtime hours

The employee number can now be accessed by:

LDA   @EMPNO

while the number of sick days can be accessed by:

LDA   @SICK

Other than the obvious convenience of not having to remember numerical displacements, this method has one great advantage. If the file is ever rearranged only the EQU's have to be changed. Had absolute numerical displacements been used, *every* reference to the file would have to be changed. This could be very tedious in a long program, and it is easy to miss a reference. The use of this scheme in the processing of a structured array is shown in example 14-5.

Example 14-5

Using the reference scheme described above, search a file of 100 employee records for the employee numbers of those whose hourly rate is $3.50 or more who have also worked more than six hours of overtime. Build a separate array of these employee numbers beginning at XFILE. The necessary definitions are:

label	inst.	operand	
EFILE	RES	500	array to be searched, 5 words/employee
FILADR	DATA	EFILE	address pointer for employee file
XFILE	RES	100	the file to be built
XFLADR	DATA	XFILE	pointer for file to be built
XCNT	DATA	0	number of employees who meet the conditions
ADR	NOP		temporary address pointer
SIX	DATA	6	comparand for overtime hours
THRE50	DATA	350	comparand for pay rate
CNT	NOP		count cell

And the program:

SEARCH	ZAR		
	STA	XCNT	zero count of employees who meet the conditions
	LDA	XFLADR	initialize address of file to be generated
	STA	ADR	. . .
	LAM	100	initialize file count
	STA	CNT	
	LDX	FILADR	address pointer to X
SLOOP	LDA	@HOURLY	hourly rate to A
	CMS	THRE50	$3.50/hour or more?
	JMP	S2	no, continue search
	NOP		yes, check the overtime
	LDA	@OVRTIM	overtime hours to A
	CMS	SIX	6 hours or more?

```
JMP    S2        no, try the next one
NOP              yes . . .
LDA    @EMPNO    get the employee number
STA    *ADR      and put it in the file
IMS    ADR       bump file pointer
IMS    XCNT      and the number who met the
                 conditions
AXI    5         set X pointer to next file
IMS    CNT       last employee?
JMP    SLOOP     no, get the next one
. . .
```

In the above example the main employee file, EFILE, was accessed by a pointer held in X, while the file being built, XFILE, was referenced by indirect addressing. While the opposite arrangement would also work, this one was used because of the ease of incrementing the structured file address in X by the use of AXI   5. The other file address never requires an increment greater than 1 so it can be handled by IMS.

15 Table Reference Schemes—Address Computation

In the earlier discussion of subroutines the terms argument and function were introduced to describe the numbers put into and received back from a subroutine. The example used in that chapter was of a square root subroutine, the argument being the number whose square root was to be taken while the function was the resultant square root. Subroutines like this can be constructed for any mathematical or logical function for which some method exists for calculating the value of the function from the argument. Trigonometric functions are another example.

In the above cases an analytic method exists for deriving the function from the argument. In many situations, though, no satisfactory means can be found for doing this and it is necessary to use the argument to "look up" the function in a table of function values. There is, for example, no way to compute a person's bank balance from his account number or his street address from his phone number. While names and phone numbers bear a relation to one another there is no way to derive one from the other. In such cases as this the argument and function are set up in tabular form. The argument table is then searched until a match is found. The function is extracted from the corresponding position in the function table.

The telephone book is such an arrangement. Access to phone numbers is simplified by the special circumstance that users of the phone book have a knowledge of the alphabet, and the phone book is arranged alphabetically. If it were not arranged alphabetically the entire book would have to be searched for a name (the argument) in order to find a phone number (the function). A second type of table reference is that in which, while the function itself cannot be computed from the argument, its position in a table of functions can be computed. In this case the argument is used to compute a *table displacement*. This displacement is used to reference the proper function value in the table of function values. This is often the case even when the function can be computed, but the time required to compute it is not tolerable. High speed, low precision, trigonometry is a case in point. Rather than compute the sine or cosine of an angle by the conventional series methods, it is much faster to look it up in a table. The table requires memory space, of course, and this is what limits the precision of such a method. Another case of this situation is shown in example 15-1.

Example 15-1

A program is required which will take an integer between 1 and 10 inclusive and return the 3/2 power of the integer as an answer. This can be computed directly by cubing the integer and taking the square root of this cube. Time constraints forbid this approach and a table lookup is necessary. The table of values of the function is:

label	*inst.*	*operand*
FTABLE	DATA	1,2,5,8,11,14,18,22,27,31
FADR	DATA	FTABLE address pointer

The table is accessed by using the integer argument as an address displacement. This is done by simply adding it to the address of the first table entry. Since the integers run from 1 to 10 this produces an address one greater than the required address. The computed address is thus decremented and used as a pointer to access the function value, as:

LDA	ARG	integer argument to A
ADD	FADR	plus the table address
DAR		decrement
TAX		move computed address to index
LDA	@0	and pick up the function value

There are several shorter ways to do this. The above is shown only for clarity. We could get rid of the DAR by specifying:

FADR	DATA	FTABLE−1

instead of the above specification. Another way to get rid of the DAR is to make use of the fact that a number can be decremented while it is being transferred from one register to the other. Thus DAR and TAX can be combined into DAX, i.e., move the contents of A to X and decrement X.

The other table lookup situation, that in which it is not possible to use the argument to determine a displacement, requires that a table of arguments be searched. When the input argument is found its *position* in the table of input arguments is used to compute a displacement which is then used to access the function in the function table. If argument and function are of identical length the displacements in the two tables are identical. This type of search is shown in example 15-2.

Example 15-2

In a data entry application two ASCII characters are read by an input routine. These characters are the initials of the typist who is entering data into the system. The input from each typist is routed to a separate buffer area in memory. The argument in this case is the word containing the typist's initials. The function is the address of the buffer area into which this typist's data are to be routed. The argument table consists of eight words, each containing the initials of a typist. The table is a set of eight addresses. The argument table is specified:

```
ARGTAB   DATA  'AA'      initials of first typist
         DATA  'BG'      initials of second typist
         DATA  'RN'      etc.
         DATA  'SW'
         DATA  'TR'
         DATA  'HS'
         DATA  'KW'
         DATA  'WW'      initials of eighth typist
ARGADR   DATA  ARGTAB    address pointer for argument
                         table
```

...

The function table is specified

```
FUNTAB   DATA  B1        address of first data buffer
         DATA  B2        address of second data buffer
         DATA  B3        etc.
         DATA  B4
         DATA  B5
         DATA  B6
         DATA  B7
         DATA  B8        address of eight data buffer
FUNADR   DATA  FUNTAB    address pointer for function
                         table
```

...

If the input initials are in location CHECK the program is:

```
SEARCH   LDX   ARGADR    argument table pointer to
                         index

         LAM   8
         STA   CNT       initialize table count
```

```
S2        LDA    @0          pick up item from argument
                             table
          XOR    CHECK       form logical difference
          JAZ    EUREKA      zero if identical, found the ar-
                             gument
          IXR                not yet, increment argument
                             table pointer
          IMS    CNT         last argument in table?
          JMP    S2          no, try the next one
          . . .
```

If control reaches this point the initials were not in the argument table. If the JAZ   EUREKA was executed, it is necessary to isolate the table displacement so it can be used to access the corresponding entry from the function table. This is done by subtracting the address of the first word of the table from the pointer in X at the time the match was found, as:

```
EUREKA    TXA                move pointer to A
          SUB    ARGADR      subtract table origin
```

Now we have a number between zero and seven in A. Adding this displacement to the origin of the function table gives the address of the function table item to be retrieved from the table, as:

```
          ADD    FUNADR      add address of function table
                             origin
          TAX                move to index
          LDA    @0          and pick up the function
          . . .
```

A more elegant way to perform this search involves the compound addressing mode discussed in an earlier chapter—indexed indirect addressing. In this mode, it will be recalled, the contents of the index register are added to the contents of a pointer held in the scratchpad portion of memory to form an effective address. The address of the pointer in scratchpad is specified in the displacement portion of the instruction as an absolute address, $0 - 255_{10}$. The pointer words in scratchpad should point to the locations immediately *before* the first item in the table to be accessed, as:

```
ARGADR    DATA ARGTAB-1
```

and

```
FUNADR    DATA FUNTAB-1
```

The reason for this is that we will use the X register as both a table displacement and a counter. Since X cannot be tested directly for a negative or positive condition but only for zero or nonzero, we want the search loop to stop when X becomes zero. The last access and comparison are done when X = 1. If all of this seems a bit obscure, it is well worth the reader's time to understand it, since the result is more compact than that of the last example. The program in the example can be rewritten:

```
                LXP   8          positive count/displacement to
                                 index
     SEARCH     LDA   *@ARGADR   pick up item from argument table
                XOR   CHECK      form logical difference as before
                JAZ   EUREKA     zero if identical
                DXR              decrement index for next try
                JXN   SEARCH     do it again if X not yet zero
                ...
```

Like the other example, if control reaches here the initials are not contained in the argument table. If the JAZ   EUREKA is executed, the function value is accessed by:

```
     EUREKA     LDA   *@FUNADR   pick up function value
                ...
```

This solution requires only half the number of instructions as that of the earlier example. It does require the use of pointer words in the scratchpad area, which must be done with some care. Certain locations in scratchpad have dedicated hardware uses as will be explained in the chapter on interrupts. Nonetheless, this method produces a very compact result and should be considered if scratchpad space is available for the pointers. Note that the search is performed from the highest to the lowest table address. This is the opposite of the previous example.

Now we will discuss the most elegant way of all to solve problems like this, the SCM instruction. SCM is in many ways the ultimate "whistles and bells" minicomputer instruction, since it is capable of performing a table search all by itself. It is a complex instruction which is a little more difficult to understand than the simple ones but is well worth the effort. Its operation involves comparison of the contents of the A register to a *series* of memory locations, with different actions taken depending on whether or not one of the memory words matched the contents of A. The entire search is done with a single execution of the SCM instruction, the end of the instruction coming when a match is found or the table is exhausted.

The precise operation of SCM is as follows. A pointer in the scratchpad area is defined to contain the address of the table to be searched, minus one, i.e., it contains the address of the word *immediately preceding* the first word of the table to be searched. The X register contains the number of items in the table to be searched. The search operates by using indexed indirect addressing to form the address of the comparand. The contents of X are added to the contents of the scratchpad pointer to form an effective address. X is then decremented and the comparand is fetched from the effective address. The order of these steps is important to understanding the use of SCM. First the effective address is computed from the scratchpad pointer and the displacement in X, then X is decremented, and finally the comparand word is fetched from memory. This order of operations means that the X register has *already* been decremented at the time the comparison is made. If a match is found the SCM instruction ceases and the instruction following the SCM is executed. If the entire table is searched without finding a match the instruction which follows the SCM is skipped. The best way to gain some understanding of this is through an example. In example 15-3, we'll solve the same problem as the previous example but use the SCM instruction this time.

Example 15-3

Using the same argument and function tables as before solve the same problem using SCM. If no match is found in the argument table execute a JMP to location RINGER. First we define the address pointers in the scratchpad:

```
ARGADR    DATA  ARGTAB-1  origin of argument table minus
                          one
FUNADR    DATA  FUNTAB    origin of function table
          ...
```

The function table pointer FUNADR points directly to the beginning of the table rather than one location below it. This is because X will have already been decremented when the match is found. We could re-increment it to access the function if the pointer pointed to the word below the first function value, but this saves an instruction. The program for the search is:

```
LXP   8            table size in X
SCM   ARGADR       scan the argument table
JMP   $+2          found it, get the function
JMP   RINGER       no match in table, exit
LDA   @*FUNADR     fetch the function, finished
```

This requires only five instructions and is much faster than the previous method. The special circumstances of this search allow one more economy to be made though. The arguments are all ASCII characters, and ASCII characters have ones in their high positions. A word containing two ASCII characters, therefore, will have a one in what would be the sign bit if the word contained a numerical quantity. The addresses in the function table always have zero in the sign bit. The sign bit of an address pointer is set only to indicate a further indirect level. Since all of the addresses in the function table are direct their sign bits are zeros. This means that all of the arguments are negative while all of the functions are positive. This allows the above to be rewritten in a simpler form:

```
LXP    8            as before
SCM    ARGADR       as before
LDA    *@FUNADR     explained below
JAM    RINGER       . . .
```

If the SCM found a match in the table, it executed the instruction which follows it, the LDA   *@FUNADR, and the A register now contains a function value which is positive. If the SCM failed to find a match in the table the instruction following SCM was skipped, and the A register still contains the original argument, which is negative. The success of the SCM can therefore be tested by the JAM instruction. One instruction has been saved.

The use of SCM allowed the table to be searched in less than *one-third* of the number of instructions required for our original example using simple indexed addressing.

Scanning a block of memory for items of a specific value often arises in another context—that of determining the *number* of items in an array which have some value. This is solved easily with SCM. Since the execution of SCM stops when a match is found, a count word can be incremented by an IMS instruction when this happens. As the X register has already been decremented when this occurs, the displacement contained in it will be nonzero if the entire table has not yet been searched. In fact the decremented X register plus the contents of the scratchpad pointer are the effective address of the *next* item to be compared if X is not zero. The SCM can thus be re-executed with this count to *continue* the table search after a match has been found, the condition for re-execution being that X is not yet zero. This is shown in example 15-4.

Example 15-4

Search the 1000 word block of memory which begins at location BLOCK and determine the number of words which contain the value -74_{10}. The scratchpad address pointer is:

BLOCKA   DATA BLOCK-1

while the program, anywhere else in memory, is:

```
            ZAR
            STA    NCNT        zero number of −74's
            LDX    N           size of array to be scanned
            LAM    74          number to be searched for
LOOKUP      SCM    BLOCKA      scan the array
            IMS    NCNT        a hit, increment the count
            JXN    LOOKUP      if X not yet zero finish the scan
            ...
NCNT        NOP
N           DATA   1000
BLOCK       RES    1000
```

The full utility of this type of search will be better understood after byte mode addressing has been discussed.

It is frequently necessary to search an array for values which lie in some specified range. In this case we cannot use SCM since it can detect only identical matches. One way to execute this type of search is shown in example 15-5.

Example 15-5

Search the 1000 word array beginning at NUMBRZ and determine the number of array items having values between −7 and +38. Using indexed, indirect addressing, we have:

```
NADR        DATA   NUMBRZ−1 the address pointer in scratch-
                            pad
            ...
```

and the program, anywhere else in memory:

```
            LDX    N           array size to X
            ZAR
            STA    NCNT        zero the hit counter
LOOKUP      LDA    *@NADR      pick up array item
            CMS    HILMT       greater than +38?
            CMS    LOLMT       or less than7?
            JMP    NEXT        yes, forget it
            NOP
            IMS    NCNT        number in range, bump the
                              counter
NEXT        DXR                decrement index
            JXN    LOOKUP      do it again if index not ex-
                              hausted
```

```
            ...
HILMT       DATA   38
LOLMT       DATA   −7
            ...
```

with the other counts and blocks defined as before. When this has been executed the number of values which fell between −7 and +38 inclusive will be contained in NCNT.

This last example leads naturally to another class of table reference and array handling problems, that of constructing the frequency distribution of a set of values. The frequency distribution is an accounting of the manner in which a set of values is distributed over an interval. A common use of frequency distributions is for the construction of histograms, a kind of bar graph which shows how many values in a set fell between subintervals of the total interval over which the values fell. One application of frequency distribution is the notorious "grading curve," known to generations of college students. In constructing one of these curves the scores on a test are classified into subintervals of the total interval 0 to 99. These subintervals are typically 5 points. The scores from 0 to 4 fall into the first subinterval, 5 to 9 into the second, 10 to 14 in the third, and so forth, with 95 to 99 falling into the twentieth . This array of subtotals is then graphed, the length of the bar being proportional to the number of scores which fell in the interval represented by the bar. The grader then makes a statistical judgment (i.e., a guess) at what ought to be a passing grade and draws a line on the graph. The actual automatic drawing of the graph will be shown in Chapter 20. Our interest here is in the construction of the numerical frequency function on which the graph is based, as shown in example 15-6.

Example 15-6

A table of 500 test scores is located at SCORES. Each of the test scores is between 0 and 99. A twenty word array beginning at location FREQ has been set to all zeros. Find the number of scores which fell into each 5 point interval as described above.

The number of the interval into which a given score falls can be computed by dividing the score by 5. This division yields a quotient between 0 and 19. This quotient is the table offset of the word which is to be incremented. The division is to be performed by an external subroutine called by:

```
JST    DIV
DATA   DVSR
```

The DATA   DVSR is an address pointer to the location containing the actual divisor as described in a previous chapter. The frequency function is constructed by:

label	inst.	operand	
	LDA	SCRADR	
	STA	SCRPTR	create temporary address pointer
	LDA	COUNT	
	STA	CNT	−500 to temporary count
FREAKY	LDX	*SCRPTR	pick up score from array
	ZAR		zero A (single precision dividend)
	JST	DIV	divide score by 5
	DATA	DVSR	. . .
	TXA		move quotient, 0-19, to A
	ADD	FRQADR	generate address in frequency array
	TAX		move to index
	IMS	@0	This increments the cell whose address was computed above by adding the 0-19 quotient to the base address of the frequency array.
	IMS	SCRPTR	increment address pointer
	IMS	CNT	last score?
	JMP	FREAKY	no, get the next one
	. . .		
SCRADR	DATA	SCORES	SCORE array address pointer
SCRPTR	NOP		temporary address pointer
COUNT	DATA	−500	array size
CNT	NOP		temporary count cell
DVSR	DATA	5	
FRQADR	DATA	FREQ	frequency array address pointer
SCORES	RES	500	score array
FREQ	RES	20	the frequency array

When the above has been executed the FREQ array contains the frequency distribution of the values in the SCORE array. If lines whose length was proportional to the numbers in the FREQ array were drawn on paper, the result would be the *histogram* of these values.

Another common kind of table reference problem is that in which argument and function are of different lengths, e.g., the argument is two words long and the function one word long. This is a special case of a technique which will be developed in Chapter 16. To illustrate the general idea involved, consider example 15-7.

Example 15-7

Five subroutines exist somewhere in memory. Their names are SUBONE, SUBTWO, SUBTHR, SUBFOR, and SUBFIV. Input from the teletype keyboard, performed elsewhere, is in the form of a string of four ASCII characters occupying two memory words. These two word arguments are contained in the table whose origin is at INTAB. The table of subroutine addresses is contained in the array XVCTR. Write a program to determine which of the arguments FUZZ, DAVE, LOVE, GENE, or BARF was typed, and cause the execution of SUBONE for FUZZ, SUBTWO for DAVE, etc. If the character string is not in the argument table execute a jump to location ILLEGL.

The tables are:

label	inst.	operand	
INTAB	TEXT	'FUZZ'	argument table
	TEXT	'DAVE'	
	TEXT	'LOVE'	
	TEXT	'GENE'	
	TEXT	'BARF'	

and

XVCTR	DATA	SUBONE	function table
	DATA	SUBTWO	
	DATA	SUBTHR	
	DATA	SUBFOR	
	DATA	SUBFIV	

An array of subroutine addresses like the above has a special name in the common parlance of programmers. Such an array is known as a *transfer vector*.

While there are a number of different ways to solve this, we will use simple indexed addressing for clarity. In this case the address pointers are:

ARGPTR	DATA	INTAB

```
FUNPTR    DATA  XVCTR
```

If the character string typed in has been stored in locations HIHALF and LOHALF we have:

	LAM	5	
	STA	CNT	initialize count
	LDX	ARGPTR	argument array pointer to index
XLOOP	LDA	HIHALF	first two characters to A
	XOR	@0	form logical difference
	JAN	NEXT	zero only if first halves are identical
	LDA	LOHALF	first two equal, try second two
	XOR	@1	form logical difference
	JAN	NEXT	zero only if second halves identical
	TXA		found it, move pointer to A
	SUB	ARGPTR	subtract out argument table origin. At this point the number in A is *twice* the number of the argument which matched the input character string because the arguments are each two words long. As each entry in the argument table is twice the length of the corresponding entry in the function table, we must divide the argument table displacement computed above by two. This is easily done by:
	LRA	1	
	ADD	FUNPTR	now add the function table origin
	TAX		and move the computed function table address to the index
	LDA	@0	now load the function, i.e., the address of the subroutine to be executed
	STA	ADR	save in temporary pointer
	JST	*ADR	and execute the subroutine
	JMP	END	finished
NEXT	AXI	2	bump the argument pointer by

```
                        the length of one entry, two
                        words
     IMS    CNT         have we tried the last argu-
                        ment?
     JMP    XLOOP       no, try the next one
```

If control reaches this point the argument table was exhausted without finding a match, therefore the next instruction per specification of the problem is:

```
     JMP    ILLEGL
```

Before passing on to the next topic something further should be noted about the last example. Obviously it could have been made shorter by the use of indexed indirect addressing rather than the simple indexed mode which was used, but there is another way in which it could have been made shorter. After the function address had been computed and moved back to X the retrieval of the necessary subroutine address and the execution of the subroutine was done by:

```
     LDA    @0
     STA    ADR
     JST    *ADR
     . . .
```

The address of the subroutine was retrieved and stored for use as an indirect pointer by the JST. If the word ADR is included, this used four words to accomplish the job. It will work, but the following will do just as well:

```
     LDX    @0
     JST    @0
```

and takes only two words. Loading the X register this way replaces the address contained in X with the *contents* of that address. Indexed addressing behaves with JST just as it behaves with any other memory reference instruction. An indexed JST's effective address is that contained in the index, plus the displacement portion of the JST itself, which is zero in this case.

16

Units of Memory Smaller than a Word—Byte Mode Addressing

The elementary addressable unit of computer memory is the word whose length is fixed in the hardware design. Many types of data require less than a word, however, and the practice of using a full word to store these items is wasteful of memory. A number whose length is 12 bits wastes 4 bits if a full word is used to store it. A 1000 word array of such numbers wastes a full 250 words of memory. The retrieval of information units less than a word long is accompanied by programming overhead which requires memory space itself and time for execution, and it is this overhead which limits the circumstances in which data may be "packed."

The problem to be solved is the packing of units of arbitrary length into 16 bit words, and their retrieval when needed. For this purpose it is useful to think of memory as being composed of a string of bits upon which we can impose any structure we like. The access to this string of bits is via instructions which can only function on word boundaries. The problem reduces to one of determining which word or words in the array contains the subunit of information required. If the subunit is five bits long, the first word contains the first three subunits and the high bit of the fourth, while the second word contains the four remaining bits of the fourth subunit, the fifth and sixth subunits and the high two bits of the seventh. If both words and subunits are numbered from zero, the first three array words look like this:

```
     word zero              word one              word two

XXXXX XXXXX XXXXX X    XXXX XXXXX XXXXX XX    XXX XXXXX XXXXX XXX
  0th   1st   2nd      3rd   4th   5th       6th   7th   8th  etc.
 unit  unit  unit     unit  unit  unit      unit  unit  unit
```

The problem is to determine which word or words contain the desired five bit unit and extract it as a single unit, even if it runs over a word boundary. The number of the word which contains the high bit of the required unit is easy to find, namely:

$$\text{word number} = \frac{5 \times (\text{unit number})}{16}$$

The product $5 \times$ (unit number) is simply the number of bits in the buffer which precede the high bit of the sought unit. Dividing this number by 16 gives the word number as there are 16 bits per word. Using the above

165

formula, the number of the word containing the high bit of the 4th unit is $(5 \times 4)/16 = 1$ with a remainder of 4. The quotient, 1, is the word number. The remainder, 4, is the number of bits to the left of the high bit of the desired unit. As it is usually desired to work with numbers which are *right justified,* meaning that the lowest significant bit occupies the low bit of the register, the number must be shifted right. This shift is easily computed to be:

$$16 \text{ bits } - \text{ unit size } - \# \text{ of bits to left of unit}$$

In order to execute a shift whose count is filled in by the program, something must be understood about the binary nature of shifts in the Alpha machines. In a single register shift, ARA, ALA, LRA, LLA, RRA, RLA, the instruction specification is in the upper thirteen bits of the instruction word, and the count occupies the low three bits. The instruction:

> LRA   3

assembles to the actual binary instruction:

> 0001001111010   010
> the LRA   the
> instruction   shift
>   count

Note that while the source instruction specified a shift of three places, the count portion of the binary instruction specifies two. The count of the binary instruction is one less than the actual number of places shifted. It is not possible to specify a count with a shift of zero. Some older programmers are accustomed to using shifts with zero counts to transfer an algebraic sign from one register to another, but that *doesn't* work on the Alpha machines. An LRA 8 assembles to:

> 0001001111010   111

Again note that the shift count is a seven in the binary when the source instruction specifies 8. Long shifts and rotates, LLR, LLL, LRR, LRL, use the same shift count scheme—the shift count in the binary instruction is one less than the number of places actually shifted—but four bits are allowed for the shift count. This allows a maximum shift of 16 places. An LLL   16 instruction assembles to the binary:

> 000110110000   1111

the right most four bits being the shift count. Such shifts can be constructed with a little care by the program itself, inserted in the string of instructions and executed, as shown in example 16-1.

Example 16-1

The double word contained in Q and $Q + 1$ is to be shifted left by the number of places indicated by the number in the A register. Write the program to do it.

label	inst.	operand	
	CMS	SIXTN	greater than 16?
	JAG	$+2	no, greater than zero?
	JMP	NOSHFT	illegal shift count, exit
	DAR		shift count OK, decrement
	IOR	INST	form the shift instruction
	STA	$+3	store it in line
	LDA	Q	load high word
	LDX	Q+1	load low word
	HLT		and execute the shift
	STA	Q	restore the double word to memory
	STX	Q+1	
NOSHFT	...		

The constants are defined as:

SIXTN	DATA	16	
INST	LLL	1	skeleton shift instruction

The instruction at INST is never executed as is. It is only the skeleton from which the real shift instruction is built by "ORing" it with the decremented shift count. The HLT instruction is likewise never executed since it is overlaid by the constructed LLL instruction.

The above illustrates a class of techniques whose principal trick is to have the program construct its own instructions. This practice is usually frowned upon as an error can lead to unpredictable results, but when carefully done it allows efficient performance of some tasks which would be clumsy with conventional methods.

The retrieval of five bit subunits from a packed buffer is shown in example 16-2.

Example 16-2

Integer data are packed into five bit subunits in the buffer which begins at TABLE. Write a subroutine to retrieve the five bit subunit whose number is in X on entry. The subunit should be right adjusted in the A register on return.

Constants are defined as:

label	inst.	operand	
SHIFT	LLL	1	skeleton shift instruction, as shown above
N	EQU	5	unit size, explained below
SIZE	DATA	N	constant related to the above, explained below
TORG	DATA	TABLE	address pointer to packed table
TABLE	RES	...	the packed data table
	...		

The retrieval program is:

GRAB	NOP		the entry point
	ZAR		
	MPY	SIZE	form # of bits preceeding required subgroup. After a multiply the X register would normally be shifted right one bit, but since we next want to shift it left 12 bits, we combine both shifts into one, namely:
	LLL	11	leaves the number of the word containing the high bit of the desired unit in A and the number of bits in this word to the *left* of the high bit in the upper four bits of X.
	ADD	TORG	displacement + table origin pointer
	EAX		and swap to X. Now the number of bits to the left of the desired high bit is in the upper four bits of A. It is moved to the lower four in one instruction by:
	RLA	5	if this number is zero no shift is necessary
	JAZ	$+3	skip the shift. If it was nonzero
	DAR		form the instruction by

	IOR	SHIFT	"oring" the decremented shift count with the skeleton instruction . . .
	STA	OP	then store it in line . . .
	LDA	@0	pick up word containing high
	LDX	@1	bit and the next if the unit spanned two words
OP	HLT		overlaid by the constructed shift inst. At this point the desired subunit is in the left most 5 bits of A. It is moved to the required position by the instruction:
	LLR	16-N	This is an 11 bit shift, explained below. The required 5 bit item is now contained in the low five bits of A the upper 11 bits of A are all zeros.
	JMP	*GRAB	return to calling program

The peculiar definition of N in the example above had a purpose. If the reader has not guessed it already, the above subroutine could be used to extract data units of *any* length less than 16 by reassembling the routine with a different value of N defined by the EQU. The assembler will compute and fill in the proper operand for the LLR   16−N instruction. This illustrates a general method for unpacking data which overlap word boundaries.

Packing information into odd sized units involves the same general principles. The word address of the highest bit is computed as before along with the number of bits to the left of the high bit. The unit to be inserted into the buffer is moved all the way to the left of the A register and saved. The word containing the high bit and the next one are loaded into A and X and both registers rotated by the amount necessary to bring the required unit position into the high bits of A, i.e., by the number of bits to the left of the high bit. The buffer character is then masked out with an AND and the new character ORed into position. This result is then rotated right into the original position and stored. This process is shown in example 16-3.

Example 16-3

Write a subroutine to pack five bit units into a word buffer which begins at TABLE. The five bit unit to be inserted is in A on entry. The unit number is in X.

label	inst.	operand	
	label	*inst.*	*operand*
PACK	NOP		entry point
	LLA	8	move the 5 bit unit to the left most
	LLA	3	five bits of A
	STA	CHAR	and save
	ZAR		
	MPY	SIZE	compute bit address of high bit
	LLL	11	Since the low order result of multiplication needs to be right shifted one bit, this instruction should normally be LRX 1. We want the high order 12 bits of the product in A, however, i.e., the product divided by 16 or the word number. This could be done by moving X to A with a TXA and the division done by a LLR instruction. The whole job is accomplished by the single LLL 11.
	ADD	TORG	add table bias
	STA	ADR	and save the word address
	EAX		swap the address to X and bring the shift count into the high bits of A
	RLA	5	move shift count to low bits of A
			Note: On the Alpha machines a zero instruction functions as a NOP. If the count is zero no shifting will be done. The STA's which follow put NOP's into the shift locations.
	STA	OP1	
	STA	OP2	
	JAZ	GO	skip if zero shift count
	DAR		otherwise decrement
	IOR	LRL	form long left rotate instruction
	EMA	OP1	store in first shift and retrieve count again

	DAR		decrement . . .
	IOR	LRR	form right rotate instruction
	STA	OP2	store in second shift
GO	LDA	@0	pick up word containing high bit
	LDX	@1	and the next one
OP1	NOP		this is overlaid by a long left rotate
	AND	MASK	mask out the old unit
	IOR	CHAR	merge unit
OP2	NOP		overlaid by long right rotate
	STA	*ADR	save first word
	IMS	ADR	bump pointer
	STX	*ADR	save second word
	JMP	*PACK	and return
CHAR	NOP		
SIZE	DATA	5	
ADR	NOP		
LRL	LRL	1	skeleton left rotate instruction
LRR	LRR	1	skeleton right rotate instruction
MASK	DATA	:7FF	mask to remove old unit
TORG	DATA	TABLE	address pointer to packed table

. . .

The sharp-eyed reader might note that some economies could have been made in both of the preceding examples. In the second example, for instance, both of the STA instructions which follow the RLA are not necessary. The second could be eliminated by specifying JAZ   GO−1, which is an STA   OP2 instruction. Also, the DAR instructions in both examples could be dispensed with by predecrementing the skeleton instructions. Instead of specifying the LRL skeleton as:

    LRL   1

which assembles to :1900, we could have specified:

    DATA   :18FF

which is one less than :1900. Then, instead of using IOR to form the instruction we would use an ADD without the DAR instruction preceding. Other situations can be found in both examples which would make the program shorter or "tighter" as they say in the trade. The examples were written as they were for clarity. For some unit sizes, such as 4 bits and 8 bits, special shortcuts can be found, but the addressing of information units other than the "natural" one, the word, involves an amount of programming overhead which limits the use of this artifice to situations not requiring great speed and for which the block of information is large enough to justify the memory used by the program.

Eight bit memory units are the most common of all subdivisions of the computer word. Eight bit units arise very commonly in communication with character-oriented peripheral devices. By reason of its widespread use the eight bit unit has come to have a special name, the *byte*. Since the need to handle bytes arises so often in computer applications, special hardware has been provided in the Alpha machines to aid in the task, the so called *Byte Mode*. Byte mode is used by executing the SBM (*Set Byte Mode*) instruction. Thereafter the computer's memory reference instructions (with some exceptions) address memory in eight bit units rather than words. The effective address of an instruction is computed as a word address. As the word contains two bytes, a further specification is required to determine whether the left or right byte in the word is the required one. For this reason byte mode instructions cannot specify relative backward addressing. The part of the instruction word occupied by this specification in normal word mode addressing is required to carry the left-right information in byte mode.

Indirect and indexed addressing in byte mode make use of a *byte pointer* carried in memory or the X register. This byte pointer is simply the word pointer shifted left one bit. The low bit of a byte pointer is a zero for left hand bytes and a one for right hand bytes. The assembly program provides for the creation of byte pointers by means of the BAC (*Byte Address Constant*) pseudo operation, used as:

```
BPTR        BAC   DOG+1
```

This creates a byte pointer containing the byte address of the right hand byte of location DOG. Note that the added constant 1 adds one *byte* to the address, not one word. As the byte pointer occupies all 16 bits of the pointer word there is no room for specification of further levels of indirect addressing. Byte mode indirect addressing is therefore limited to a single level.

The assembly program recognizes byte mode addressing by the "B" which is added to the instruction mnemonic, as:

```
            SBM                 byte mode indicator on
            LDAB   KARL         pick up the byte
            ...
KARL        DATA  'AB'
```

Keep in mind that the word KARL must be defined after the instructions which reference it to avoid indirect addressing. If KARL were defined before the instructions which reference it, the assembly program would generate an indirect addressing link automatically to allow the reference. If the backward reference were already indirect, the extra indirect link is impossible, since only one direct level is allowed. This condition is flagged as an error by the assembly program. The JMP, JST, and IMS instructions are excluded entirely from byte mode addressing and function the same way whether or not the byte mode indicator is on. On the older Alpha 16 (not the LSI machine) the Scan instruction is also excluded from byte mode.

The uses for byte mode addressing are as numerous as the applications which handle data of this length. The remainder of this chapter will be devoted to illustrating a few of these. The first is a problem which arises in writing compiler programs. One of the elementary syntactical checks performed by compilers is to see whether the statement written by the programmer has unmatched parentheses. In languages like FORTRAN and BASIC a statement must contain as many left parentheses as right. The BASIC statement:

$$120 \quad \text{LET } Y = (A + B) * (A - B)$$

is considered to be in error because it contains more left parentheses than right. The correct statement is:

$$120 \quad \text{LET } Y = (A + B) * (A - B)$$

The programs which process these statements into strings of machine executable instructions must check for such syntactical errors before proceeding. A method of checking for matching parentheses is shown in example 16-4.

Example 16-4

Write a program to check for unmatched parentheses in a 72 character BASIC or FORTRAN statement. The statement is in ASCII characters beginning at location NEXT and is packed two characters per word.

label	inst.	operand	
	LDX	NXTADR	address pointer to index
	ZAR		
	STA	LEFT	zero parenthesis counts
	STA	RIGHT	...
	LAM	72	
	STA	CNT	initialize character count
	SBM		byte mode indicator on
PCHECK	LDAB	@0	pick up character

```
        CAI    '('         is it a left parenthesis?
        IMS    LEFT        yes, bump left count
        CAI    ')'         is it a right parenthesis?
        IMS    RIGHT       yes, bump right count
        IXR                increment byte address point-
                           er
        IMS    CNT         last character?
        JMP    PCHECK      no, get the next one
        SWM                yes, byte mode off
        LDA    LEFT        left parenthesis count to A
        SUB    RIGHT       minus right parenthesis count
        JAN    TILT        counts unequal, an error
        . . .
LEFT    NOP                left parenthesis count
RIGHT   NOP                right parenthesis count
CNT     NOP                character counter
NXTADR  BAC    NEXT        byte address pointer
NEXT    RES    36          36 word buffer (72 characters)
        . . .
```

Manipulation of bytes or characters is also a common task in cryptography, the art of codes and ciphers. The purpose of a cipher is to conceal the contents of a message from all but its intended recipient and the construction of ciphers is an ancient practice. One of the simpler encipherment schemes is called the substitution cipher. In this scheme one letter of the alphabet is substituted for another in order to garble the message being transmitted. The recipient of the message, knowing the substitution scheme can reverse the process and recover the original message. A trivial example of this is the reversal of the alphabet "end for end," Z being substituted for A, Y for B, X for C, and so forth. In this scheme the word CAT is enciphered to XZG. The process of message encipherment is shown in example 16-5.

Example 16-5

Write a program to encipher messages by the substitution method outlined above. The table of letter equivalents is contained in an array at location SUBS. The message to be enciphered is 72 characters long and begins at location PLAIN. Place the enciphered message in the 72 character array at CIPHER.

label	inst.	operand	
	LAM	72	set up character count

```
           STA   CNT        ...
           LDA   PPTR       message address byte pointer
           STA   IN         to temporary pointer
           LDA   CPTR       enciphered message address
                            byte pointer
           STA   OUT        to temporary pointer
           SBM              byte mode on
L1         LDAB  *IN        pick up message character
           SWM              switch back to word mode
           ADD   SPTR       add substitution string pointer
           TAX              move to index. If the first
```

character had been a "C" the index would now contain the address of the first character in the substitution table plus the numerical value of the character C, i.e., a :C3. We want the index to point to the third character in the table of substitutes, so we subtract out :C1.

```
           SXI   :C1
           SBM              back to byte mode
           LDAB  @0         pick up cipher character
           STAB  *OUT       and store in enciphered string
           IMS   IN
           IMS   OUT        increment   the   character
                            pointers
           IMS   CNT        last message character?
           JMP   L1         no, do it again
                 ...
CPTR       BAC   CIPHER     cipher string address pointer
PPTR       BAC   PLAIN      message text address pointer
SPTR       BAC   SUBS       substitution  table  address
                            pointer
IN         NOP
OUT        NOP
CNT        NOP              temporary cells
SUBS       TEXT  'ZYXWVUTSRQPONMLKJIHGFEDCBA'
```

The above string determines the substitution scheme, in this case a simple reversal of the alphabet.

```
CIPHER     RES    36        72 character cipher buffer
PLAIN      RES    36        72 character message buffer
           . . .
```

Ciphers like the one in the above example are mere historical curiosities nowadays, since they are easily broken by the tool of frequency analysis. This is a very simple technique which involves counting the number of occurrences of the various letters in the enciphered message to give clues to the real identities of the enciphered characters. A simple count of the letters used in the text of this page will show that the letter E occurs much more frequently than K, P, or V. In an enciphered message of any length this "natural" frequency of letters emerges very quickly and gives the cipher scheme away. Once a few letters are deciphered by frequency analysis the remainder can be gotten very quickly from context.

The "breaking" of a substitution cipher by frequency analysis is shown in example 16-6.

Example 16-6

Write a short program to determine the frequency of appearance of the 26 characters of the alphabet. The numbers of occurrences are to be left in the 26 word array beginning at FREAK. The enciphered message to be scanned begins at ENIGMA. The message is 1000 characters long.

label	inst.	operand	
	LDA	EADR	initialize pointer
	STA	IN	
	LDA	M1000	initialize count
	STA	CNT	
	LDX	FADR	this is a *word* address pointing to the frequency array. It is held in X so that there will be no necessity to switch back to word mode to fetch it from memory when needed.
	SBM		byte mode on
L1	TXA		move frequency array address to A
	ADDB	*IN	address plus character value
	EAX		swap combined address to X, save origin in A
	SXI	:C1	same as previous example

```
          IMS    @0          increment the cell
          IMS    IN          bump message pointer
          IMS    CNT         last message character?
          JMP    L1          no, do it again
          ...
EADR      BAC    ENIGMA      enciphered message byte
                             pointer
FADR      DATA   FREAK       frequency table pointer
IN        NOP                temporary address pointer
M1000     DATA   -1000       array count
CNT       NOP
          ...
```

When the above has been executed the frequencies of occurrence of the letters of the enciphered message will be in locations FREAK through FREAK+25. The use of the FREAK table is now straightforward. The arrays themselves are defined:

```
FREAK     RES    26          frequency array
ENIGMA    RES    500         1000 character message buffer
          ...
```

As primitive as the above cipher seems today, it was used for secret communication in the early days. It is believed that messages enciphered by a method similar to this were the medium used by Mary Stuart (Queen of Scots) to communicate with her forces in Scotland during her imprisonment by her cousin, Elizabeth I of England. The messages were intercepted by Elizabeth's security chief, Sir Francis Walsingham, and easily deciphered. The evidence thus gained was used at Mary's treason trial and led directly to her execution, though there is some speculation that the messages themselves were frauds manufactured by Walsingham himself.

Mary Stuart's experience would seem to indicate that a simple substitution cipher is not good enough, and as cryptography grew more sophisticated better methods were evolved. In the search for an encipherment method which would not yield so easily to analysis, cipher experts derived what has become known as a polyalphabetic cipher. This type of cipher completely obscures the natural frequency of the letters in the enciphered message and, therefore, renders the tool of frequency analysis unusable. Encipherment by this method involves the use of a "key" in conjunction with the message to be sent. This key should be random and used only once, but the practical difficulties involved in transmitting the key or keys undetected to a receiver at a distance usually dictate that they come from some standard book, copies of which are available to both sender and receiver.

Polyalphabetic encipherment is a very simple process. The message to be enciphered and the key are laid out side by side, with all blanks removed. Suppose the message to be sent is NEED MONEY, and the key chosen is the word PALPITATION. The encipherment is done by taking the ordinal position in the alphabet of corresponding characters from the message and key and adding them. For the message and key chosen above, the first key character is P, the 16th letter of the alphabet, and the first message character is N, the 14th letter. The 16 and 14 are added to produce 30. Since the 30 is greater than 26 we reduce it by 26 to get a 4. The enciphered character is therefore D, the 4th letter of the alphabet. The entire message is enciphered as follows:

KEY		PLAINTEXT		CIPHERTEXT		
P	16	N	14	30 − 26 =	4	D
A	1	E	5		6	F
L	12	E	5		17	Q
P	16	D	4		20	T
I	9	M	13		22	V
T	20	O	15	35 − 26 =	9	I
A	1	N	14		15	O
T	20	E	5		25	Y
I	9	Y	25	34 − 26 =	8	H
O	15		—			—
N	14		—			—

The message NEED MONEY has thus been reduced to DFQTVIOYH, which is gibberish. The decipherment process is equally simple. The number of the key character is subtracted from the number of the cipher-text character. If the result is negative or zero 26 is added, and the result is the number of the plaintext character. Since this process is so simple machines existed to perform it long before the days of computers. It was the breakdown of one of these machines which prevented the Japanese Embassy in Washington from delivering a declaration of war to the U.S. State Department on December 7, 1941. The declaration was supposed to have been delivered half an hour before the Pearl Harbor attack to lend a semblance of legality to it. The breaking of such a cipher led directly to the death of the Japanese Admiral Yamamoto during the war. Routine monitoring of Japanese military radio traffic yielded the Admiral's travel itinerary and time schedule. The Admiral was known to be a compulsively punctual individual. With his schedule known, American planes were waiting to intercept his transport. To the Admiral's misfortune he was exactly on time and perished as his transport was shot down. A full account of this incident and the polyalphabetic and other cipher and code methods is given in the book *The Codebreakers* by Kahn.

In doing polyalphabetic encipherment by computer a number of simplifications can be made. It is unnecessary to keep the alphabetic tables because the ASCII codes for the alphabetic characters form an ascending sequence of numbers from :C1 through :DA. If the upper two bits are removed from these codes, the remaining bits form a number between 1 and 26. Encipherment consists of reducing the corresponding characters from the key and the message, or "plaintext," to numbers between 1 and 26, and adding them. If the sum is greater than 26, it is reduced by 26 and ASCII code bits merged with the result. This forms the enciphered or "ciphertext" character. Deciphering is just the reverse process. The "stripped" key character is subtracted from the "stripped" ciphertext character. If the result is zero or negative, 26 is added to it. When the ASCII code bits are merged with this number the result is the "plaintext" character. The machine implementation of the process, using byte mode arithmetic and logical instructions is shown in example 16-7.

Example 16-7

Write two programs, one to encipher and the other to decipher, by the polyalphabetic cipher methods described above. Key and plaintext are both to be considered one line (72 characters) long. The key is located at KEYTXT and the plaintext begins at PLNTXT. The ciphertext result is to be left in memory beginning at CFRTXT. Since three arrays of characters are being addressed, the best method is to use indirect indexed addressing. This works in byte mode just as it does in word mode. We begin by creating the necessary scratchpad pointers, as:

label	inst.	operand	
KEYPTR	BAC	KEYTXT	byte pointer to key
PLNPTR	BAC	PLNTXT	byte pointer to plaintext
CFRPTR	BAC	CFRTXT	byte pointer to ciphertext
	...		

and the programs, beginning with the encipherment:

NCIPHR	ZXR		zero byte address displacement
	SBM		byte mode indicator on
N1	LDAB	@*PLNPTR	plaintext character to A
	ADDB	@*KEYPTR	plus key character
	ANDB	MASK	strip ASCII code bits off
	CMSB	TWTY6	greater than 26?
	JMP	$+2	no, skip it

```
            SUBB   TWTY6      yes, reduce it by 26
            IORB   BITS       merge ASCII code bits
            STAB   @*CFRPTR   store ciphertext character
            IXR               increment address displace-
                              ment
            CXI    72          last character
            JMP    $+2         yes, continue with program
            JMP    N1          no, get next character
            . . .
DCIPHR      ZXR               zero byte address displace-
                              ment
            SBM               byte mode indicator on
D1          LDAB   @*KEYPTR   key character to A
            ANDB   MASK       strip it
            STAB   T          and save it . . .
            LDAB   @*CFRPTR   ciphertext character to A
            ANDB   MASK       strip it
            SUBB   T          subtract key
            JAG    $+2        skip if greater than zero
            ADDB   TWTY6      add 26 if minus or zero
            IORB   BITS       merge ASCII code bits
            STAB   @*PLNPTR   store plaintext character
            IXR               increment address displace-
                              ment
            CXI    72          last character?
            JMP    $+2         yes, skip out and continue
            JMP    D1          no, get next character
```

Note that the following constants are required by the two programs above. Particularly notice that they are created in the *left* half of the word. Both halves of the word can be used but the constants are shown as below for clarity in the example.

```
MASK        DATA   :3F00
TWTY6       DATA   :1A00
BITS        DATA   :C000
T           NOP
KEYTXT      RES    36          72 character buffer areas
PLNTXT      RES    36
CFRTXT      RES    36
            . . .
```

17 Conversion of Input Numbers to Binary

The table at the end of Chapter 13 shows a unique binary code for every functional key on the teletype keyboard. The purpose of this chapter is to show how strings of input characters can be manipulated to produce the binary equivalent of the decimal or hexadecimal numbers represented by these input strings.

The ASCII codes for the numbers 0 through 9 have the binary equivalents of these decimal numbers "buried" in them. The code for 5, for example, is:

$$1011\ 0101_2 = B5_{16}$$

The "stripping off" of the upper four bits is a simple task, i.e.:

```
        LDA    CHAR      ASCII character to A
        AND    MASK      mask off the unwanted bits
        ...
MASK    DATA   :F
        ...
```

This leaves only the problem of how to combine the binary equivalents of a string of digits to form a binary number. Stripping the digits 1, 7, and 5, for example, yields:

$$0001\ 0111 \quad \text{and} \quad 0101$$

What is required is the binary number:

$$10101111_2 = 175_{10}$$

The most obvious way to convert the three digits is to multiply them by their decimal place values and add the results, i.e., the 0001 by 1100100_2 (100_{10}), the 0111 by 1010_2 (10_{10}) and the 0101 by 1, as:

$$
\begin{aligned}
0001 \times 1100100 &= 1100100 \\
0111 \times 1010 &= 1000110 \\
0101 \times 0001 &= \underline{+0000101} \\
&10101111
\end{aligned}
$$

The multiplication itself can be done either by the MPY instruction discussed in Chapter 11 or by a software sequence. A software multiply by 100_{10} is:

```
        ALA    2              times 4
        STA    T1             save result
        ALA    3              times 32
        STA    T2             save this too
        ALA    1              times 64
        ADD    T1             add what we saved
        ADD    T2             . . .
        . . .
```

which depends upon the fact that $100 = 64 + 32 + 4$. A software multiply by ten has been given in a previous chapter; it is:

```
        ALA    1              times 2
        STA    T              save it
        ALA    2              times 8
        ADD    T
        . . .
```

which depends on the fact that $10 = 8 + 2$ as explained before. While such schemes work well and are a necessity on computers not equipped with multiply hardware, the task is better accomplished in the Alpha machines with the MPY instruction. If the three digits 1, 7, and 5 are stored in locations D1, D2, and D3 respectively, an easy solution is:

```
        ZAR
        LDX    D1             hundreds digit to X
        MPY    HUNDRD         times one hundred
        LRX    1              format product
        STX    T1             save hundreds
        LDX    D2             tens digit to X. A is still zero
        MPY    TEN            times ten
        LRX    1              format product
        TXA                   move tens product to A
        ADD    T1             form tens plus hundreds
        ADD    D3             add units
        . . .
HUNDRD  DATA   100
TEN     DATA   10
        . . .
```

This is straightforward enough, though it can be made shorter. The reader may recall from the discussion of the MPY instruction that it is necessary to zero the A register before multiplication to prevent the contents of A from being added to the product. This property of MPY is usually a nuisance, since it involves an extra step for normal multiplication, but we can make use of it here since we are forming the sum of a series of products. The above sequence can be rewritten:

LDA	D3	units digit to A
LDX	D2	tens digit to X
MPY	TEN	form ten times tens digit plus units digit. At this point the product is contained completely in X, shifted left one bit. For the next step we want to add this product/sum to the product of one hundred times the hundreds digit. To format X requires an LRX 1 instruction. To move the contents of X to A requires a TXA. Both of these instructions can be replaced with a single LLL 15, as:
LLL	15	format and move to A
LDX	D1	hundreds digit to X
MPY	HUNDRD	form final product/sum
LRX	1	format X
...		finished, binary number is in X

If the binary number is greater than the capacity of one word, this last procedure cannot be used, of course, since the partial result being added will be double precision. Still the above is useful for single precision numbers.

An even greater simplification can be achieved by treating multiplication by the higher powers of ten as repeated multiplication by ten, i.e.:

$$N \times 100 = N \times 10 \times 10$$

and

$$N \times 1000 = N \times 10 \times 10 \times 10$$

and so forth. This is utilized by initially setting a result cell to zero. Each entry to the convert routine with a new digit causes the result cell to be multiplied by ten and the new digit added. This product/sum then replaces the result cell. A subroutine which uses this scheme is shown in example 17-1.

Example 17-1

Write a subroutine to perform decimal to binary conversions. Entries are to be made with the successive digits, highest to lowest, in the A register. The result is to be preset to zero by the calling routine before the first entry:

label	inst.	operand	
	label	*inst.*	*operand*
BCON	NOP		entry point
	LDX	RESULT	load former product/sum into X
	MPY	TEN	multiply by ten and add new digit
	LRX	1	format X
	STX	RESULT	save new result
	JMP	*BCON	
RESULT	DATA	0	result cell, prezeroed
TEN	DATA	10	
	...		

Another program could use the above to read and convert a 4 digit number from the keyboard as follows:

	ZAR		
	STA	RESULT	zero result cell
	LAM	4	
	STA	CNT	set up digit count
FETCH	JST	RKB	get digit from teletype
	CMS	NINE	legal numeric?
	CMS	ZERO	...
	JMP	TILT	illegal, go tell him
	NOP		
	AND	EF	mask off ASCII code bits
	JST	BCON	convert and add new digit
	IMS	CNT	four digits yet?
	JMP	FETCH	no, get another one
	...		program continues here
NINE	DATA	:B9	
ZERO	DATA	:B0	
EF	DATA	:F	
CNT	NOP		
	...		

The really useful mode of operation for such a program is that in which the program can handle any number of digits up to some limit, i.e., the keyboard operator should not have to type 0003 to enter a 3. To do this we insert a terminating condition into the program so that a transfer is made to CONT either upon exhaustion of the count *or* upon encountering some special character in the input string. This is shown in example 17-2.

Example 17-2

Write a subroutine which is used by a calling program by:

JST	KREAD	jump to keyboard read routine
STA	BIN	store binary number input
...		

The routine should recognize negative numbers and accept input from one to four digits long, terminating either on the fourth digit or a blank, whichever comes first. In the case that no digits are typed, just the terminating blank, return should be made with a zero result and overflow on. If illegal characters are typed the routine should print "??" and start the process over.

label	*inst.*	*operand*	
KREAD	NOP		entry point
	ARM		
	STA	STRG	set positive/negative trigger
	LAM	4	
	STA	CNT	initialize count
	ZAR		
	STA	RESULT	initialize result
	STA	DIGITS	and digit count
	JST	RKB	get character from keyboard
	CAI	'+'	plus sign?
	JMP	RN	yes, get the number
	CAI	'−'	minus sign?
	STA	STRG	yes, set trigger for negation
RN	JST	RKB	get character
	CAI	' '	terminating character (blank)?
	JMP	END	yes, wrap it up
	CMS	NINE	no, legal numeric character?
	CMS	ZERO	...
	JMP	TILT	no, go type "??"
	NOP		
	AND	EF	mask out ASCII code bits
	JST	BCON	convert and add
	IMS	DIGITS	bump digit count
	IMS	CNT	last digit?
	JMP	RN	no, get the next one
END	LDA	RESULT	pick up result
	IMS	STRG	negative?
	NAR		yes, do it
	LDX	DIGITS	pick up digit count

```
ROV                      overflow off for normal return
JXN     $+2              test for significance
SOV                      set OV if null result
JMP     *KREAD           and return
...
```

The constants NINE, ZERO, and EF are defined as before. Setting STRG to −1 on entry causes a skip when the IMS   STRG is executed unless the first character was a minus. If the minus was found, the ASCII code minus sign is itself stored in STRG. Since the code is not a −1 the skip is not taken in this case and the result is negated.

Conversion of fractions to binary is somewhat different, though equally straightforward. The digits of the fraction are converted as if they were integer digits, and the result divided by the appropriate power of ten, i.e., if there were three digits in the fraction the integer result is divided by 10^3. Note that in this division the binary integer forms the *high* order dividend. As an example consider the fraction 0.123_{10} or

$$0.000\ 1111\ 1011\ 1110_2$$

with the left most bit being the sign and the radix point located immediately to the right of the sign. If the decimal integer 123 is taken as the high dividend (the low dividend being zero) the actual value of the binary dividend considered as a double precision number is 123×32768 or 4030464. This number, 4030464, when divided by 1000 yields 4030 as a quotient. The integer 4030 in binary is:

$$0000\ 1111\ 1011\ 1110_2$$

which is exactly the desired result. The programmer should keep in mind that the conversion of fractions involves approximation. While the integer 123 can be represented exactly by a binary integer, the fraction .123 cannot be represented exactly. The decision to round up or down will depend on circumstances, but the cumulative effects of precision loss must be kept in mind when working with such numbers. Precision loss can be a deceptive thing. If the binary approximation to 1/10 is added ten times, the result is *not* one but .9997558. While the 15 bit magnitude of the word can hold a little more than four decimal digits equivalent precision, the loss of precision is great enough over only 10 additions to cause an error in the fourth place of the sum.

What is usually required is not either pure integer or pure fraction input, but a combination, i.e., the ability to convert numbers such as 323.83 or −66.57. To do this the techniques discussed above are combined to produce a decimal interpretation routine which will accept and convert numbers in a "free" format. Of necessity, the example is rather complex and lengthy. If the reader will take the time to understand it, though, he will be rewarded with a general knowledge of how such input conversions are attacked.

Example 17-3

Using the previously discussed RKB and PRT routines to perform character reading and printing, construct a general input conversion routine for decimal numbers. The routine should accept and correctly convert integers, fractions, or numbers composed of both integer and fraction. In particular, the accepted format should include:

+1   or   1   or   +1.0   or   1.0   or   1.

all of these converting to the same binary integer in two's complement notation. Results are to be returned to the calling program with the integer portion in A and the fraction in X, in proper double precision format, *with the sign of the X register vacated*. The integer portion of a number may be as large as 32767, while the fraction may have from one to four digits. The range of numbers which can be converted is to be 32767.9999 to −32767.9999.

This problem will be solved by treating the integer and fraction portions separately, the break being made when a decimal point is encountered in the input string. The routine is used by executing:

```
JST    INPUT      get the number
JMP    ERROR      error, garbage typed in
STA    INTEGR     save the integer part
STX    FRACTN     save the fraction part
...
```

Numbers are to be typed as a continuous string, with the end of the number being signified by either a blank or the fourth fraction digit, whichever comes first. If no digits are typed, only the terminating blank, overflow returns on to indicate the null condition. The normal return is to the second instruction after the calling JST. The fraction is converted by dividing by a power of ten which depends on the number of fraction digits typed. Since the address of the divisor in the DVD instruction is held in the second word of the instruction, it is initialized at the beginning of the routine and incremented to point to the next highest power of ten each time a fraction digit is typed. The required subroutine is:

label	inst.	operand	
INPUT	NOP		entry point
	LDA	DADR	
	STA	DVD+1	initialize fraction divisor address
	ZAR		
	STA	RESULT	zero cumulative result cell
	STA	DIGITS	and the digit counter
I1	STA	SIGN	and the plus/minus flag
I2	JST	RKB	get a character
	CAI	'+'	plus sign?
	JMP	I2	yes, ignore it, number is assumed positive
	CAI	'−'	minus sign?
	JMP	I1	yes, set plus/minus flag and get another character
	JMP	$+2	no, it can only be '.', blank or numeric
I3	JST	RKB	get a character
	CAI	'.'	decimal point?
	JMP	FRC	yes, go process the fraction
	CAI	' '	no, was it the end of the number?
	JMP	IEND	yes, integer only, process it
	JST	CON	no, test for numeric and convert
	JMP	I3	get the next integer digit
FRC	ZAR		
	EMA	RESULT	get the integer and zero the work cell
	STA	INTGR	save the integer part
	LAM	4	
	STA	FCNT	set up fraction digit count
F1	JST	RKB	get the fraction digit
	CAI	' '	end of the number?
	JMP	FEND	yes, process both parts
	JST	CON	no, test for numeric and convert
	IMS	DVD+1	increment fraction divisor address pointer
	IMS	FCNT	last allowed fraction digit?
	JMP	F1	no, get another one
	JMP	FEND	yes, process both parts

Control reaches the following section when no decimal point has been encountered, i.e., the input number is pure integer.

IEND	LDX	SIGN	pick up plus/minus flag
	LDA	RESULT	and binary integer
	JXZ	$+2	was there a minus sign?
	NAR		yes, negate the number
	STA	INTGR	and save it
	ZXR		zero the fraction
	JMP	F2	and go make the null test

Control reaches the following section when a blank is encountered after a decimal point has been typed, i.e., when there is a fractional part of the number.

FEND	LDA	RESULT	pick up the converted fraction digits
	ZXR		zero the low order dividend
DVD	DVD	$-$	This symbol is equivalent to zero. It simply means that the *assembled* address pointer in the second word of the DVD instruction is zero. It has been previously filled in with a pointer to a table of divisors, with the pointer being incremented to point to the appropriate power of ten each time a new fraction digit was encountered.
	LDA	SIGN	pick up plus/minus flag
	JAZ	F2	is the input number positive?
	LDA	INTGR	no, complement it in double precision
	NXR		
	CAR		
	LLX	1	clear the low order sign
	LRX	1	
	JXN	$+2	carry to high order?
	IAR		yes, do it
	STA	INTGR	and replace the integer part
F2	LDA	DIGITS	did he type anything at all?
	ROV		
	JAN	$+2	yes, leave OV off
	SOV		no, a null entry, turn it off

	LDA	INTGR	pick up the integer part, the fraction is still in X if there was one
	IMS	INPUT	increment the return pointer past the error return
TILT	JMP	*INPUT	and return . . .

A jump directly to TILT skips over the incrementation of the return pointer. Control thus goes to the instruction immediately after the calling JST, the error return.

The working cells and constants are:

RESULTS	NOP		binary convert result cell
DIGITS	NOP		input digit counter
SIGN	NOP		plus/minus flag
INTGR	NOP		integer cell when there is a fraction
DADR	DATA	$+1	divisor table address pointer
	DATA	1	
TEN	DATA	10	this cell does double duty as a multiplier
	DATA	100, 1000, 10000	
			remainder of divisor table
NINE	DATA	:B9	ASCII comparands for legality check
ZERO	DATA	:B0	. . .
EF	DATA	:F	ANDing mask
FCNT	NOP		fraction digit counter

The actual binary converter, which also performs the ASCII legality check is:

CON	NOP		entry point
	CMS	NINE	
	CMS	ZERO	legal numeric?
	JMP	TILT	no, take the error return
	NOP		
	AND	EF	yes, strip off the superfluous bits
	LDX	RESULT	multiply by 10 and add new digit
	MPY	TEN	. . .

```
LRX    1              reformat product
JAN    TILT           integer > 32767, error, return
                      to JST+1
STX    RESULT         and save it
IMS    DIGITS         bump the digit count
JMP    *CON           and return . . .
```

Besides decimal numbers, computer input is often intended to specify bit patterns. For such specifications it is clumsy to have to convert the desired bit pattern to decimal before typing it in, so facilities are often required which will allow direct binary or hexadecimal input. Direct binary input, such as might be used to set a group of computer controlled switches is shown in example 17-4.

Example 17-4

Write a subroutine which will convert a binary number read from the keyboard as a string of ASCII ones and zeros to internal binary form. The routine should read up to 16 bits terminating either on the 16th bit or a blank character. If less than 16 bits are read the result should be right adjusted. If a character other than 1, 0, or blank is encountered the routine should type "??" and start over again.

label	inst.	operand	
BINARY	NOP		entry point
	LAM	16	
	STA	CNT	initialize count
	ZXR		zero X to develop number
B1	JST	RKB	get the character
	CAI	' '	end of the string?
	JMP	END	yes, exit
	SOV		OV on in case it's a one
	CAI	'0'	was it a zero?
	JMP	OFF	yes, shift in a zero bit
	CAI	'1'	was it a one?
	JMP	RLX	yes, rotate in a one bit
	LDA	QMA	neither, garbage
	JST	PRT	print "??"
	JMP	BINARY+1	and start over
OFF	ROV		turn OV off
RLX	RLX	1	rotate the bit in
	IMS	CNT	last bit?

```
          JMP   B1           no, get another one
END       TXA                move result to A
          JMP   *BINARY      and return
CNT       NOP
QMA       DATA  $+1          address pointer for error print
          TEXT  '??'         error message
```

Hexadecimal input is equally simple except that the input characters must be checked for validity in two ranges, 0-9 and A-F. The conversion of the A-F characters is made a little more complicated because A does not immediately follow 9 in the sequence of ASCII characters. It is thus not possible to simply mask out the upper four bits of the A-F characters to get the binary number 1010 through 1111. With a little thought though, the problem is easily solved. Suppose we have already verified that the input character is valid, i.e., it is in the A-F range. The binary code for the ASCII character ''A'' is:

$$1100\ 0001$$

with the characters B through F following in immediate sequence. If, before masking off the upper four bits, we were to add a binary nine to the ASCII code, as:

$$
\begin{array}{ll}
1100\ 0001 & \text{the ASCII ''A''} \\
+0000\ 1001 & \text{the binary nine} \\
\hline
1100\ 1010 &
\end{array}
$$

If we now mask out the upper four bits of this result:

$$
\begin{array}{ll}
 & 1100\ 1010 \\
\Lambda & 0000\ 1111 \\
\hline
 & 0000\ 1010
\end{array}
$$

which is exactly the required result. The use of this method is shown in example 17-5.

Example 17-5

Write a subroutine to read one to four hexadecimal characters from the keyboard and return the result in the A register. The input string is to be terminated on either the fourth character or a blank, whichever comes first. Characters which do not represent legal hexadecimal should produce the message ''??'' and the input reattempted.

label	inst.	operand	
HEXIN	NOP		entry point

```
         LAM    4
         STA    CNT          initialize character count
         ZAR
         STA    VALUE        and start with zero result
H1       JST    RKB          get the character
         CAI    ' '          end of number?
         JMP    END          yes
         CMS    NINE         no, was it 0-9?
         CMS    ZERO         ...
         JMP    TRYALF       no, maybe A-F
         NOP
         JMP    ZIPOFF       yes' mask the character
TRYALF   CMS    F            was it A-F?
         CMS    A
         JMP    ZILCH        no, garbage
         NOP
         ADD    BENIGN       yes, add binary nine
ZIPOFF   AND    LOFOUR       mask off high four bits
         EMA    VALUE        swap with the old result
         LLA    4            move it left four bits
         IOR    VALUE        merge the new hex digit
         STA    VALUE        and put it back
         IMS    CNT          last digit?
         JMP    H1           no, get another character
END      LDA    VALUE        pick up the result
         JMP    *HEXIN       and return
BENIGN   DATA   9
NINE     DATA   :B9
ZERO     DATA   :B0
F        DATA   :C6
A        DATA   :C1
LOFOUR   DATA   :F
CNT      NOP
VALUE    NOP
```

With the information in the examples in this section the reader should have no trouble constructing input conversion routines to suit any purpose. The importance of absolute error checking of all input cannot be stressed too strongly. If a single possibility for an error to slip through exists, it will happen sooner or later if the program is used to any extent. In many cases the error checking will have to include some consideration of the plausibility of what has been entered, beside the raw legality checks shown in this chapter. If the numbers being entered were control parameters for a nuclear reactor, no great imagination is required to predict the eventual consequences of unchecked input. This instance may seem dramatic, but the cost of an error can be very high in industrial and medical processes even when the consequences are not so apocalyptic as with a nuclear reactor.

18

Conversion of Binary Numbers to Output Form

In the previous chapter methods were discussed by which data are converted from external form to the binary form suitable for processing by the arithmetic orders of the computer. In this chapter we will be discussing methods for performing the opposite process—conversion of numbers from internal binary to the decimal or other external form necessary for human examination.

Conversion of binary integers to decimal is generally done by one of two possible methods, the choice depending on whether the computer being used has a hardware divide facility. If no divide instruction is present the digits of the decimal number are generated by subtraction of the successively lower powers of ten. In this scheme the conversion begins by subtracting ten thousand from the positive integer as many times as possible before the result is negative. The number of such successful subtractions is the ten thousands digit of the decimal number. To generate the thousands digit one thousand is subtracted from what remains as many times as possible, and so forth. A converter which works by this method is shown in example 18-1.

Example 18-1

Write a program to convert the positive binary integer in A to a string of ASCII digits beginning at byte location DECIML+1. Since five decimal digits will be generated the last one will occupy the right most byte of the word at word location DECIML+2.

label	inst.	operand	
	LXM	5	begin with number in A, initialize digit count
	STX	CNT	. . .
	LDX	DADR	
	STX	BADR	initialize byte address of decimal string
	LDX	PADR	
	STX	TADR	and address pointer for decimal power table
L1	ZXR		zero X to receive decimal digit

195

```
L2        SUB   *TADR      can we subtract this power of
                           ten?
          JAM   NXT        no, store the digit
          IXR              yes, increment decimal digit
          JMP   L2         and try to subtract again
NXT       ADD   *TADR      add the power of ten back in
          AXI   '0'        add the ASCII code bits to the
                           character in X
          SBM              byte mode on
          STXB  *BADR      store decimal character in
                           string
          SWM              byte mode off
          IMS   BADR       increment byte pointer
          IMS   CNT        last digit?
          JMP   L1         no, get the next one
          . . .
CNT       NOP              digit counter
DADR      BAC   DECIML+1   byte pointer to decimal digit
                           string
BADR      NOP              temporary byte pointer
DECIML    RES   3, '00'    decimal string begins as all
                           zeros
PADR      DATA  $+1
          DATA  10000      table of powers of ten
          DATA  1000       . . .
          DATA  100        . . .
          DATA  10         . . .
          DATA  1          . . .
TADR      NOP              temporary table pointer
```

The example just shown will convert a positive binary integer to decimal with leading nonsignificant digits being zero. No provision is made for negative numbers or for the location of the algebraic sign of a negative number. One way in which this convert can be modified would be to set a trigger which depended on the sign of the binary number, using the trigger to set the character '+' or '−' in the unused first byte of location DECIML. This would yield a negative decimal number which looked like:

$$-00255$$

whereas the desirable form of the number is −255, i.e., without leading nonsignificant zeros, and with the sign immediately to the left of the most significant decimal digit. The placing of a character to the left of the most significant digit has another significance though. In writing checks by computer it is imperative that the currency symbol ($) be written immediately to the left of the highest numeric digit so the amount of the check cannot be increased by addition of a digit. The solution to both of these problems will be shown in the next example.

The second method for converting binary to decimal, and the preferable one, is used when the computer has a hardware divide instruction. While the DVD instruction on the Alpha machines is somewhat clumsy, it is adequate to this purpose. The idea in converting by division is to generate the digits by dividing by ten, with the remainder of the division to begin the digit sought. If the binary number 111111 (63_{10}) is divided by 1010_2 the result is:

$$0110 \quad \text{remainder } 0011$$
$$1010 \;) \; \overline{111111}$$

the remainder being the low digit of the decimal number. An ASCII digit is easily formed from this by adding or ORing the necessary bits, as

$$\begin{array}{ll} 0000\ 0011 & \text{the remainder} \\ \underline{1011\ 0000} & \text{an ASCII zero} \\ 1011\ 0011 & \text{an ASCII '3'} \end{array}$$

This process generates the digits from lowest to highest, a bit inconvenient from an addressing point of view, but not a disability. The quotient of the division forms the dividend for the next stage. This is a little more clearly shown if we convert the number 100000001_2 (257_{10}). Dividing the first time we get:

$$11001 \quad \text{remainder } 0111$$
$$1010 \;) \; \overline{100000001}$$

The remainder 0111 is used to form the decimal units digit. Using the quotient 11001 as the new dividend we have:

$$0010 \quad \text{remainder } 0101$$
$$1010 \;) \; \overline{11001}$$

the 0101 being the tens digit. The quotient 0010 is used as the new dividend:

$$0 \quad \text{remainder } 0010$$
$$1010 \;) \; \overline{0010}$$

This remainder forms the hundreds digit. As the quotient is now zero the conversion is finished, and the three BCD digits 0010, 0101, and 0111 are the decimal equivalent of the original binary number.

A subroutine to convert binary integers to ASCII-decimal is shown in example 18-2.

Example 18-2

Write a subroutine to convert any binary integer, including the maximum negative number, to its correct decimal-ASCII representation. The converted number should be right adjusted with no leading nonsignificant zeros and the algebraic sign should be in the character immediately to the left of the most significant digit. The subroutine is to be called by:

label	inst.	operand	
	LDA	BNUM	binary integer to A register
	JST	ICON	jump to convert routine
	DATA	AREA	address of 3 word buffer in which result is to be left
	...		
AREA	RES	3	
	...		

The subroutine is:

ICON	NOP		entry point
	STA	NUMBER	save the input number
	LDX	*ICON	fetch result buffer word address
	IMS	ICON	increment return pointer
	SIN	5	explained in chapter 21
	EMA	DB	save argument and fetch blanks
	STA	@0	set result to all blanks
	STA	@1	...
	STA	@2	...
	EMA	DB	restore blank and fetch argument
	LLX	1	form byte address of result buffer
	AXI	5	and set it to end of buffer. This byte address now points to the last byte of the result area, i.e., the units position of the decimal number to be generated.
	STX	BADR	save byte address in temporary pointer
	ZXR		form trigger for maximum negative number

JAP	I1	was the number positive?
NAR		no, negate it
JAP	I1	is it positive yet?
CAR		no, maximum negative number, form ones
XRM		complement and set skip trigger

At this point the trigger in the X register is set to -1 if and only if the argument was -32768. This trigger will be used to control the incrementation of the units digit.

I1	STX	TRG	save the trigger
	TAX		move dividend to X
LLX	LLX	1	format X for the division
	ZAR		set high order dividend zero
	DVD	TEN	and divide by 10. The quotient is now in X and remainder in A.
	STX	DVDND	save the quotient
	IMS	TRG	units digit of maximum negative number?
	JMP	$+2	no, skip the incrementation
	IAR		yes, increment this digit only
	AAI	'0'	add the necessary ASCII code bits

The completed ASCII digit is now in A ready to be stored in the string. For this purpose BADR is moved to X. It was initialized to point to the low (units) decimal digit.

	LDX	BADR	byte address pointer to X
	SBM		byte mode on
	STAB	@0	store the digit
	SWM		byte mode off
	DXR		decrement the byte pointer
	STX	BADR	and replace it
	LDX	DVDND	reload the old quotient. This forms the new dividend for the next division as per the discussion above.
	JXN	LLX	if dividend is nonzero there are still higher order digits to convert, try again.
	LDA	NUMBER	convert finished, get the origi-

nal binary number. It will be noticed that the result pointer BADR was decremented and replaced before it was determined that no further division was necessary. It therefore points to the position of the next higher order decimal digit if there had been one. This is also the position we want for the algebraic sign. In this exercise a plus sign will be left as blank. Only the minus sign will be specified.

	JAP	I2	skip this if the argument was positive
	LXP	'−'	load a minus sign if it was negative
	SBM		byte mode on
	STXB	*BADR	place the sign in the decimal number
	SWM		byte mode off
I2	JMP	*ICON	and return . . .
NUMBER	NOP		argument save cell
DB	DATA	' '	blanks for buffer initialization
BADR	NOP		temporary result byte pointer
TRG	NOP		maximum negative number trigger
DVDND	NOP		temporary dividend save cell
TEN	DATA	10	divisor

Binary fractions are converted by multiplication of the fraction by ten to produce the successive BCD digits. As an example take the fraction:

$$0110\ 0000\ 0000\ 0000_2 = .75_{10}$$

Multiplying this single precision fraction by ten will produce the double precision result:

A   X

0000 0000 0000 0111   0100 0000 0000 0000

The portion of this result which falls in the A register, a 7, is the high order digit of the result. An ASCII character can be formed from this by a suitable

IOR or AAI instruction as shown in the previous example. Taking the low order portion of the product, i.e., the:

$$0100\ 0000\ 0000\ 0000$$

and multiplying it by ten yields the double precision product:

A	X
0000 0000 0000 0101	0000 0000 0000 0000

Again, the high order product, a 5, is the next digit of the decimal fraction. This process can be continued until the low order result is a zero, indicating that there are no more digits to be converted.

A more typical requirement is for some fixed number of digits. A routine which converts a positive binary fraction to a decimal fraction is shown in example 18-3.

Example 18-3

Write a short program segment which will convert the positive binary fraction held in the X register to a five digit ASCII decimal fraction at location DFRC. The decimal fraction is to be preceeded by a decimal point.

label	inst.	operand	
	LAM	6	total number of characters to be stored
	STA	CNT	to temporary count
	LDA	BADR	move byte pointer to temporary cell
	STA	T	...
	LAM	'.'	pick up decimal point
	JMP	L2	and place it as the first character
L1	ZAR		zero A to prepare for multiply
	MPY	TEN	multiply fraction by ten
	LRX	1	format low order product
	AAI	'0'	add the ASCII code bits
L2	SBM		byte mode on
	STAB	*T	place the character
	SWM		byte mode off
	IMS	T	increment byte pointer
	IMS	CNT	last digit?
	JMP	L1	no, do it again

```
        . . .
CNT     NOP                 character counter
T       NOP                 temporary byte pointer
TEN     DATA  10            multiplicand
BADR    BAC   DFRC          byte pointer to character buf-
                            fer area
DFRC    RES   3
        . . .
```

Fractions are almost never considered as isolated numbers but as part of an integer-fraction combination. As might be expected the case of the maximum negative number causes trouble in a twos complement fraction. Consider the binary fraction:

$$0111\ 1111\ 1111\ 1111$$

This represents the maximum positive fraction—adding a one to the low position of this number would cause its value to become the integer one. Now consider the twos complement of this number:

$$1000\ 0000\ 0000\ 0001$$

This represents, by definition, the negative of the above positive binary fraction. But subtracting a low order bit from it yields a still more negative number, namely:

$$1000\ 0000\ 0000\ 0000$$

which, again by definition, cannot have a value other than unity. To see this another way, add the binary fraction 0100 0000 0000 0000 to itself:

$$
\begin{array}{l}
0100\ 0000\ 0000\ 0000 \\
+0100\ 0000\ 0000\ 0000 \\
\hline
1000\ 0000\ 0000\ 0000 \quad \text{plus overflow}
\end{array}
$$

The result is invalid. The value of the original fraction was $.5_{10}$ and adding it to itself produced a number which was not a fraction, i.e., a one. Now take the twos complement of the above fraction, i.e., 1100 0000 0000 0000 and add it to itself:

$$
\begin{array}{l}
1100\ 0000\ 0000\ 0000 \\
+1100\ 0000\ 0000\ 0000 \\
\hline
1000\ 0000\ 0000\ 0000 \quad \text{and } no \text{ overflow}
\end{array}
$$

This means that an unrestricted binary fraction cannot be safely converted as pure fraction, it might have the value -1! It is for this reason that an allowance must be made for an integer part when converting fractions. The process of converting an integer-fraction combination is shown in example 18-4.

Example 18-4

Write a subroutine which will convert the integer in A and the fraction in X to ASCII-decimal. The radix point is considered to be between the registers, the X register contents being pure fraction. The input is considered to be a true double precision number, with the low order sign zero. The subroutine is called by:

label	inst.	operand	
	LDA	INTGR	integer part to A
	LDX	FRCTN	fraction to X
	JST	DCON	jump to converter
	DATA	BFR	word address of 6 word buffer which is to receive the ASCII-decimal string.

. . .

The result is to be left in a 12 character string, including sign and decimal point beginning at BFR. There are to be five fraction digits to the right of the decimal point.

DCON	NOP		entry point
	LLX	1	clear low order sign, just in
	LRX	1	case he forgot, and turn off overflow
	STA	SIGN	save integer part in algebraic sign
	JAP	D1	proceed if positive . . .
	NXR		
	LLX	1	otherwise double negate,
	LRX	1	turn off overflow
	CAR		and complement A
	JXN	$+2	a zero low order half?
	IAR		yes, increment high order
D1	STA	TRG	and save in maximum negative number trigger
	JOR	D2	overflow off if all OK
	ARM		no, maximum negative number
	STA	TRG	set trigger
	LRA	1	and set A to maximum positive number
D2	STX	FRACT	save fraction
	STA	INT	and positive integer
	LDX	*DCON	pick up buffer address

	IMS	DCON	and increment return pointer
	LDA	DB	blanks to A
	STA	@0	set entire result to blanks
	STA	@1	...
	STA	@2	...
	STA	@3	...
	STA	@4	...
	STA	@5	...
	LLX	1	form byte address
	AXI	5	of low integer digit
	STX	IPTR	and save . . .
	AXI	1	and of decimal point before first fraction digit
	STX	FPTR	and save it . . .
	LDX	INT	ready integer part for conversion
D3	ZAR		zero high order dividend
	LLX	1	predivide formatting shift
	DVD	TEN	and divide
	STX	DVDND	save old quotient/new dividend
	IMS	TRG	low digit of maximum negative number?
	JMP	$+2	no
	IAR		yes increment it
	AAI	'0'	add the ASCII code bits
	LDX	IPTR	integer digit byte pointer to X
	SBM		byte mode on
	STAB	@0	store the digit
	SWM		byte mode off
	DXR		decrement pointer
	STX	IPTR	and replace
	LDX	DVDND	load new dividend
	JXN	D3	finished if zero, otherwise try again
	LDA	SIGN	pick up original integer
	JAP	CFRC	and skip if it was positive
	LXP	'−'	otherwise place the minus sign
	SBM		byte mode on
	STXB	*IPTR	store the character
	SWM		byte mode off
CFRC	LAM	6	initialize character count for fraction convert

```
            STA   CNT       ...
            LAP   '.'       pick up the decimal point
            LDX   FRACT     and the fraction in X
            JMP   L2        and skip to place the point
    L1      ZAR             zero for multiply
            MPY   TEN       multiply by ten
            LRX   1         post multiply formatting shift
            AAI   '0'       add the necessary code bits
    L2      SBM             byte mode on
            STAB  *FPTR     place the point or fraction digit
            SWM             byte mode off
            IMS   FPTR      increment fraction digit
                           pointer
            IMS   CNT       last fraction digit?
            JMP   L1        no, generate another one
            JMP   *DCON     yes, finished with convert, re-
                           turn
SIGN        NOP             algebraic sign save cell
TRG         NOP             maximum negative number
                           trigger
FRACT       NOP             binary fraction
INT         NOP             binary integer
IPTR        NOP             temporary integer digit
                           pointer
FPTR        NOP             temporary fraction digit
                           pointer
DVDND       NOP             save cell for dividend during
                           integer convert
TEN         DATA 10         multiplier/divisor for both
                           converters
CNT         NOP             fraction digit counter
DB          DATA  ' '       blanks for initializing buffer
```

Using the routine in the example just given a number can be converted and printed on the teletype by:

```
            LDA   INTGR     integer to A
            LDX   FRCTN     fraction to X
            JST   DCON
P           DATA  ALLSIX    address pointer to result area
            LDA   P         pick up pointer to print
            JST   PRT       previously discussed print routine
            ...
```

```
ALLSIX    RES  6              result buffer
          DATA '\ \'          remember the backslashes for
                              PRT!!
          . . .
```

The final exercise in this chapter will be devoted to conversion of binary to hexadecimal form. The problem of conversion to hexadecimal output form reduces to that of splitting the 16 bit word into 4 bit groups and processing each group to form the proper ASCII character. If the 4 bit group is in the range 0-9 the problem is trivial. The necessary bits to form ASCII code can be merged with the 4 bit group using IOR or AAI as shown before. For groups from 1010_2 through 1111_2 there is the problem of generating the corresponding A-F ASCII characters. The 0-9 characters are formed by merging :BO with the 4 bit code, as:

$$\begin{array}{ll}
0000\ 1001 & \text{a nine} \\
\underline{1011\ 0000} & \text{a :BO} \\
1011\ 1001 & \text{the ASCII character}
\end{array}$$

The problem of turning 1010_2 into $1100\ 0001$ is solved easily by adding seven to the 4 bit group before adding the :BO, but only if the group is in the 1010 to 1111 range. An individual 4 bit group can be processed by:

```
          . . .              4 bit group in A
          CMS  NINE          greater than 9?
          JMP  $+2           no, normal
          ADD  SEVEN         yes, add a seven
          ADD  BZERO         and the ASCII code bits
          . . .
NINE      DATA 9
SEVEN     DATA 7
BZERO     DATA :BO
```

A very short program which takes advantage of this trick is shown in example 18-5.

Example 18-5

Write a subroutine which will convert the binary A register to 4 ASCII-hexadecimal characters in A and X. This subroutine is to be called by the following sequence:

```
label     inst.    operand

          LDA  BIN           binary number to be con-
                             verted to A

          JST  HEX
```

```
          STA    FIRST2      save two high characters
          STX    LAST2       save two low characters
          . . .
HEX       NOP                entry point
          LXM    4
          STX    HCNT        initialize digit count
```

Shift instructions are now used to "split" the 4 bit groups apart over A and X, with 4 zero bits to the left of each group. This is shown schematically in the comments columns below. D means a 4 bit group, X means irrelevant contents and O means zero. Before the shifts the contents of the registers are:

```
                             A     X
                             DDDD  XXXX
          LLR    4           ODDD  DXXX
          LRX    4           ODDD  ODXX
          LLR    8           OOOD  DDOD
          LLA    4           OODO  DDOD
          LLL    4           ODOD  DODO
          LRX    4           ODOD  ODOD
```

The operation is now performed in the registers, testing the *high* eight bits of the A register to see whether it is ten or greater. If so, a seven is added to the *high* byte of A. The entire double register is then rotated left eight bits. Since the overflow bit is involved in this rotation only the high seven bits of the character just tested appear in the low part of X, the low bit staying in the overflow bit. At this point we add the ASCII code bits to the character just tested with an AXI instruction. Since the character is still shifted one bit to the right of its "normal" position, the operand of the AXI is not :BO, but half of this, :58. After all four characters are processed this way a single long left rotate brings both registers into the normal position and the conversion is complete.

```
C         CMS    TEN         compare high half of A
          JMP    $+3         less than ten, skip
          NOP                greater than ten
          ADD    SEVEN       or equal to ten, add a seven
          LRL    8           rotate both registers left one
                             byte
          AXI    :58         and add :B0/2
          IMS    HCNT        last digit?
          JMP    C           no, do it again
          LRL    1           yes, move to compensate for
                             overflow
```

```
            JMP    *HEX        and return
HCNT        NOP                digit counter
TEN         DATA   :A00        a ten in the high eight bits
SEVEN       DATA   :700        and a seven in the high eight
                               bits
            ...
```

19

Processing Data Stacks—Special Instructions

In an earlier chapter an example was given which involved the movement of data in a way which simulated the movement of railroad cars on a piece of track of fixed length, i.e., capable of holding a fixed number of cars. In the earlier example the data themselves, identifiers for the cars, were physically moved. The first data location was made to correspond to the first car, the second address to the second car, and so forth. The example involved only four data items and the most straightforward solution to it was to physically move the items themselves with the base location of the block or stack of data remaining unchanged.

When the number of data items becomes large, and under certain other circumstances, it becomes profitable to modify address pointers rather than move the data themselves. In this type of data management the ordinal position of data items in a stack is determined relative to a beginning address given in an address pointer called a *stack pointer*. Entering an item into a data stack is called *pushing* it onto the stack, and withdrawing an item is called *popping* it from the stack. Data stacks may be organized to behave in many different ways but the two principal modes of organization result in what are called LIFO (*Last In First Out*) and FIFO (*First In First Out*) stacks.

The FIFO stack behaves like the railroad track section described in the earlier example. Pushing an item onto one end of a fixed length stack pops an item from the other end. The FIFO stack thus mimics the behavior of many physical situations: railroad cars on a fixed piece of track, boxes on a conveyor, cars in a tunnel, etc. The essential characteristic here is that the stack can hold a fixed number of items. The contents of the stack may change but the length of the stack does not. A frequent use of these structures in programming industrial problems is to simulate delays due to routing in material flow problems.

LIFO stacks behave somewhat like the spring loaded tray delivery devices found in cafeterias. Trays are loaded into the device from the top, the last tray loaded being the first available on the top of the stack. This kind of stack can only be accessed from the top.

To aid in the handling of data stacks computer manufacturers have recently begun to provide special instructions which perform part of the address management work of stack handling. The reader should clearly understand that these instructions do nothing which cannot be accomplished by the normal instructions of the computer—in many cases more efficiently.

Stack instructions mimic the normal memory reference instructions of the computer in their mnemonic forms but not at the binary level. Unlike byte handling, stack handling involves the use of separate instructions rather than a mode which can be switched on and off. Stack instructions involve three words, two words for the instruction itself and one for the stack pointer. They are indicated at the assembler level by appending an "S" to the normal memory reference mnemonic—LDAS instead of LDA, SUBS instead of SUB. The double word instruction contains two elements, the instruction specification itself in the first word and an address pointer which specifies the location of the stack pointer in the second word. *NOTE* that the second word is *not* the stack pointer but an address which tells where the stack pointer is located. There are four modes in which stack instructions can be executed. They are:

1. Direct access

   The word whose address is specified by the stack pointer is accessed. This amounts in effect to double level indirect addressing—the address word of the instruction is used to access the stack pointer, and the stack pointer is used to access the memory word. There is no particular advantage to this arrangement. The stack instruction:

   LDAS ADR

   requires three words—two for the instruction and one for the stack pointer ADR, whereas the normal instruction:

   LDA   *ADR

   uses only two words, one for the instruction and one for the pointer ADR which is identical to the stack pointer in the previous instruction.

2. Autodecrement

   The stack pointer is decremented and the operand accessed through this decremented pointer. If the stack pointer points to ADOLPH before the instruction is executed it is decremented to point to ADOLPH−1, and the contents of ADOLPH−1 are accessed. The autodecrement form of the instruction is specified by a minus sign in the operand field following the stack pointer name, as:

   ADDS ADOLPH,−

   Note the comma which separates the stack pointer name from the minus sign. Keep in mind that the decrementing is done *before* the access. This is a different order from:

3. Autoincrement

   The stack pointer is used to access the operand in memory, and *then* the stack pointer is incremented. The use of this feature is shown in example 19-1.

Example 19-1

Use the ADDS instruction to form the sum of the ten numbers in the stack which begins at SNOW.

label	inst.	operand	
	LDA	RAIN	initialize stack pointer
	STA	SPTR	...
	LXP	10	count to X
	ZAR		zero A to receive sum
SUMM	ADDS	SPTR,+	the + sign for autoincrement
	DXR		decrement count
	JXN	SUMM	do it again if count nonzero
	...		
RAIN	DATA	SNOW	address pointer to stack
SPTR	NOP		active stack pointer
SNOW	RES	10	
	...		

The autoincrement feature has eliminated the necessity for separate incrementation of an address pointer held in X or a memory word. It should be remembered that though ADDS is written as a single instruction it generates *two* machine words. The above should be compared to the same function performed by ordinary indexed addressing, i.e.:

	LDX	RAIN	address pointer to X
	LAM	10	
	STA	CNT	initialize count
	ZAR		
	ADD	@0	form sum
	IXR		bump address
	IMS	CNT	last one?
	JMP	$-3	no, do it again

This uses the same number of memory words as the previous code. Also consider the use of indexed indirect addressing:

	LXP	10	
	ZAR		
	ADD	*@RAIN	
	DXR		

```
        JXN     $-2
        . . .
```

with RAIN being defined in scratchpad as:

```
RAIN          DATA SNOW-1
```

which is considerably shorter.

4. Indexed

   In this form the contents of the stack pointer are added to the contents of the index register to form the effective operand address. This resembles indexed indirect addressing in the manner in which the effective address is computed, except that it requires one word more than the indexed indirect mode—the second word of the instruction—and the pointer need not be in scratchpad. If scratchpad space were at a premium this mode might be useful.

A LIFO stack is managed by use of the LDAS and STAS (or LDXS and STXS) instructions in opposite modes, i.e., LDAS   PTR,− and STAS   PTR,+ or LDAS   PTR,+ and STAS   PTR,−. In either case alternate execution of load and store instructions pops and pushes items from the stack. Any accounting which concerns stack size or limits must be performed separately.

The nominal reason for the existence of special hardware to perform these push and pop functions is to aid in the construction of subroutines which are recursive or reentrant and to aid in the composition of certain types of operation/operand strings which arise in compiling higher level languages such as COBOL and FORTRAN. Failure to become proficient in the use of these operations will have no particular effect on the performance of most programmers. This subject will arise again briefly during the discussion of interrupt processing, but beyond this the subject and the special instructions can be safely ignored.

20 Communication With the Real World—Input and Output

A computer performs its function by manipulating data which originate in the real world and expressing the results of those manipulations to the real world. Information comes into computers from the real world in an almost limitless variety of ways—keystrokes, switch closures, motions, or other changing conditions within some external device. Likewise information is presented to the real world in a variety of forms by the computer —numbers printed, curves drawn, voltages adjusted, etc. The huge variety of devices and modes by which information is transferred between the computer and the real world precludes any attempt to discuss even a significant fraction of them in a book like this. The object of this chapter and the next one is to acquaint the reader with the common requirements for transmission of information between computers and real world devices in general.

Broadly, there are two distinct categories of information transmission—transmission initiated by the computer and that initiated by the external device. The second category, transmission initiated by the external device, will be discussed in the next chapter. The topic of this chapter will be those transmissions which are initiated by the computer and are solely under the control of the computer.

In computer controlled transmission of data the computer performs three distinct types of functions. These functions are combined in fairly obvious ways to control the orderly flow of information between computer and real world device. The functions are:

1. *Control.*

   Pulses are sent from the computer to the real world device to cause it to perform certain actions. The actions initiated by these control pulses vary with the nature of the device and the control code used. The mnemonic instruction used in Alpha machines to send control pulses to peripheral devices is SEL (Select) or varients of SEL such as SEA or SEX. For example, the instruction:

   SEL   TTY+3

   where the symbol TTY has the value :38, will cause the teletype tape reader to begin driving paper tape through its read station. This instruction by itself does *not* cause data to be brought from the teletype tape reader to the computer. The tape reader simply moves tapes past the

213

read station until commanded to stop by another SEL instruction, namely:

SEL   TTY+4

There is no particular scheme of sense in the numbers used in these Select codes. Both device and computer are wired in such a way that if the proper instructions are issued the desired action will take place. It is up to the programmer to know which codes perform appropriate actions for the device in question.

2. *Sense*.

These functions allow the computer to test the status of a device external to itself, typically to determine whether the device is ready to transfer data to the computer or to accept a transfer of data from the computer. Tests made using the sense functions cause a program skip of one instruction if the condition being tested is met. In the Alpha machines there are two basic sensing instructions, SEN and SSN, testing for the true and false states of the tested condition respectively. As an example, the teletype can be tested to determine whether or not it is ready for a data transfer by:

SEN   TTY+1

in which TTY has the same meaning as before. If the teletype is ready for the data transfer the instruction which immediately follows the SEN will be skipped. Using SEN and a jump a two instruction loop can be built which, in effect, waits until the transfer is possible, i.e.:

SEN   TTY+1
JMP $-1

If the teletype is not ready control passes to the instruction which follows the SEN, which jumps back to the SEN. The computer thus "hangs" in this two instruction loop until the transfer is possible. This procedure does *not* transfer the data; it only causes a pause until the transfer can be made.

3. *Data transfer functions*.

These cause data to be moved between computer and peripheral device. The basic data transfer instructions in the Alpha machines are INA or INX, meaning *IN*put to A or X, and OTA or OTX, meaning *OuT*put from the A or X registers to the peripheral device.

Each peripheral device is connected to the computer by a collection of electronics known as an *interface*. An interface is usually but not always specific to a given device, i.e., a different type of electronic interface is required to drive a teletype from that required for a relay output register. From the programmer's point of view the interface is part of the peripheral device. Computer and peripheral device communicate only through the interface.

Input/output instructions of all types—control, data transfer, and sense—are composed of three distinct parts. These parts are:

1. *The instruction specification.*

This is held in the upper eight bits of the sixteen bit instruction word. It specifies the nature of the instruction, i.e., one of the three types described above and such further information as may be necessary to the particular instruction. In data transfer instructions this includes the direction of the transfer, in or out, the source or destination register, A or X, and various special features of the transfer. For sense instructions it will specify whether the instruction skip is to be made on a true or false condition. For control instructions (SEL) this portion can specify various options which will be left to the later discussion.

2. *The device address.*

This is a five bit binary number which specifies which peripheral device is involved in this instruction. This number is unique to the peripheral device concerned. It represents a sort of "password" recognized only by the device concerned. This means that instructions addressed to a digital input register cannot affect a line printer or card reader. This device address should not be confused with a memory address. The device address is a means of referring to a specific peripheral device and no other.

3. *A function code consisting of three bits which further specifies the operation of the instruction.*

This function code is interpreted by the interface to the peripheral device and the action of each function code is determined by the wiring in the device interface. Since the variety of specific functions is so great there is no systematic scheme to function codes even in standard peripheral devices, though code 4 has been standardized for SEL instructions to mean reset, as that term is interpreted for each device.

The above described parts of the input/output instructions are located in the instruction word in the manner indicated schematically below:

$$iiiiiiii \quad ddddd \quad fff$$

in which i stands for instruction specification, d for device address, and f for function code. The eight bit instruction specification allows easy handling in hexadecimal, but the five and three division of device address and function code is clumsy. For this reason it is convenient to use an assembly program artifice to generate the device address and function code. It will be recalled that the expression:

```
TTY        EQU    :38
```

appeared without explanation in an earlier chapter. The bare five bit device address for the teletype is 00111_2. If this is expressed in an eight bit group with the low three bits set to zero, it is:

$$0011\ 1000$$

This would correspond to the operand of an I/O instruction which had the expression TTY or TTY+0 as its operand. Using the above EQU artifice allows the programmer to write expressions like TTY+4 as I/O operands and let the assembler do the necessary composition of the operand field. The instruction:

```
SEL    TTY+4
```

assembles to:

$$0100\ 0000\ 0011\ 1100$$

when TTY is defined as shown above.

Before leaving this subject it should be noted parenthetically that it is also possible, and valid, to specify device address and function code as absolute numeric operands, i.e.:

```
SEL    :3C
```

or

```
SEL    60
```

These forms both produce a result identical to the SEL   TTY+4 above, but do not show the clear division between device address and function code, beside making program changes more complicated. With this piece of formatting strategy out of the way we can proceed to the main business of explaining computer controlled input and output.

Perhaps the most frequent and elementary output task is the printing of a teletype character. This is accomplished by executing the instruction:

```
OTA    TTY
```

with the ASCII code for the desired character in the low eight bits of the A register. To print the character "D" on the teletype page printer it is only necessary to execute:

```
LAP    'D'              character D to A register
OTA    TTY
```

As the teletype requires about 1/10 second to print a character a series of characters could be printed by arranging a suitable pause between the OTA instructions. Since it requires at least a tenth of a second to push the RUN button on the computer this could be done with HLT instructions. The word FROG could be printed by:

```
LAP    'F'
OTA    TTY
HLT
LAP    'R'
OTA    TTY
HLT
LAP    'O'
OTA    TTY
HLT
LAP    'G'
OTA    TTY
HLT
```

Inserting an HLT instruction to cause a pause is no way to do the job, of course, but it will work. The problem reduces to finding some way to waste time until the teletype is ready to accept another character from the computer without stopping the computer. It could be done by loading a number or series of numbers into the A register and counting down to zero or contriving some combination of IMS instructions which would waste the required amount of time, but this would depend on the specific timing of the given teletype interface. It was noted earlier that a variation of about 20 percent can be expected in teletype speeds.

A better way is to use a facility which is built into the interface for this purpose. Very simply, this facility provides a flag which can be tested by the SEN instruction. The flag is set (on) when the device is ready for data transmission and reset (off) when the device is not ready. The flag is known as a *Buffer Ready Flip Flop*, one of those terms dear to hardware engineers and incomprehensible to everybody else, and it is abbreviated to BRFF in the manufacturers literature. We will refer to it here simply as a ready flag. Using this ready flag we can perform the above task without stopping the computer by:

```
LAP    'F'        ASCII 'F' to A register
OTA    TTY        and print it
SEN    TTY+1      this tests the ready flag
JMP    $-1        jump back if not ready
LAP    'R'        ready, load the R
OTA    TTY        print the R
SEN    TTY+1      and wait 'til it's finished
JMP    $-1        . . .
LAP    'O'        ready, load the O
OTA    TTY        and print it
```

```
SEN    TTY+1          wait 'til it's finished
JMP    $−1            . . .
LAP    'G'            ready, load the G
OTA    TTY            and send it out
SEN    TTY+1          test and wait . . .
JMP    $−1            until finished
...                   then resume the program
```

All of this repetition is not necessary, of course, as the procedure shown can be formalized easily into a subroutine for printing characters on the teletype (see example 20-1).

Example 20-1

Write a subroutine to print the character which is in the A register on entry on the teletype page printer. The subroutine should not return control to the calling program until the character has been printed and the teletype is ready to accept another character. The character to be printed is in the low eight bits of the A register.

label	inst.	operand	
PCHAR	NOP		entry point
	OTA	TTY	send the character out
	SEN	TTY+1	test the ready flag
	JMP	$−1	and wait 'til it's finished
	JMP	*PCHAR	finished, return
	...		

Note that the subroutine in example 20-1 makes no mention of word or byte mode. It will work in either mode, since no memory references are made. This is an advantage as the "natural" mode for working with characters in byte mode. The use of the above subroutine is shown in example 20-2.

Example 20-2

Write a short program segment to type a message located at MSGE using the PCHAR subroutine.

label	inst.	operand	
	LAM	18	18 characters in the message
	STA	CNT	initialize count
	LDX	MSGADR	byte pointer to index
	SBM		byte mode on
PLOOP	LDAB	@0	pick up the character

```
        JST    PCHAR       go print it
        IXR                increment the byte pointer
        IMS    CNT         last character
        JMP    PLOOP       no, get the next one
        SWM                restore word mode
        . . .
MSGADR  BAC    MSGE
MSGE    TEXT   'THE SKY IS FALLING'
        . . .
```

A still more useful form of the **PCHAR** subroutine would supply a line feed automatically every time a carriage return was typed, as shown in example 20-3.

Example 20-3

Write a character print subroutine which will combine the functions of carriage return and line feed to make the teletype behave as if it were an ordinary typewriter in this respect.

label	inst.	operand	
CHOUT	NOP		entry point, meaning CHaracter OUT
	OTA	TTY	send the character out
	SEN	TTY+1	wait 'til it's finished
	JMP	$−1	. . .
	CAI	:8D	was it a carriage return?
	JMP	$+2	yes, supply the line feed
	JMP	*CHOUT	no, return
	LAP	:8A	load the line feed
	JMP	CHOUT+1	and send it out

The reader may recall that this is the identical routine given at the end of Chapter 13. The routine which followed **CHOUT** in that chapter, PRT, can be reexamined now in the light of what has just been done.

Getting data into the computer from a peripheral device usually involves conditioning the device in some way to initiate the transfer. To read a character from the teletype tape reader for example requires that the tape reader be set in motion. There are two possible ways this can be done —read a single character and then stop the reader, or start the reader and move the tape continuously. The tape reader can be made to advance one tape frame by:

```
        SEL    TTY+2
```

or it can be made to run continuously by:

SEL   TTY+3

In either case, execution of the SEL instruction resets (turns off) the ready flag (BRFF). The need for this is obvious, since to have the ready flag on at the beginning would cause the SEN instruction to skip before the tape frame had actually advanced. The procedure for reading paper tape from the teletype is shown in example 20-4.

Example 20-4

Write a short subroutine to read one character from the teletype paper tape reader and return with the character read in the A register.

label	inst.	operand	
RTF	NOP		entry point (*R*ead *T*ape *F*rame)
	SEL	TTY+2	ready flag off, advance the reader
	SEN	TTY+1	data ready to be read yet?
	JMP	$−1	no, wait
	INA	TTY	yes, read the character
	JMP	*RTF	

Before leaving this last example it is worth noting that while the ready flag is turned on by the data becoming available it is turned off by the act of transferring the data, i.e., by the INA. This is necessary when reading a block of data in the continuous mode, as is shown in example 20-5.

Example 20-5

Write a program segment to read a 50 word block of data from the teletype paper tape reader, leaving it packed two bytes per word beginning with location INPUT.

label	inst.	operand	
	LAM	100	50 words = 100 bytes
	STA	CNT	initialize count
	SEL	TTY+4	initialize teletype interface. Function code 4, as noted before, is the reset code. If the reader is in motion it is stopped, and the ready flag is turned *on*.

			This property of function code 4, turning the ready flag on, will be important in a later example.
	SEL	TTY+3	this starts the reader moving and turns the ready flag *off* in preparation for the reading of data
	LDX	BADR	byte address of INPUT to index
	SBM		byte mode on
LOOP	SEN	TTY+1	ready to read data yet?
	JMP	$−1	no, wait
	INA	TTY	yes, read it and turn the ready flag *off*
	STAB	@0	store it in the buffer area
	IXR		increment the pointer
	IMS	CNT	last byte read?
	JMP	LOOP	no, read another one
	. . .		
BADR	BAC	INPUT	byte pointer to INPUT
INPUT	RES	50	. . .

Reading data from the teletype keyboard involves a process which is very similar to the step read of the earlier example. In this case the reader is not started, but a SEL instruction is executed to "prime" the keyboard for input. This instruction is SEL   TTY+1. To read a character typed on the keyboard:

	SEL	TTY+1	ready flag *off*, prime keyboard
	SEN	TTY+1	has he typed it yet?
	JMP	$−1	no, keep waiting
	INA	TTY	yes, get the character he typed and turn off the ready flag

. . .

Before leaving the subject of keyboard input one other point must be covered. With the teletype under computer control just striking the key does *not* cause the character associated with that key to be printed. The ASCII code for the key becomes available to the computer as just shown, but the character is not printed automatically. Since it is usually desirable (but not always) that the material being typed be visible on the teletype page some solution must be found to this. The one which comes immediately to mind is to simply type the character back, i.e., when the key is struck read the data and immediately send it back to the teletype printer by means of a routine like PCHAR or CHOUT. This works and the method is still used on some computers, but it involves the difficulty that there are two data transmissions, which doubles the time required for each character. It also poses the danger that the typist will strike the next key before the computer has been able to "echo" the previous character, with gibberish as the result. To get around this problem while still leaving open the possibility of "blind" or unprinted typing, an "autoecho" mode has been provided which forces the character to be printed as it is being typed. This autoecho mode is turned on by executing:

    SEL   TTY

or

    SEL   TTY+0

before the typing begins. With this information the reader will now be able to understand the workings of the RKB routine given in Chapter 13.

In summary of what has been discussed to this point, there are three distinct steps involved in input to the computer:

1. Given that the device is in a known state (e.g., after a reset has been issued), a command must be issued to initiate the type of input required (keyboard, paper tape, etc.). This command is in the form of a pulse from the computer to the peripheral. In the Alpha series machines this pulse is created by the execution of a SEL instruction. The specific identity of the pulse sent to the peripheral device is determined by the function code used with the SEL instruction.

2. Sufficient time must be allowed to pass to permit the peripheral device to perform whatever is necessary to ready itself to transmit data. This time may be specific, as the time required to move a paper tape one frame, or it may be indefinite, as when waiting for a key to be struck by an operator. In either case, the peripheral device signals its readiness to transmit data by setting a ready flag called the Buffer Ready Flip Flop. This ready flag is tested by a SEN instruction in the Alpha machines, this test causing the instruction after the SEN to be skipped when the ready flag is set (on).

3. The actual transmission of data from the peripheral to the computer. This transmission is accomplished by an INA or one of the other input transmission instructions. If the transmission involves data less than one word in length the input data are *right* justified, i.e., byte data will appear in the *low* eight bits of the register.

Output is equally simple, consisting of the following steps:

1. Given that the device is not already in the process of transmitting data

and is in a known state, the data are presented by the computer to the peripheral device by means of an OTA or equivalent instruction with the appropriate function code.

2. A delay is effected to give the peripheral device sufficient time to act upon the data which has been sent to it. In the case of the teletype given in the examples this delay is sufficient to allow the character represented by the output ASCII to be actually printed. Like the delay on input this delay is implemented by means of the SEN instruction.

Again, in either of the above cases the ready flag (BRFF) signals the readiness of the device for another transmission. The ready flag is turned off by the transmission of the data, via INA or OTA. It is significant that the computer is completely tied up while waiting for the transmission to be completed when input or output is done in this way. The processor is "hung" in the two instruction loop formed by the SEN and JMP $-1 while waiting for the ready flag to signal the end of transmission. This means that it cannot perform any other task until the ready flag has been turned on. In the case of tape this involves only a tenth of a second or so, but for keyboard input the wait is *indefinite*, and if the computer is supposed to be performing other tasks on a schedule, temperature monitoring of a nuclear reactor, for example, those tasks are neglected until the data transfer is complete. Obviously this kind of data transfer process is not workable in situations in which the computer cannot be "hung up." A way out of this bind exists, however. The hardware of any modern computer, including the Alphas, provides a means by which the ready flag can be monitored automatically while the processor goes about its necessary business. This activation of this hardware feature will cause no action until a data transfer is ready to be made. It will then "notify" the program of the fact. This facility, called the interrupt system, will be discussed in Chapters 21 and 22.

Before going into some of the more exotic forms of printed output, we will consider another kind of peripheral device, a relay output register. These devices provide a set of relay contacts available to the real world which can be selectively opened and closed under computer control. By connecting the controls of real world devices to these contacts the devices may be operated under computer control. Some of the devices contain as many as 64 relays on a single option card, but the one available with the Alpha contains only 32. The relays of the output register can be addressed in either eight or sixteen bit groups as the programmer desires. The status of a group of relays is set by sending a byte or word from the computer with zeros in positions where open relays are required and ones in the positions of those relays which are to be closed. The usual device address of the relay output register is :1C. Writing this number in the left most five bits of an eight bit byte, we have:

$$1110\ 0000_2 = E0_{16}$$

References to the relay output register can now be made symbolically by defining this device address as:

RCOM   EQU   :E0

and this convention will be used through the remainder of this discussion. The relay output register is initialized, i.e., all relays are opened by using function code 4 with a SEL, i.e.:

SEL   RCOM+4

Individual relays are closed by execution of an output instruction with the appropriate bit or bits set to ones in the register whose contents are transmitted to the RCOM. The relays are numbered 0-31 from right to left. To close relay 0, the right most relay, the low bit of A is set and sent to the RCOM, as:

LAP   1   low bit of A is one, all others are zeros

OTA   RCOM+4   output to the lower 16 relays

. . .

The choice of the upper 16 or lower 16 relays is determined by the function code, in this case a 4. Note that the use of function code 4 here has no relation to its use with the SEL order. To set (close) relay 16, i.e., the right most relay of the second group of 16, the instructions would be:

LAP   1   low bit of A is one, all others are zeros

OTA   RCOM+5   output to the upper 16 relays

. . .

Several things should be understood about these last two examples. First, the choice of the lower or upper group of 16 relays was made by the choice of the function code, 4 or 5. Also, only the lowest relay of each group was closed, since only the low bit of A was set to a one when the OTA was executed. Finally, *all* the other relays were opened because all bits but the lowest one were zeros, i.e., a one bit causes a relay to close or to remain closed, and a zero bit causes the relay to open or remain open. Since individual relays must be controlled without disturbing the status of other relays in the same group, some data management at the bit level is required.

First, there is the problem of getting the bit into the right position in the A register. Given that we have the number of the relay we want to close in the A register, there are any number of ways to solve this problem. The most obvious one that comes to mind is:

```
            TAX                     move relay number to X
            ZAR                     all A register bits zero
            SOV                     and the overflow bit on
MOVE        RLA     1               now rotate left one bit. This brings
                                    the one bit from the overflow into
                                    the low bit of A the first time
                                    through and moves it into succes-
                                    sively higher bits of A on succes-
                                    sive passes.

            JXZ     OUT             if count is zero exit
            DXR                     otherwise decrement and rotate
                                    again
            JMP     MOVE            . . .
            . . .
```

This rotates the A register and overflow bit left the required number of times to place the bit in the desired position, given that the original number was 0-15. It may take a fairly long time to execute, however, and there is a better way.

The reader may recall the earlier discussion of the formats of shift orders, particularly long shifts. The shift count is contained in the low four bits of a long shift instruction, the actual number of shifts being one greater than the count in the binary instruction. This can be utilized for a shortcut solution to the above problem. We can use the relay number as a shift count to rotate a bit into the correct position in one operation instead of the repeated operations shown above. This is a more elegant solution to the problem, and it looks like this:

```
            . . .                   relay number in A, 0-15
            IOR     LSHF            form the rotate instruction
            STA     $+3             store the instruction in line
            ZAX                     zero both registers
            SOV                     and turn overflow on
            NOP                     this is overlaid by the long rotate
            STX     BIT             and save the result
            . . .
LSHF        LRL     1               skeleton shift instruction
            . . .
```

Even with this problem solved though, we still have the problem of how to turn the selected relay on without turning everything else in the relay group off. This is solved by keeping a "relay status word" in memory into which individual bits are "ORed" without influencing the other bits in the word. It is this relay status word which is output to the RCOM rather than an individual bit. To maintain such a word requires that *all* control of relays be done through a common subroutine. Since there are 32 relays, the relay management subroutine will have to keep two status words, one for the upper group and one for the lower. The logic of the method just shown can be extended easily to apply to a 32 bit double word, as shown in example 20-6.

Example 20-6

Write a subroutine which will accept a number in the range 0-31 in A and produce as its function a single bit set in the double word formed by A and X. The low bit of X is considered to be bit 0 of the double word and the sign bit of A is bit 31.

The routine should be called by:

label	inst.	operand	
	LDA	NUMBER	relay number to A
	JST	RLYNO	. . .
	JMP	DSASTR	error return, relay number not 0-31
	. . .		normal return

The routine is:

label	inst.	operand	
RLYNO	NOP		entry point
	STA	BIT	save the relay number
	CMS	THTY1	greater than 31?
	JMP	$+2	no, test for less than zero
	JMP	*RLYNO	yes, error return
	JAM	$−1	OK if positive
	ZXR		
	SOV		this positions the one bit "below" the low bit of the X register in case the relay number is less than 16. Now test the relay number for range . . .
	CMS	SIXTEEN	less than 16?
	JMP	$+4	yes, leave the bit where it is
	NOP		greater
	SAI	16	or equal, subtract 16, and
	RRX	1	move the bit to the position just "below" the upper word. Now we have a number in the

```
                                      0-15 range in A and a one bit in
                                      either overflow or the sign bit
                                      of X.
              IOR    ROT              form the long left rotate
              STA    $+2              store the instruction in line
              ZAR                     high word to zero, and execute
              NOP                     the rotate.
              IMS    RLYNO            increment the return pointer
              JMP    *RLYNO           and return
BIT           NOP
THTY1         DATA   31
SXTEEN        DATA   16
ROT           LRL    1                skeleton instruction
              . . .
```

Using the routine just shown it is fairly easy to create a pair of management routines for the RCOM, as shown in example 20-7.

Example 20-7

Using subroutine RLYNO write a pair of subroutines, RON and ROF, to turn individual relays of a 32 bit RCOM on and off respectively. The user of these routines should be able to turn a relay on by:

label	inst.	operand	
	LDA	RNMBR	relay number to A
	JST	RON	go turn it on
	JMP	ERROR	bad relay number
	. . .		

or off by:

	LDA	RNMBR	relay number to A
	JST	ROF	go turn it off
	JMP	ERROR	bad relay number
	. . .		

The relay turn on routine is:

RON	NOP		entry point
	JST	RLYNO	check validity and get the appropriate bit
	JMP	*RON	garbage, take the error return
	IOR	UPPER	merge bit with upper relay word

STA	UPPER	and update the word in memory
OTA	RCOM+5	and turn the upper relay(s) on
EAX		now swap for the lower word
IOR	LOWER	and merge the lower bit(s)
STA	LOWER	and update the word in memory
OTA	RCOM+4	and turn the lower relay(s) on
IMS	RON	increment return pointer
JMP	*RON	and return

The relay turn off routine is:

ROF	NOP	entry point
	JST	RLYNO	check validity and get the appropriate bit
	JMP	*ROF	garbage, take the error return
	CAR		now complement to form a double word mask
	CXR		this mask will be used to "AND" out the bit to be turned off
	AND	UPPER	mask upper
	STA	UPPER	update word in memory
	OTA	RCOM+5	turn off the relay
	EAX		swap for lower word
	AND	LOWER	mask out the bit to be turned off
	STA	LOWER	update the word in memory
	OTA	RCOM+4	turn off the relay
	IMS	ROF	increment return pointer
	JMP	*ROF	and return
UPPER	DATA	0	status word for relays 16-31
LOWER	DATA	0	status word for relays 0-15
	...		

The routines just shown will allow orderly management of the status of the RCOM. The presumption in the use of relays to switch real world devices on and off is that electronic speeds are not required in the switching, and that the devices being switched will remain in the on or off state for a fairly long time relative to the speed of the computer itself. The small reed relays used in an RCOM have closing times on the order of 3 milliseconds, enough time for thousands of computer instructions to be executed in the interval between the issuance of the closing command and the actual closure of the relay. Situations do arise, however, in which it is necessary for the program to be sure that a relay is actually closed before proceeding with the main task. It is in connection with this requirement that sense instructions are used with the RCOM. Two ready flags are available for testing, one associated with the lower 16 relays and one with the upper. Successful testing of these flags does *not* assure the program that the relay has actually closed, only that enough time has elapsed that it should be closed. The ready flag for the lower 16 relays is tested by:

```
SEN    RCOM+0
JMP    $-1
```

while the flag for the upper 16 relays is tested by:

```
SEN    RCOM+1
JMP    $-1
```

In some applications data are transferred between computer and the real world in high speed "bursts." If the data must be transmitted at a rate higher than the computer can handle with the ordinary input/output facilities the computer will be unable to keep up. This situation arises fairly commonly. Deformation data from a mechanical part which is being destructively tested is one example. In cases like this a hardware device exists to provide the extra "boost" required by the computer to handle the transmission. These are the *Direct Memory Access* (DMA) devices. Though there are some fine hardware distinctions between the various DMA type devices, they have one common characteristic—data are transmitted directly between the outside world and the memory of the computer. The data do *not* pass through the registers of the machine as shown in the examples so far in this chapter.

In some ways DMA devices can be considered to be small computers themselves. Their capabilities are limited to the management of incoming and outgoing data, but they require none of the main computer's time to perform their function. The activities of the DMA are controlled by the computer. Typically the computer sends the DMA a count of words or bytes to be transmitted and the memory address from which this transmission should begin. After this everything is automatic with the DMA setting a ready flag when the entire block of data has been transferred. Whether the computer proceeds with other work or waits, testing the DMA ready flag until the transmission is finished, the movement of the data happens at a much higher rate than would be possible by transfer through the registers.

For intermediate speed situations in which the transfer of data through the computers registers is too slow but which do not require the great speed of the DMA, the Alpha machines have two peculiar, but useful, hardware features called block input/output and automatic input/output. These two features are implemented as six separate instructions. The instruction pair which performs the fastest transmission is BIN and BOT, meaning *B*lock *IN*put and *B*lock *O*u*T*put. Block instructions can be used *only* to transmit word data, not bytes. They will *not* pack or unpack byte data. Also, they transmit the block of information beginning at the highest address and going toward the lowest. Their use is best understood by an example. A ten word "stream" of data can be sent to a peripheral device by:

```
LXP    10              positive word count to X
BOT    DVC+FC          output the block
DATA   BFR−1
```

in which DVC is the device address, and FC is the function code which would be used in a SEN instruction to sense the true state of the ready flag for this peripheral. BFR−1 points to the word whose memory address is one less than the lowest address of the ten word block. The data are retrieved from memory from highest to lowest, however, with the first transmitted word occupying the high memory address. On input, if the data are to be processed in the order in which they are received the array must be reversed in memory, or an addressing mode used which will allow processing in this direction. Reversing the array in memory is possible, and this kind of task should be well within the capability of readers who have carefully worked through the earlier examples in this book. It does take time, however, and the time required for this reversal might well negate the time savings made by using the block instructions. To process the list from highest to lowest use can be made of indexed indirect addressing, as described earlier in this book. This compound addressing mode will allow the items to be accessed from highest to lowest, with termination occurring when the contents of the index have been decremented to zero.

A powerful facility is available in the Automatic Input and Output instructions. Though the real power of this method cannot be shown until the interrupt system is understood (Chapter 21), their general method of operation can be shown here. There are four instructions in this group, AOT and AOB for output and AIN and AIB for input. These are complex multiword instructions, but well worth the effort required to learn their use. Suppose it were necessary to print:

HELP HELP!!

on the teletype. The normal means of doing this would be to form a byte address in memory or the X register, this address pointing to the string of characters to be printed. A negative count of characters would be kept and incremented with the termination of printing occurring when the count was exhausted. The AOB (*A*utomatic *O*utput *B*yte) instruction will do *all* of these things in a single instruction. The count and byte address are still kept in memory but the incrementation of both is accomplished by the AOB instruction, as well as the skip when the count becomes zero. Further, the data transmitted do *not* go through the registers but travel directly from memory to the peripheral, in this case the teletype. AOB transmits one byte each time it is executed, turning the ready flag off as it does so. The AOB instruction is followed immediately in memory by a count word and a byte address pointer. The count word contains the *negative* of the number of bytes to be transmitted. The byte pointer points to the byte address immediately below the first byte to be transmitted. If ten characters were to be printed beginning at location FRENCH, for example, the sequence would be written:

AOB	TTY	the Auto Output Byte instruction
DATA	-10	the byte count
BAC	FRENCH-1	the byte pointer

The sequence of events is as follows. First, the byte address pointer is incremented and used to access the byte from memory. This incrementation is the reason that the byte pointer points to the byte location one before the first character to be printed. The byte is then sent to the teletype with the ready flag being simultaneously turned *off*. Finally, the count is incremented. If the result of the incrementation is a zero the instruction which follows the address pointer is executed. If the incrementation does not produce a zero the instruction after the address pointer is skipped. Note that this is just the opposite order from that taken by an IMS instruction. The best way to begin to understand the use of AOB is by an illustration (see example 20-8).

Example 20-8

Using the AOB instruction, write a program to print the message HELP HELP!! on the teletype.

label	inst.	operand	
	SEL	TTY+4	this resets the interface and turns the ready flag *on*. This will allow the SEN which immediately follows to skip to the AOB immediately and send out the first byte.
X	SEN	TTY+1	ready flag on?
	JMP	$-1	no, wait
	AOB	TTY	yes, increment the byte pointer, get the character, send it out and turn the ready

```
                                   flag off. Then increment the
                                   count. If the count is now zero
                                   go to J1. If it isn't go to J2.
              DATA   -11           11 characters in the message
              BAC    T-1           message byte pointer
J1            JMP    $+2           exit to here on zero count
J2            JMP    X             and go here on nonzero count
              . . .
T             TEXT   'HELP HELP!!'
              . . .
```

Such a capability as this has a great number of uses. To illustrate one of these the reader will recall a method given in a previous chapter for the construction of the frequency function of a list of student test scores. It is often useful to have a plot of this function. Data in pictorial form are more meaningful than a simple list of numbers. The plot of a frequency function is known as a histogram, and its purpose is to show by a brief examination what fraction of the scores fell between some particular limits. Using the AOB instruction it is very easy to type out such a graph. Using the asterisk as a plotting character, a full teletype line is set up in memory containing all asterisks. This is preceded by enough space to contain any labeling that may be required at the left side of the graph. In the example which will be derived here the labeling consists of the score interval and the number of scores which fell in that interval. We begin by assuming that the frequency function has already been constructed as a table of numbers in memory by the method discussed earlier. The data could be shown in tabular form (see table 20-1).

What we really want is a sort of bar graph (see table 20-2).

The basic plotting method is to adjust the number of asterisks printed to the count of scores which fell in the interval represented by the line. For

Table 20-1
Frequencies of Test Scores

Score	Number of Scores in This Interval	Score	Number of Scores in This Interval
0-4	0	50-54	9
5-9	1	55-59	13
10-14	1	60-64	12
15-19	1	65-69	16
20-24	2	70-74	17
25-29	1	75-79	17
30-34	3	80-84	13
35-39	3	85-89	11
40-44	5	90-94	8
45-49	8	95 up	3

Table 20-2
Histogram of Scores

```
 0     0 |
 5     1 |*
10     1 |*
15     1 |*
20     2 |**
25     1 |*
30     3 |***
35     3 |***
40     5 |*****
45     8 |********
50     9 |*********
55    13 |*************
60    12 |************
65    16 |****************
70    17 |*****************
75    17 |*****************
80    13 |*************
85    11 |***********
90     8 |********
95     3 |***
```

clarity here we will presume that the no count can be greater than the allowed space on the teletype line, minus whatever space is required for labeling. If the frequency function is already constructed and left in memory beginning at location VECTOR, then the histogram and associated numerical data shown above can be constructed as shown in example 20-9.

Example 20-9

Write a program to plot the histogram of the frequency function which begins at location VECTOR. Each plotted line is to be labeled at the left with the first score of the interval it represents and the number of scores which fell in the interval. Numerical conversions should be done by using the ICON converter routine developed in Chapter 18.

label	inst.	operand	
HSTGRM	LAM	20	
	STA	LCNT	set up line count
	LDA	VADR	
	STA	VPTR	and address pointer to vector
	ZAR		
	STA	NUMBER	initialize interval labeling number
BEGIN	LDA	NUMBER	pick up interval labeling number

	JST	ICON	convert to decimal-ASCII
	DATA	NAREA	in this buffer
	LDA	*VPTR	# of scores in the interval to A
	JST	ICON	convert to decimal-ASCII
	DATA	PAREA	leave the result here
	LAM	18	−(# of label characters + one border character (I))
	SUB	*VPTR	minus number of asterisks to be plotted
	STA	CNT	initialize count of AOB instruction
	LDA	PBFRA	initialize AOB address pointer
	STA	ADR	. . .
	SEN	TTY+1	teletype busy?
	JMP	$−1	yes, wait
	SEL	TTY+4	OK, initialize and set ready flag on
SENSE	SEN	TTY+1	teletype busy?
	JMP	$−1	wait
	AOB	TTY+0	print the character
CNT	DATA	0	preinitialized count
ADR	DATA	0	preinitialized byte address pointer
	JMP	$+2	do this if the count goes to zero
	JMP	SENSE	and this if it doesn't
	LDX	NUMBER	pick up interval label number
	AXI	5	bump for next interval
	STX	NUMBER	and save it
	IMS	VPTR	increment data pointer
	IMS	LCNT	and line counter, last line?
	JMP	BEGIN	no, do the next line
	. . .		continue program
NUMBER	NOP		interval label number
VADR	DATA	VECTOR	address pointer to data array
LCNT	NOP		line counter
VPTR	NOP		temporary data array pointer
PBFRA	BAC	CRLF−1	byte output pointer
CRLF	DATA	:8D8A	carriage return and line feed
NAREA	RES	3	ASCII interval label space
	DATA	' '	two blanks
PAREA	RES	3	ASCII # of scores in interval
	DATA	' I'	blank and "I" for left border
	RES	27, '**'	54 asterisks
	. . .		

Automatic input from byte oriented devices is done in a similar way. The *A*uto *I*nput *B*yte instruction is followed by a count and byte address. The ready flag is turned off and the device started. When the first byte of data is available the ready flag turns on and the sense instruction skips to the AIB. This cycle is repeated until the count is exhausted. The use of AIB is shown in example 20-10.

Example 20-10

Write a subroutine using the AIB instruction which will read and store input from the teletype tape reader. This subroutine is entered with the number of bytes to be read in the A register and the byte address (not the byte address minus one) in the X register. Data are to be read from the teletype tape reader and stored from the given byte address up.

label	inst.	operand	
TELERD	DATA	0	entry point
	JAZ	END	zero byte count, forget it
	JAM	$+2	already minus?
	NAR		no, negate it
	STA	BCNT	and save in AIB byte count
	DXR		form byte address minus one
	STX	PTR	and save in AIB byte pointer
	SEL	TTY+4	reset interface
	SEL	TTY+3	start reader, turn BRFF off
T1	SEN	TTY+1	data ready yet?
	JMP	$-1	no, wait
	AIB	TTY	read the character
BCNT	DATA	0	preinitialized count
PTR	DATA	0	preinitialized byte pointer
END	JMP	*TELERD	return when finished
	JMP	T1	otherwise keep reading
	...		

In case it has escaped the reader's notice, there has been no mention of byte mode in the AOB and AIB examples. These instructions create their own byte mode and function independently of the mode of the computer at the time of their execution.

The same kind of data transfer can be performed with word oriented peripherals by the use of the AIN and AOT instructions. These instructions work in essentially the same way as their byte counterparts shown in the examples above, except that the count is a word count and the pointer is a word pointer. As with the byte instructions, the word pointer contains the address of the word *below* the first word involved in the transmission.

Before leaving this subject it must be stressed that not all of the available input/output instructions have been discussed. This would be the function of a machine reference manual rather than a book of this type. What has been attempted is to cover the principles of data transmission using simple instructions in easily understood examples. When this much has been mastered the reader should have no trouble understanding the more exotic instructions available on the Alpha and other computers.

21

Responding to Events in the Real World—The Interrupt System

In Chapter 20 the relation between computer and peripheral device was that of master and slave. The computer completely dominated and directed the activities of the peripherals, with devices being started and stopped at the convenience of the program. The assumption existed that computer responsibilities other than those of input and output could wait until the input and output were finished.

One need not look far to find examples of situations in which this scheme of things is unworkable. The nuclear reactor situation cited previously is one. Consider also the situation of a computer whose duties involved response to missile attack being kept from its monitoring function while waiting for operator input of some minor parameter, such as the name of the duty officer at a shift change. Clearly there are classes of situations in which external circumstances must dictate the activities of the computer, the normal flow of work through the machine being scheduled around these unpredictable external events. A possible means for doing this was suggested in the last chapter, namely the automatic monitoring of ready flags with some kind of notification given to the operating program that an external event has occurred. With this facility the computer would be able to devote its attention almost exclusively to its main responsibility, taking time to transfer data or record an external event only when a peripheral was ready to transfer or the event actually occurred.

The computer facility for performing this automatic ready flag monitoring is called the *interrupt system*, and the external event which brings it into play is said to cause an *interrupt*. The precise sequence of events involved in an interrupt will be detailed a little later, but the idea is fairly simple. Given that all the conditions for the occurrence of an interrupt are met, the interrupt causes the current activity of the computer to be suspended so that a subprogram, called the *interrupt service routine*, can be executed. This interrupt service routine performs whatever is appropriate to the situation which caused the interrupt—transfer of data, incrementing a counter, or whatever—and then causes the previous activity of the computer to be resumed as if nothing had happened. The interruption of a program follows certain well-ordered rules. An interrupt cannot occur in a circumstance which would cause disruption of the program being interrupted. With the exception of SCM this means that interrupts cannot occur during the execution of an instruction, only after the instruction has

237

finished. If an interrupt request appears during an ADD instruction, for example, the ADD instruction is finished before the interrupt is recognized.

When an interrupt does occur a definite sequence of steps is executed. First, the computer suspends the fetching of the next instruction from memory. The program counter still points to the next instruction to be fetched, but the step is not carried out. Next, the peripheral device is interrogated by the CPU, asking in effect, "From what location should I fetch the next instruction?". The peripheral interface responds with a number which is the address of the instruction to be executed when this particular interrupt occurs. This does *not* change the program counter. The instruction is fetched from the location specified by the peripheral interface and loaded into the I register. The instruction in the I register is then executed. If this instruction was of the type which does not change the program counter, i.e., anything but a JST or one of the jumps, the execution of the interrupted program is immediately resumed as if nothing had happened. The only effect on the operating program has been a pause long enough to execute the interrupt instruction. As an example of this kind of interrupt processing, take the simple problem of turning the overflow light on and then off after ten seconds. To time the ten seconds a CPU option known as a *real time clock* will be used. The term real time clock is a misnomer, since the device does not keep time but only generates interrupts at given intervals. It can be wired in a number of ways to produce different intervals but is most commonly connected to produce 100 interrupts per second, one each 10 milliseconds.

The real time clock interrupt instruction is located at memory address :18. To be sure that the load program does not relocate this instruction elsewhere, we precede the instruction with the pseudo operation:

ABS   :18

ABS means absolute, and its use insures that the instruction which follows the ABS will be located at :18.

Since the real time clock does not transfer data to the computer, no subroutine is necessary to input data or perform other service tasks. All that is required is a notation that an event (the passage of 10 milliseconds) has occurred. For this purpose the interrupt service routine, as defined above, is reduced to a single instruction, IMS. The operation of the real time clock interrupt is shown in example 21-1.

Example 21-1

Using the real time clock (RTC) interrupt, write a program which will turn on the overflow light, keep it on for exactly ten seconds, then turn it off and stop. The RTC interrupt instruction is fixed in location :18 by:

label	inst.	operand
	ABS	:18
	IMS	BEATS
BEATS	DATA	0

The occurrence of an RTC interrupt instruction causes the CPU to suspend the execution of the in-line instructions of the program below and execute the IMS in location 18. Since this occurs every 10 milliseconds the number in location BEATS is a measure of how much time has passed since the program began. The program can be located anywhere in memory. The operation of the interrupt does not depend on the location of the program being interrupted. After the IMS in location :18 has been executed the program below continues as if nothing had happened. The program is:

	SEL	RTC+4	this instruction resets the RTC interface in much the same way that function code 4 was used to reset the teletype interface. Any RTC interrupts that might be waiting are cleared.
	SEL	RTC	this instruction "arms" the RTC interrupt. This will be explained shortly.
	SOV		overflow light on
	EIN		this instruction turns the computer interrupt system on. It will be explained shortly.
LOOP	LDA	BEATS	pick up contents of BEATS
	CMS	THOU	1000 interrupts yet? Since there are 100 interrupts each second, 1000 interrupts = 10 seconds.
	JMP	LOOP	not yet, keep trying
	NOP		
	ROV		ten seconds up, turn it off
	HLT		and stop
	...		
THOU	DATA	1000	comparand

```
\  RTC          EQU    :40              RTC device address. This is  \
                                        the same kind of device ad-
                                        dress definition as used in the
                                        teletype example:
                                        TTY  EQU  :38.
              . . .
```

The three instructions beginning at LOOP form a loop from which there is no escape until the value of BEATS reaches 1000.

Having given this example, it is now necessary to specify the conditions which must be fulfilled for an interrupt to occur. The conditions are:

1. The interrupt system of the computer must be turned on. The interrupt system is turned on and off by means of the EIN and DIN instructions, meaning *E*nable *IN*terrupts and *D*isable *IN*terrupts. Except for power failure interruption, no interrupt can occur from any source unless the interrupt system has been turned on. When this interrupt system is on it is said to be *enabled*. When it is off it is said to be *disabled*. These two terms, enabled and disabled, are specific and apply to the computer interrupt system as a whole and not to any particular peripheral or device, and they will be used this way in this book.

2. The device which is to interrupt must have its interface specifically conditioned in a way which will allow it to cause interrupts if the system as a whole is enabled. This conditioning involves setting a bit in the interface. On the Alpha machines this bit is called the *word transfer mask*. For the sake of generality and applicability to other systems we will use the term *arming bit*. When the arming bit (word transfer mask) is on the device is said to be *armed*. When the arming bit is off the device is *disarmed*. These two terms, armed and disarmed, are specific to the devices to whose interfaces the arming bits belong. They have nothing to do with the enabling and disabling of the interrupt system.

3. The ready flag of the interrupting device must turn on.

In summary, an interrupt can occur if and only if:

1. The interrupt system is enabled, and
2. The device is armed, and
3. The ready flag of the armed device turns on.

If any of the above conditions is not met there will be no interrupt. It is too obvious to require statement that no interrupt can occur if the computer is halted.

In the last example an IMS was used to increment a cell which was tested by the program for a threshold value. IMS is a very useful interrupt instruction when the interrupt is being used to count events. If the computer were being used as a traffic monitor with passing cars blocking a light beam which in turn caused the interrupt, the IMS could be used to count cars. This is a situation in which no data are transmitted. We are not interested in the identities of the passing cars, only in the fact that they are passing. When IMS is used as an interrupt instruction it has two special properties. First, it *never* causes a skip. It will be recalled that IMS causes a program skip when the incremented cell goes from − 1 to zero under normal conditions. When it is used as an interrupt instruction this skip is suppressed. Something happens in place of the skip which will be explained in the next chapter, but there is no skip.

Second, under normal circumstances incrementing a memory cell from :7FFF to :8000 will cause the overflow bit to be turned on. This is not true when IMS is an interrupt instruction. Overflow is never turned on. The reason for these differences in the behavior of IMS should be fairly obvious. To perform a skip would disrupt the interrupted program. The program counter does not change when IMS is the interrupt instruction and to increment the program counter for a skip would cause an instruction in the interrupted program to be skipped, with unpredictable effect. The story is the same with overflow. If the interrupted program were using overflow at the time of the interrupt, disturbance of OV would cause disruption of the interrupted program. For devices such as the RTC which do not require the transmission of data, execution of the interrupt instruction (i.e., the IMS) also turns off the ready flag. This is important, as it must be turned off before it can be turned on again to cause the next interrupt.

To use the RTC to keep an actual time-of-day clock is a different kind of problem. In this case the interrupt instruction cannot be a simple IMS, as there are different types of time intervals to be incremented, seconds, minutes, and hours. What is required here is an actual interrupt service routine which can perform the necessary manipulation to manage the clock, i.e., an actual interrupt service routine. The interrupt service routine is entered like any other subroutine—by a JST instruction. This time, however, the JST is the interrupt instruction. Like IMS, JST has a special characteristic when used as an interrupt instruction, namely *it disables the interrupt system*, just as if the program had executed a DIN instruction. This is true of *no* other instruction, only JST. It does *not* disarm the device causing the interrupt, the device stays armed, but the interrupt system is disabled. This is to allow sufficient time for the interrupt service routine to turn off the ready flag which caused the interrupt in those devices in which it is not automatically turned off. It follows that the interrupt service routine *must*, repeat *must*, turn the interrupt system back on before returning control to the interrupted program. Failure to do this means that no other interrupt can occur again, from this device or any other. The failure to turn the interrupt system back on after an interrupt serviced by a JST is one of the two most common programming errors in dealing with interrupts.

The second most common programming error is associated with the status of the interrupted program. Since the interrupts occur at points in the program which cannot be predicted, the contents of the various operating registers and indicators cannot be predicted. It is the responsibility of the interrupt service routine to save and restore the status of these registers and indicators before returning control to the interrupted program. The failure to do so is the other most common error, and it causes chaos in the interrupted program. Suppose, for example, that the operating program were computing payroll figures and had just computed the size of your check, say 22487 for $224.87, when the interrupt occurred. The interrupt service routine, instead of saving this 22487 that it found in the A register, returned control to the payroll program with a 1 in A. The payroll program, unaware of the interrupt, goes on to type out your paycheck, $0.01—that kind of chaos. This is the kind of error which is called "computer error" by accounting departments, but it is actually programmer error.

The procedure for saving the machine status is fairly straightforward if the special facilities for this task are used. First, it is necessary to save the contents of the A and X registers. Since the computer *may* be in byte mode at the time of the interrupt, a simple STA and STX will not do the job, as they would save only the low eight bits of each register under these conditions. A special instruction is available for use in this situation. Its use is:

```
ISVCE    NOP               entry point to interrupt service
                           routine
         SIN   2           explained below
         STA   ASAVE       save A register contents
         STX   XSAVE       save X register contents
         . . .
```

The SIN 2 does not refer to a duet of electronic perversions but is a mnemonic for *S*uppress *IN*terrupts. Since the executions of the JST interrupt instruction turned the system off, interrupt suppression is of no interest here. What is of interest is another property of SIN, namely that it forces the computer into word mode for the number of instructions specified in its operand field. This allows the STA and STX to be executed in word mode, saving the full 16 bit contents of A and X. After the two instructions have been executed the computer returns to the mode it was in at the time the SIN was executed, in this case the same mode as at the time of the interrupt. The overflow bit and byte mode indicator can be saved by the special instruction SIA or SIX, meaning *S*tatus *I*nput to *A* or *X*. These instructions bring the overflow bit and byte mode indicator (and other status bits) into A or X, from which they can be stored in memory. The execution of SIA or SIX also forces the computer unconditionally into word mode. The status can be restored by loading the saved status word from memory and executing SOA or SOX, for *Status Output from A or X*. This restores OV and the byte mode indicator to the same condition as when the SIA or SIX was executed. The whole sequence of saving registers and status is:

label	*inst.*	*operand*	
ISVCE	NOP		entry point to interrupt service routine
	SIN	2	suppress byte mode for two instructions
	STA	ASAVE	save A contents
	STX	XSAVE	save X contents
	SIA		status bits to A
	STA	STATUS	save the status
	...		(interrupt service program)
	LDA	STATUS	saved status to A
	SOA		restore OV and byte mode
	SIN	2	force word mode for two instructions
	LDA	ASAVE	reload A
	LDX	XSAVE	reload X
	EIN		reenable the interrupt system!!!!!
	JMP	*ISVCE	and return to interrupt program

This sequence saves and restores the entire status of the computer at the time of the interrupt and allows the interrupted program to resume execution as if the interrupt had not occurred. It only remains to clarify the operation of the JST as an interrupt instruction. As was stressed previously, the occurrence of the interrupt and the loading of the interrupt instruction into the I register does not change the program counter P. It still points to the next instruction to be executed in the interrupted program. If the interrupt instruction is a JST, it is this value which is saved in the entry point location of the interrupt service routine. The return address pointer in the entry point of an interrupt service routine is thus the old program counter, and an indirect jump *through* this location will allow the interrupted program to resume execution with the instruction which would have been fetched if the interrupt had not occurred.

Now we turn to the problem of keeping a time-of-day clock. The basic logic is shown in example 21-2.

Example 21-2

Write an interrupt service subroutine to keep a binary time-of-day clock, with seconds, minutes, and hours in separate words in memory. Presume that the initialization of the clock and the enabling of the interrupt system have been done elsewhere in the operating program. The interrupt instruction is:

label	inst.	operand	
	ABS	:18	
	JST	*$+1	the interrupt instruction
	DATA	CLOCK	address pointer to interrupt service subroutine

The interrupt service routine is:

CLOCK	NOP		interrupt service entry point
	SIN	2	suppress byte mode
	STA	AR	save A
	STX	XR	save X
	SIA		read status in
	STA	STATUS	and save it
	IMS	BEATS	increment # of clock beats
	LDA	BEATS	pick it up
	CAI	100	one second gone yet?
	JMP	$+2	yes, skip
	JMP	END	no, reload and return
	ZAR		
	STA	BEATS	reset beat counter to zero
	IMS	SECOND	and increment seconds
	LDA	SECOND	pick up seconds
	CAI	60	one minute up yet?
	JMP	$+2	yes, skip
	JMP	END	no, reload and return
	ZAR		
	STA	SECOND	...
	IMS	MINUTE	and increment minutes
	LDA	MINUTE	pick up minutes
	CAI	60	one hour up yet?
	JMP	$+2	yes, skip
	JMP	END	no, reload and return
	ZAR		
	STA	MINUTE	reset minutes counter to zero
	IMS	HOUR	and increment the hours

```
            LDA    HOUR        pick up hour
            CAI    24          a full day elapsed?
            JMP    $+2         yes, skip
            JMP    END         no, reload and return
            ZAR
            STA    HOUR        reset hours counter to zero
END         LDA    STATUS      load the status
            SOA                and restore it
            SIN    2           force word mode for two in-
                               structions
            LDA    AR          reload A
            LDX    XR          reload X
            EIN                enable the interrupt system!!!
            JMP    *CLOCK      and return to interrupted pro-
                               gram
BEATS       DATA 0             beat counter
SECOND      DATA 0             seconds counter
MINUTE      DATA 0             minutes counter
HOUR        DATA 0             hours counter
AR          DATA 0             A register save
XR          DATA 0             X register save
STATUS      DATA 0             status save
            ...
```

The value of this binary clock can be printed at any time by converting HOUR, MINUTE, and SECOND to decimal-ASCII. A word of caution is due here, however. Since the values of the intervals printed may change at any time, they should be copied into another area before conversion or nonsense may result in the printout. This is one of the immediate results of the introduction of an extra dimension into the programming process—time.

Next we turn attention to another type of interrupt—that in which data are to be transferred. This type of interrupt bears directly on the previously cited problem of a monitoring process which cannot be stalled waiting for input. To address this directly we will use the teletype in an interrupt driven mode. The teletype is a complex device—it can transfer data in either direction but if the ideas underlying data transfer to and from it are mastered, most other devices are easily understood as special cases. Teletype interrupts are armed by a SEL instruction with function code 5. This causes the arming bit (word transfer mask) to be turned on in the teletype interface. The entire arming/enabling sequence for the teletype is:

```
            SEL    TTY+4       reset teletype interface
            SEL    TTY+0       enable auto echo
```

```
SEL   TTY+5        arm teletype interrupt
SEL   TTY+1        ready flag off, set in keyboard
                   mode
EIN                enable the interrupt system
...
```

with TTY being defined as before. After this sequence has been executed striking a key on the teletype will cause the instruction in memory location 2, the teletype interrupt location, to be executed. Unlike the real time clock, execution of the teletype interrupt instruction does *not* turn the ready flag off, except for the special cases to be covered in Chapter 22. This means that for the purposes being discussed here the interrupt instruction must be a JST to an interrupt service subroutine which will turn the flag off. The interrupt instruction is specified therefore as:

```
ABS   2         location of interrupt instruction
JST   *$+1      the interrupt instruction
DATA  TSVCE     address of teletype interrupt ser-
                vice
...
```

The servicing of teletype input interrupts is shown in example 21-3.

Example 21-3

Write a teletype interrupt service routine which will accept a decimal-ASCII integer from the keyboard, convert it to binary and place the result in location CONST. The process should terminate on either the fourth typed digit or a blank, whichever comes first. After the conversion is done the routine should be left in such a condition that it can be reexecuted by typing another number. Ignore all non-numeric characters. Begin by assuming that the teletype arming/enabling sequence has been executed elsewhere and that the interrupt location has been initialized as shown above.

label	inst.	operand	
TSVCE	NOP		entry point, teletype interrupt service
	SIN	2	save status sequence, as explained
	STA	AR	above . . .
	STX	XR	...
	SIA		...
	STA	STATUS	...
	INA	TTY	this reads the character from

			the teletype *and* resets the ready flag
	CAI	' '	end of input?
	JMP	EUREKA	yes, move the result
	CMS	NINE	check for numeric validity
	CMS	ZERO	. . .
	JMP	RELOAD	non-numeric, ignore it
	NOP		
	AND	EF	mask out code bits
	STA	T	and save new digit
	LDA	RESULT	multiply old result by ten
	ALA	1	. . .
	STA	RESULT	. . .
	ALA	2	. . .
	ADD	RESULT	. . .
	ADD	T	add new digit
	IMS	CNT	last digit?
	JMP	RELOAD	no, reload and return
EUREKA	ZAR		yes, load new result and zero for next pass
	EMA	RESULT	. . .
	STA	CONST	place result in CONST cell
	LAM	4	reload count
	STA	CNT	
RELOAD	LDA	STATUS	restore status for return to
	SOA		interrupted program
	SIN	2	. . .
	STA	AR	. . .
	STX	XR	. . .
	EIN		turn the interrupt system back on!!!!!
	JMP	*TSVCE	and return to interrupted program
NINE	DATA	:B9	
ZERO	DATA	:B0	
T	NOP		
CNT	DATA	−4	
RESULT	DATA	0	
EF	DATA	:F	
AR	NOP		
XR	NOP		
STATUS	NOP		
	. . .		

There is one fine point about interrupt service routines which should be made clear before we proceed. The execution of the JST as an interrupt instruction stores the value of the old program counter in the entry point of the interrupt service routine, and loads the program counter with the address of the first executable instruction of that routine. Except for the fact that the JST is executed "out of line," so to speak, this is entirely normal behavior. The reader should consider what would happen if the device being serviced were sufficiently fast that another interrupt could occur while the computer was still executing the interrupt service routine. The execution of EIN would enable this interrupt to be recognized, but the value of the program counter stored by the interrupt JST would be within the interrupt service routine itself. This would mean that the original return address was destroyed and replaced by a return address within the interrupt service routine itself. The service routine would, therefore, be in a "loop" of sorts from which it could not recover, the original return address having been destroyed. To prevent this from happening the EIN instruction is wired in a special way, so that the interrupt system is not actually enabled until the instruction *after* the EIN is executed. It is thus guaranteed that at least one instruction after the EIN can be executed without disturbance by other interrupts. For the teletype interrupt this is not applicable, but for high speed devices it could become a consideration.

Just as the computer cannot be hung up waiting for input, the same considerations preclude a hang up waiting for output. The output of a block of information can also be done under interrupt control. The difference between output and the input just shown is that the first output datum must be sent out under computer control. In the case of the teletype the first character is sent out with the next following when the ready flag turns on to cause the interrupt. Succeeding characters are then sent to the interface as each interrupt occurs until the interrupt service routine recognizes the end of the output string, either through the exhaustion of a count or the recognition of some special terminating character such as the backslash used previously in this book.

It should be clearly understood that a teletype interrupt always causes the execution of the same interrupt instruction in the same location, whether the interrupt was caused by input or output. It is up to the programmer to keep track of the source of interrupts. In the case of the teletype this is not difficult as keyboard or tape input is not done at the same time as output. Though the device is bidirectional, it cannot be transmitting in both directions simultaneously. The specific use of the teletype interrupt for output is shown in example 21-4.

Example 21-4

Write a subroutine which will initiate the printing of a string of characters on the teletype and service the teletype interrupts as they arise, sending out one character each time an interrupt occurs until the end of the string is reached. The output string should be preceded by a carriage return and line feed, and the end of the string is signalled by a backslash. The program entry point to this routine is to be called PRT. The interrupt entry point is to be called ILOC. PRT is entered with the word address of the beginning of the character string in the A register. The interrupt instruction is first specified as:

label	*inst.*	*operand*	
	ABS	2	
	JST	*$+1	interrupt instruction
	DATA	ILOC	address of interrupt service

The PRT and ILOC routines are located elsewhere in memory. They are:

PRT	NOP		program entry point
	LLA	1	form byte address
	STA	ADR	and save it for the interrupt service routine
	LAP	:8D	pick up carriage return to begin string output
	OTA	TTY	and send it out
	STA	LAST	then save the character
	JMP	*PRT	and return to calling program

After this has been executed the program can go on its way doing whatever work needs to be done as the main function of the system. Each time the ready flag turns on an interrupt will cause the service routine at ILOC to be executed.

ILOC	NOP		interrupt service entry point
	SIN	1	suppress byte mode for one instruction
	STA	AR	and save the A register
	SIA		read the status and force word mode
	STA	STATUS	save the status
	LDA	LAST	pick up last character sent out
	CAI	:8D	was it a carriage return?
	JMP	$+2	yes, supply the line feed
	JMP	GO	no, get character from string
	LAP	:8A	pick up line feed

```
          JMP   OUT        and send it out
GO        SBM              byte mode on
          LDA   *ADR       pick up character
          SWM              byte mode off
          IMS   ADR        increment character byte
                           pointer
          SEL   TTY+1      turn ready off, just in case
          CAI   '\'        is this the end of the string?
          JMP   RLD        yes, terminate
OUT       OTA   TTY        output the character
          STA   LAST       and record last character sent
                           out
          LDA   STATUS     load status
          SOA              and restore it
          SIN   1          suppress byte mode
          LDA   AR         reload A register
          EIN              reenable the interrupt sys-
                           tem!!!
          JMP   *ILOC      and return to interrupted pro-
                           gram
```

The reader may recognize that the routine in the above example performs exactly the same function as the PRT routine given in Chapter 13. The only difference between the previous PRT and this one is that the computer is not "stalled" in the interrupt driven example. After the first character has been sent out the performance of normal work can resume, with the interrupt system "stealing" the few cycles necessary to send out another character when the teletype is ready for it.

Before concluding this chapter it should be noted that there are differences in the interrupt system of the various computers now available. Some do not allow the specification of the interrupt instruction—a JST is assumed to be the interrupt instruction, and the interrupt location in memory contains the address of the interrupt service routine, not an instruction. In a number of others there exists a so-called priority system under which the interrupt system is not disabled when an interrupt JST is executed. In these systems only interrupts of lower priority than the one being processed are disabled. This leads to the interruption of the interrupting routine by a yet higher priority interrupt. This second interrupt routine may then be itself interrupted by a still higher priority interrupt, and so on. This leads to no particular complication unless there is some subroutine which is used by the interrupt service routines on more than one level. To see what happens, suppose that both interrupt levels 1 and 2 used the SQRT subroutine given earlier in this book. If the first interrupt happened on level 2 and the level 2 interrupt service routine were executing SQRT at the time another interrupt, this time from level 1 arrived, the SQRT routine would be interrupted. The level 1 interrupt, following normal practice, would save all of the registers and status and then proceed to use SQRT itself—*thereby destroying all of the partial results of the level 2 execution which were in memory*. When the level 1 interrupt had been serviced, control would return to SQRT to finish executing the level 2 interrupt service. Since the temporary cells which contained the level 2 partial results had been destroyed, the answers returned to the level 2 interrupt service routine would be nonsense, and the result of the level 2 interrupt service would be unpredictable.

Techniques exist for the writing of subroutines which are capable of functioning under the circumstances just described. Such subroutines are said to be *reentrant*, and one of the functions of the stack instructions described in an earlier chapter is to aid in the writing of reentrant routines. For most programmers, however, time is far better devoted to finding ways to avoid situations like this rather than solving them. In the examples in this book the simple expedient has been taken of keeping the interrupt system disabled during the execution of the entire interrupt service routine. An alternative to this is to avoid having a subroutine used by more than one interrupt. In the great majority of cases one of these two solutions will take care of the problems. If the interrupts are to be kept disabled during interrupt service, the service routine itself should be kept short. If any extensive work is necessary, the service routine can set a flag which can be sensed by the main operating program, with the work being done there. If the second solution is taken, that of avoiding use of the same routine by different interrupts, it will be necessary to duplicate the routine, one copy for each interrupt using it. This consumes memory, of course, but if the program does not occupy all of memory there is no harm done. In any case the simplest solution is the best one, and exotic techniques such as reentrant subroutines almost never pay if programmer time is considered in the cost. The programmer should nevertheless be aware of the possibilities.

When the time taken to respond to an interrupt is not critical, the hardware problems are often simplified by tying several sources of interrupt to one line in such a way that an interrupt is created by a request from any one of them. It then becomes necessary for the interrupt service routine to determine which of the devices caused the interrupt. The technique for doing this is called *polling*, and it consists of no more than testing the ready flags of all the devices connected to the interrupt line. Since the interrupt is caused by a ready flag or flags turning on, they can be tested in succession by SEN instructions addressed to the different devices. In this way a software priority can be established among the devices by the order of testing. Suppose there are three devices connected to one interrupt line. An interrupt generated by any of them will cause the program to be interrupted. The polling service routine for this situation looks like this:

label	inst.	operand	
PSVCE	NOP		entry point to common service routine
	SIN	2	register and status save sequence
	STA	AR	...
	STX	XR	...
	SIA		...
	STA	STATUS	...
	SEN	DVC1+X	was DVC1 the source of the interrupt?
	JST	SVC1	yes, service this device
	SEN	DVC2+Y	or was it the second device DCV2?
	JST	SVC2	yes, service it
	SEN	DVC3+Z	or was it DCV3?
	JST	SVC3	yes, service it
	LDA	STATUS	standard status and register
	SOA		restore sequence
	SIN	2	...
	LDA	AR	...
	LDX	XR	...
	EIN		TURN THE INTERRUPTS BACK ON!!!!!
	JMP	*PSVCE	and return to interrupted program
AR	NOP		
XR	NOP		
STATUS	...		

This has the advantage that only one save and restore sequence is required. If more than one device interrupts at the same time, both are serviced in one pass. The symbols X, Y, and Z designate the function codes for testing the ready flags of DVC1, DVC2, and DVC3 respectively.

Finally, the only way to become proficient with any aspect of programming is practice—i.e., make all the mistakes and learn from them, and this applies to interrupt service programming probably more than any other technique. Interrupt service routines differ from all others in one important respect. If there is an error it is not in general possible to repeat the circumstances under which the error occurred. An interrupt, by definition, can happen at any time and an error in the interrupt service routine can disrupt any part of the interrupted program, and this fact makes the debugging of systems using interrupts more difficult. Some specific techniques for debugging such programs are given in Chapter 23.

22 Further Interrupt Service Techniques—Automatic Data Transfers

The previous chapter described techniques for the service of interrupts as single events, the beats of the real time clock, keystrokes on the teletype keyboard, or the printing of a character. It is the purpose of this chapter to treat the handling of groups of events—a number of clock beats or a series of transferred characters, for example—as a single serviceable event.

Not previously discussed is the ability of our example computer to handle interrupts in groups, with interrupt service being called for only after some number of events has occurred. To do this it will be necessary to introduce some new concepts and nomenclature. The writer notes with regret that it will not be possible to use the nomenclature of the manufacturer's manuals—these are a hopeless semantic quagmire, at least as far as the subject of interrupts is concerned. For those readers who have access to one of these machines an attempt will be made to establish a correspondence with the nomenclature of the manual, inasmuch as that is possible without destroying clarity.

The principal new concept involved in understanding group interrupt handling is that there are *two* interrupts connected with every peripheral device in the Alpha machine. The use of the first interrupt was described in the last chapter. The machine manuals call this the word interrupt, though this name is clearly not applicable to devices which transfer no data, or to devices which transfer bytes rather than words, such as magnetic tapes and teletypes. We will refer to this interrupt hereafter as the *event* interrupt. The second interrupt comes into play only when some number of event interrupts has occurred, and it signals the occurrence of this number of event interrupts. This second interrupt is called a *block* interrupt, both here and in the manufacturer's literature. The simplest way to show its use is by means of the real time clock, a device which transfers no data.

In the previous chapter an example showed the use of the event interrupt to drive a binary time-of-day clock. Each 100th of a second the event interrupt caused the execution of an interrupt service routine which basically did nothing but count the interrupts and increment the software "clock" by one second when 100 interrupts had occurred. Using the block interrupt the counting can be done automatically and the service routine shortened. The reader may recall that when IMS is used as an interrupt instruction no skip takes place when the cell being incremented goes from −1 to 0. If the block interrupt is armed, however, something else happens, namely a second interrupt, to a different interrupt location than the one used by the event interrupt.

This allows a negative number to be placed in memory and incremented by an IMS in the event interrupt location (:18 for the real time clock). When the count reaches zero, i.e., after 100 interrupts in this case, another interrupt is generated, but this time the interrupt instruction is fetched from another location in memory. For the clock this location is :1A. This *block interrupt instruction* is a JST which leads to a service routine. The service routine is therefore executed only *once* per second instead of 100 times per second, a considerable saving in overhead if only the time necessary to save and restore machine status is considered. The event and block interrupts are armed separately. This gives the programmer the freedom to use the event interrupt only, or to use both in situations which allow block interrupt use. The arming sequence for using both interrupts is:

SEL	RTC+4	reset RTC interface, disarm and clear interrupts
SEL	RTC+2	arm block interrupt
SEL	RTC	arm event interrupt
EIN		
...		

The interrupt locations are initialized to:

location

	ABS	:18	
:18	IMS	BEATS	event interrupt instruction
:19 BEATS	DATA	−100	number of event interruptions per block interrupt
:1A	JST	*$+1	block interrupt instruction
:1B	DATA	CSVCE	address of block interrupt service
	...		

Using the block interrupt, the earlier software clock routine can be rewritten:

label	inst.	operand	
CSVCE	DATA	0	entry point
	SIN	1	. . .
	STA	AR	register and status save
	SIA		. . .
	STA	STATUS	. . .
	LAM	100	reload event interrupt count
	STA	BEATS	
	IMS	SECOND	increment seconds

```
         LDA    SECOND    identical logic from previous ex-
                          ample
         CAI    60        . . .
         JMP    $+2       . . .
         JMP    RELOAD
         ZAR
         STA    SECOND
         IMS    MINUTE
         LDA    MINUTE
         CAI    60
         JMP    $+2
         JMP    RELOAD
         ZAR
         STA    MINUTE
         IMS    HOUR
         LDA    HOUR
         CAI    24
         JMP    $+2
         JMP    RELOAD
         ZAR
         STA    HOUR
RELOAD   LDA    STATUS
         SOA
         SIN    1
         LDA    AR
         EIN              don't forget to reenable!!!!!
         JMP    *CSVCE    return to interrupted program
```

The overhead associated with this routine is principally the saving and restoration of registers and status, though the reader may notice that this time only the A register was saved. Since X was not used by the service routine it is not disturbed. As the routine is executed only once per second instead of 100 times per second, the total overhead has been reduced by a factor of almost 100. The IMS still has to be executed 100 times per second, but only the IMS, not the interrupt service routine itself.

This dual level interrupt operation achieves its greatest usefulness in the transfer of data blocks between the computer and peripherals by means of the AUTO I/O instructions. In this kind of transfer the AUTO I/O instruction occupies the event interrupt location. For data transferring peripherals this is called the word interrupt location in the manufacturer's literature, even if only bytes are being transferred. For the teletype this is location 2. The block transfer instruction is at location 6, this difference of 4 locations being standard for all peripheral devices (at least so far). When the event interrupt occurs the instruction at location 2 is executed, i.e., the AUTO I/O instruction. The locations which follow the AUTO I/O instruction contain the count and pointer, just as shown previously. The block interrupt location contains a JST to a service routine to do the end of block housekeeping. As location 5 is not used it will be used here to contain the address pointer to the end of block interrupt service routine. Event and block interrupt locations look like this:

location

	ABS	2	
2	AOB	TTY	the Auto I/O instruction
3	DATA	−19	the character count
4	BAC	MSG−1	address pointer to message
5	DATA	BSVCE	address pointer to end of block service
6	JST	*$−1	end of block interrupt instruction

The above sequence, once started, will transfer the 19 character block which begins at MSG to the teletype and interrupt to location BSVCE when the last character has been transferred. The use of AOB as an interrupt instruction is shown in example 22-1.

Example 22-1

Use the AOB instruction under interrupt control to print the message:

FREE BEER!

on the teletype. Location DONE should be set initially to zero and then set to one when the message has finished printing. In this way DONE can be used as a flag which can be tested by other parts of the program to monitor teletype activity. Begin by assuming that the AOB TTY is already in location 2 and the JST *$−1 is in location 6. The message is printed by:

label	*inst.*	*operand*	
	LAM	10	number of characters in message
	STA	3	to count cell
	LDA	ADR	byte address counter
	STA	4	to address pointer of AOB
	LDA	EOBA	initialize end of block service address
	STA	5	
	ZAR		

```
        STA    DONE        set DONE to zero
        SEL    TTY+4       disarm both interrupts, turn
                           ready on
        SEL    TTY+5       arm the event (word) interrupt
        SEL    TTY+6       and the block interrupt
        EIN                enable the interrupt system
        . . .              program continues as the mes-
                           sage is being printed
```

The end of block interrupt service routine is:

```
EOB     NOP                entry point
        SEL    TTY+4       end of transmission, disarm
                           both interrupts
        IMS    DONE        set DONE to 1
        EIN                reenable the interrupt sys-
                           tem!!
        JMP    *EOB        and return to interrupted pro-
                           gram
```

The definitions of the operands used are:

```
ADR     BAC    FB−1
FB      TEXT   'FREE BEER!'
EOBA    DATA   EOB
```

The end of block interrupt can be used as a facility for "chaining" messages. Take the case of the need to print the text:

HOW'S YOUR WIFE?

followed by:

COMPARED TO WHAT?

It is sometimes useful to be able to break the text into two or more parts, with the block interrupt service routine for the first part setting up the address and pointer in the AUTO I/O instruction for the second part. This is easily done but one word of caution is in order. Though it is not made clear in the manufacturer's documentation, the execution of the block interrupt appears to disarm the word interrupt, so that it must be rearmed as part of the block interrupt service procedure. There is one other fine point about the assembly program which should also be clarified here. Since the apostrophe is used as a delimiter in TEXT statements, a special provision is necessary to generate an apostrophe as part of the text. This is done by using a double apostrophe. The string HOGAN'S GOAT is generated by:

```
TEXT   'HOGAN' 'S GOAT'
```

The problem posed above is solved in the following:

Example 22-2

Print the "chained" character string specified above by means of two executions of an AOB string. Assuming again that the AOB is already in location 2 and the JST   *$−1 is in location 6, the first part of the message (the HOW'S YOUR WIFE? part) is started by:

label	inst.	operand	
	LAM	16	length of HOW'S YOUR WIFE? string
	STA	3	to AOB count
	LDA	QA	byte pointer to AOB pointer
	STA	4	. . .
	LDA	SVA1	block interrupt service address
	STA	5	to block interrupt address pointer
	SEL	TTY+4	disarm interrupts and turn ready flag on
	SEL	TTY+5	arm event (word) interrupt
	SEL	TTY+6	arm block interrupt
	EIN		and enable the interrupt system
	. . .		program continues here

The interrupt service routines are:

SV1	NOP		entry point for first block interrupt
	SIN	1	suppress byte mode
	STA	AR	etc., as described before
	SIA		. . .
	STA	STATUS	. . .
	LAM	17	length of COMPARED TO WHAT? string
	STA	3	to AOB count
	LDA	AA	byte pointer to AOB byte pointer
	STA	4	. . .
	LDA	SVA2	second block interrupt service address
	STA	5	to block interrupt service address

```
        SEL   TTY+5        rearm the event (word) inter-
                           rupt
        LDA   STATUS       reload status and A register
        SOA                etc., as described before
        SIN   1            ...
        LDA   AR           ...
        EIN                reenable the interrupt sys-
                           tem!!
        JMP   *SV1         and return to interrupted pro-
                           gram
SV2     NOP                entry point to second block in-
                           terrupt service routine
        SEL   TTY+4        transmission complete, dis-
                           arm interrupts
        EIN                turn the interrupt system back
                           on!!!!!
        JMP   *SV2         then return to the interrupted
                           program

The various operands are:

SVA1    DATA  SV1
SVA2    DATA  SV2
AR      NOP
STATUS  NOP
QA      BAC   Q-1          byte pointer for first string
AA      BAC   A-1          byte pointer for second string
Q       TEXT  'HOW' 'S YOUR WIFE?'
A       TEXT  'COMPARED TO WHAT?'
        ...
```

This type of transmission, like DMA transmission, has the advantage that very little time is wasted in interrupt service overhead. In systems which are running close to their full capacities this could be a significant advantage. The disadvantage of this type of transmission is that it lacks the flexibility available in word-by-word or byte-by-byte transmission. AUTO I/O transmits a fixed number of data items. It cannot recognize special termination characters so that the length of transmission could be specified as so many words or until a special character is encountered, whichever comes first. Adding this capability would multiply the utility of these instructions manyfold, but such things do not seem to be in the cards for minicomputer users, at least not in the near future.

Using block interrupts for input is similar to their use for output. Instead of setting the ready flag on to start the transmission, the ready flag is turned off and the device started, with the first item being transmitted when the ready flag turns on. As with other input and output instructions, the execution of the transmission instruction, the AOB, AIB, or whatever, turns the ready flag off.

Again, there is no substitute for experience. Some useful knowledge can be gained from reading about subjects such as block interrupts, but real proficiency springs from having actually written programs to try the technique, and having kept at it until success was achieved. Nothing can replace actually doing the work and analyzing the failures.

23

Getting the Program to Run—Some Pointers on Debugging

When at long last the program has been completely written, and the various mechanical processes of assembly and loading completed, the beginning programmer faces the most frustrating and disillusioning part of the task—making the program run. The first attempt to run a newly written program will result in one of the following two outcomes:

1. An out and out catastrophe in which the program produces nothing at all or devours itself, or both.

2. A more subtle disaster in which the program appears to run but produces nonsense.

A third alternative, the program running correctly the first time, is about as probable as winning the Irish Sweepstakes and will not be considered here. Even when this *appears* to be the case a little closer look will usually show that either 1 or 2 above is actually closer to the truth. This chapter is an attempt to come to grips with the practical reality that programs contain errors, and these errors must be found and eliminated to make the program do what it is supposed to do.

To debug a program with a minimum of agony and time wasted, the debugging process must not be considered as a phase which follows the writing. Debugging properly begins before the first instruction is written, in the planning stages when the program is being laid out. The first stage of debugging is the organization of the program in such a way that errors are easily traceable later. This means that the program should be planned as a series of *short* segments, each of which performs some well defined task and which can be executed independently in an experimental way until the segment is completely debugged. This process is repeated until all segments are individually debugged. The segments are then loaded and linked together via the linking loader and execution of the entire composite program is attempted.

If the first stage has been carried out to completion, i.e., if all of the segments have really been debugged, any remaining problem must come from one of two sources, either one or more segments is not leaving its results in the location or format expected by other segments, or there has been an oversight in program planning and some essential element is missing. If the programmer is satisfied that the overall scheme is valid then the answer must lie in the location or format of the results passed from one segment to the next.

All of this sounds much more clear-cut than it really is. Errors can escape the first phase debugging of the individual segments. A program segment may produce a correct result and leave that result in the right place and format, and still cause trouble by destruction of the contents of some part of memory outside itself. If the destruction occurs in another segment the cause is not obvious. The only way to find this kind of error is to reload the program so it is in its original undamaged form, then begin to execute it in logical sequence, examining the area subject to the destruction after each segment is executed. When the destruction occurs, the offender is the last segment executed. All of this debugging should be done with the interrupt system off if possible. This separates the errors caused by straightforward programming mistakes from those caused by bad interrupt service routines.

If the source of the problem cannot be immediately found, valuable information can be gotten from loading and executing a self-destroying program several times to see if the destruction is consistent each time. If the same destruction takes place every time the problem is *probably* not related to interrupts, though this source cannot be ruled out. If the destruction is random and nonrepetitive, the interrupt service routines should be suspected. As interrupts are random events, bad interrupt service routines will disrupt the operating program at random. The single possible exception to this is the real time clock interrupt. If the program crashes immediately when it is started and always in the same place, the source is still probably an ordinary in-line programming error, but the real time clock interrupt cannot be ignored as a possibility. Since the clock is started at the same time as the computer, the first interrupt tends to take place at the same point in the program, making it look as if interrupts were not involved.

Remember in debugging that the computer is a completely literal machine which does only what you have told it to do. It has no interpretive ability and cannot know what you intended. The errors lie in the programmer's failure to specify exactly what is required. They are almost never machine malfunctions. There is a great temptation to proclaim a machine malfunction when all the obvious sources have been examined, and this diagnosis is almost never correct, even if it does save the ego momentarily. Machine error is not impossible but don't bet on it. In this writer's experience a problem has only once been actually traceable to machine error, and this experience includes some of the earliest first generation vacuum tube junkers. Everybody who was using computers in the early days has his own favorite horror story, but one of the famous ones concerns a machine malfunction on an IBM 650 which was traced to a short circuit caused by an electrocuted mouse which had wandered into the high voltage vacuum tube circuitry.

The economy of debugging is enhanced greatly if more than one bug can be found in a single pass. Debugging is an iterative process. The program is run until a bug or set of bugs is found and the corrections are made in the source programs, which are then reassembled to give corrected listings and tapes. The corrected program is then reloaded and execution attempted until the next crash, at which time the cycle is repeated. Most of the time is wasted in the reassembly, particularly if only a teletype is available as the listing device. If the number of these reassemblies can be reduced the debugging will go more quickly. The length of the segments being assembled also has a gross effect on the efficiency of the process. *Keep the segments short.*

The principal tool for debugging is a debug program, supplied as part of the standard software for almost all minicomputers. This program allows execution and modification of the program from the keyboard in a fairly convenient way. Individual memory words can be inspected and changed, portions of the program can be selectively executed, blocks of information can be moved from one part of memory to another, and searches of memory for specific values can be made. The debug program is used by typing one character commands which are followed by numerical address specifications. To print the contents of memory location :1AF3, for example, we type:

I1AF3.

The *I* means inspect, and the period enters the command. The response to this is that the contents of :1AF3 are typed as:

1AF3   F705

The first number is the address and the second the hexadecimal contents of that address. The contents can now be changed by typing the desired contents. If the contents were to be changed to :F704, for example, the entire transaction would look like this:

I1AF3.
1AF3   F705   F704.

and the change is made.

It is possible to examine and/or modify a series of locations by typing a space instead of a period at the end of the transaction. Each time the space bar is struck the next higher memory address and its contents will be typed. If the contents are to be modified, type the new contents and then press the space bar. If the contents are not to be modified simply press the space bar and the next location will be typed out. Inspection of addresses from higher to lower can be done by using a comma instead of the space bar.

The numerical address specification can be modified by appending the identity of one of the 16 pseudo registers to the number. These pseudo registers, numbered RO through RF, are a convenient means of accessing locations within a program using the displacements shown in the assembly listing. Suppose a subroutine HARRY has been loaded and relocated by the loader program at :2E3. The third word of subroutine HARRY, relative location 2 starting from zero, is at :2E5. This is fairly easy to compute mentally, but adding :3E to :2E5 mentally is not so easy. The use of the pseudo registers solves the problem. First, we set the pseudo register to the value of the beginning of the relocated routine HARRY by:

    R12E3.

Thereafter we can access any instruction or data word in HARRY by simply appending the register identification to the relative location shown in the assembly listing. To access relative location E as described above, we type:

    I3ER1.

with the result:

    0321   XXXX

The 321 is the sum of :2E3 and :3E, and XXXX represents the contents of location 321. These contents can then be modified as shown before by typing the desired contents, and the inspection continued or terminated by a blank, comma, or period.

This facility can be used to make corrections to the program being debugged by means of changing the actual binary program. If a superfluous instruction is discovered it can be eliminated by simply zeroing the instruction location. The zero is a binary NOP instruction and if the NOP will do no harm at this point in the program, work can proceed immediately to find other remaining errors. To create a binary NOP in the location discussed above, we would type:

    I3ER1

and the reply would be:

    0321   XXXX 0.

the zero and period being typed by the programmer.

A missing instruction is a little more complicated to fix, but the trick is worth learning because it can save extra assembly passes and speed debugging. Consider the following subroutine which has been relocated at :AE4:

actual location	assembly location	binary instruction		mnemonic instruction	
OAE4	0000	0000	TIMES	NOP	
OAE5	0001	9A04		STA	MPR
OAE6	0002	0110		ZAR	

OAE7	0-03	1960		MPY	MPR
OAE8	0004	OAEA			
OAE9	0005	F705		JMP	*TIMES
OAEA	0006	0000	MPR	NOP	

The routine contains an error, namely that the LRX   1 which should follow the MPY is missing. Patching this kind of error involves replacing the instruction after the MPY, namely the JMP, with a JMP to a scratchpad location which is unused. The necessary correction is then inserted in the scratchpad location *in binary*, along with duplicating the function of the instruction which was replaced by the jump into the scratchpad area. Suppose that scratchpad locations from :50 to :52 were available. The binary jump to scratchpad location :50 is :F050. It is at location :50 that we place the LRX   1 instruction. In getting to location :50 we destroyed the return JMP instruction, so its function must also be duplicated in scratchpad. What is required is an indirect JMP *through* location :AE4. Since :AE4 is not directly accessible from scratchpad the reference to it must also be indirect. This is a case where double level indirect addressing is necessary to do the job. The entire patch now consists of the LRX   1 in location :50 and a JMP indirect in location :51 through an indirect pointer which is in location :52. The indirect addressing bit of the instruction is the right most bit of the left half of the instruction. A direct JMP to location :52 would be :F052, while the indirect JMP is :F152. Since *two* indirect levels are required the indirect bit of the address pointer in :52 must also be set. The indirect bit of an address pointer is the high bit, i.e., the pointer must read :8AE4 rather than :0AE4. The entire patch looks like this:

location	contents	meaning
:50	:13A8	an LRX 1 instruction
:51	:F152	a JMP *:52
:52	:8AE4	an indirect pointer to :AE4

Using the debug program, the entire transaction looks like this on the teletype:

command	meaning
R1AE4.	set pseudo register #1 to the beginning of routine TIMES
I5R1.	print the contents of :AE9.

The response to this command is:

| OAE9 | F705 | F050. | the F050 having been typed by the programmer. Location AE9 now contains a JMP to scratchpad location :50 |

I50.   print the contents of location :50

The response is:

    0050   XXXX   13A8(space)
    0051   YYYY   F152(space)
    0052   ZZZZ   8AE4.

in which XXXX, YYYY, and ZZZZ are the now irrelevant former contents of locations :50-:52. The patch is now complete and debugging can continue with the search for further errors. Errors patched this way must still be corrected in the source program, of course, but this way several can be accumulated before an assembly pass is made. This process is admittedly tedious but much less so than repeated reassemblies.

The reason for using scratchpad for the patch is that scratchpad addressing is absolute and therefore much simpler than the relative forward and backward displacement and addressing used in the rest of memory. For this reason the program plan should leave at least a few adjacent scratchpad locations for debugging purposes.

If a program error cannot be traced down by any conventional method there is a method of last resort which can be used for tracing errors in programs which do not use interrupts. This method consists of executing one instruction at a time manually by repeated application of the RUN switch with the STOP switch on. In this way the results of every instruction can be examined directly in the registers and the error finally located. This method will not find an error caused by an interrupt service routine, since no interrupts can occur in this mode.

The most powerful debugging technique available from the debug program is known as *breakpointing*. Using this technique, parts of the program being tested are executed under debug control, with control being passed back to the debug program when the so-called breakpoint is reached. The debug program accomplishes this by replacing two of the instructions in the program being tested by a JMP and an address pointer which points back to the debug program. Two addresses are specified, A and B. The jump back to the debug program is located in the instructions which immediately follow B. Control is then transferred to address A and the program executes until it reaches B, at which point control returns to the debug program. The contents of registers are then typed out and the normal inspection facility of debug can be used to examine memory locations of interest. The technique allows a careful programmer to zero in on errors very rapidly but there is some danger involved. Should the breakpoint return instructions be located in some program location which is used as data by the program being tested, the result is not predictable. If the data word is a constant the program will attempt to use the breakpoint return instructions as a constant and generate nonsense, creating an artificial error where none may have existed before. If the program stores data in these locations the breakpoint return instructions will be destroyed and the return to the debug program will never occur, again creating an artificial error. Even with this limitation breakpointing is a powerful error tracing tool.

A good precaution to be taken when testing a new program is to fill memory with HLT instructions before loading the program. This way if control wanders outside the program area the computer will stop immediately and minimize the destruction, making the specific error easier to find. Though there are no hard and fast rules for identifying the kind of error which is causing a problem, there are some symptoms which usually relate to specific error types. A few of these are:

1. The STOP switch is pressed but the computer continues to run. This usually means an indirect addressing loop. The computer cannot stop until the instruction in progress is completed. If an indirectly addressed instruction leads to another indirect address, and thereafter to another, and finally back to the instruction which started the chain, the instruction can never be completed. The computer can be stopped by pressing reset. The value contained in the program counter will point to the trouble spot.

2. The program produces different results when executed automatically than when executed manually, one instruction at a time. This is almost always associated with an input/output timing problem. The transfer begins with a reset of the device interface and then proceeds to transfer the data. At the end of the transfer a jump back to the beginning occurs to start transferring the next block of data. The problem here is that the reset for the second block occurs while the final transmission of the first block is in progress. This reset destroys the transmission in progress. A typical manifestation of this problem is a program that will print a seven digit number in manual but only a six digit number in automatic. This kind of error can be maddening if you don't recognize it.

3. Half of an instruction or instructions destroyed. This happens when byte mode is left on when it should be off. Indirectly addressed or indexed store instructions have effective addresses half of the intended addresses. Data intended to be stored in data areas are stored in program areas, and the program begins to behave strangely as it devours itself. If you are satisfied that all of the inline SBM and SWM instructions are correct, a good place to look next is for an interrupt service routine which is returning control to the interrupted program in the wrong mode. A strong clue to this kind of error is the byte mode light being on. In almost all but communications applications the byte mode light will be off most of the time. If it is on for unusual intervals start looking for this problem in the indicated places.

4. The program looks correct, but the result isn't in memory where it is supposed to be stored. This is one of the stupid programming errors, usually the result of writing STA instead of STX or vice versa. Sometimes this happens when two program segments are merged into one in which temporary storage is shared between the formerly separate routines. This one is fairly easy to find.

5. Having loaded memory with HLTs before loading the program, a stop occurs with HLT in the I register (:0800) and some value in the program counter. When the area around the value in the program counter is examined no such HLT exists. This one is poison if you haven't seen it before. It is caused by an illegal interrupt. The Alpha machines are particularly susceptible to this because the choice of interrupt locations for most devices is not fixed as on most minicomputers, but is selectable by the wiring on the connector. There are two choices in this case. Either rewire the connector correctly, or find out where the actual interrupt address has been mislocated by the man with the soldering iron and move the interrupt service instruction there. A way to locate the actual interrupt address is to use unique halts in the possible interrupt locations. Any binary instruction in the range :0800 through :08FF will work as a halt. If scratchpad is initialized with halts whose lower half contains the scratchpad address of the halt itself, the low eight bits of the I register are the actual interrupt location when the computer stops.

The idea of debugging is to get a program that works, not necessarily an efficient one. At this stage a few extra instructions here and there don't hurt. Write using the simplest possible methods to accomplish what has to be done. When the program finally works, more elegant schemes can be substituted and the program tightened up. This way if the elegant scheme doesn't work you have something to go back to and a good idea of what failed. Make the assembler do as much of the work as possible by using EQU's for device addresses and symbol differences to generate array length counts. By doing this you will protect yourself in some measure from creating more errors while attempting to correct the first batch. Don't *EVER* use an instruction as a constant. This may be tempting when you are trying to save a memory word in a tight situation, and it may create a warm inner glow at the realization of how clever you are, but if the instruction ever changes because of a program update, it will create chaos.

From the point of view of development of programming skills, debugging is the most productive of all programming activities. No other programming activity, including reading this book, can yield so much specific hard knowledge and skill. If you run into a blank wall don't be afraid to ask for help. A fresh eye can often spot an error quickly in a situation in which your exhausted perception repeatedly glosses over it. Getting help may bruise the ego a bit, but solving the problem and acquiring the specific knowledge of the solution will build skill to a point where the bruises are not so frequent or painful.

Good luck!

Index

Index

About the Author

Walter J. Weller is a minicomputer software consultant based in Chicago, working in industrial, medical, and educational application of small computers. During the course of his work he recognized the need for a book detailing the techniques covered in this volume. Mr. Weller received the M.A. and the Ph.D. degrees from Northwestern University.